Women in the
United States Military,
1901–1995

Recent Titles in
Research Guides in Military Studies

The Peacetime Army, 1900–1941: A Research Guide
Marvin Fletcher

Special Operations and Elite Units, 1939–1988: A Research Guide
Roger Beaumont

The Late 19th Century U.S. Army, 1865–1898: A Research Guide
Joseph G. Dawson III

U.S. Military Logistics, 1607–1991: A Research Guide
Charles R. Shrader

Celluloid Wars: A Guide to Film and the American Experience of War
Frank J. Wetta and Stephen J. Curley

Military Intelligence, 1870–1991: A Research Guide
Jonathan M. House

The Militia and the National Guard in America Since Colonial Times:
A Research Guide
Jerry Cooper

The Soviet Armed Forces, 1918–1992: A Research Guide to Soviet Sources
John Erickson and Ljubica Erickson, compilers

Women in the United States Military, 1901–1995

A Research Guide and Annotated Bibliography

Compiled by
VICKI L. FRIEDL

Research Guides in Military Studies, Number 9

Greenwood Press
Westport, Connecticut • London

Library of Congress Cataloging-in-Publication Data

Friedl, Vicki L.
    Women in the United States military, 1901–1995 : a research guide
and annotated bibliography / compiled by Vicki L. Friedl.
       p.   cm.—(Research guides in military studies, ISSN
0899–0166 ; no. 9)
    Includes indexes.
    ISBN 0–313–29657–X (alk. paper)
    1. United States—Armed Forces—Women—History—20th century.
2. United States—Armed Forces—Women—Bibliography.   I. Title.
II. Series.
    UB418.W65F75   1996
    355'.0082—dc20   96–5253

British Library Cataloguing in Publication Data is available.

Library of Congress Catalog Card Number: 96–5253
ISBN: 0–313–29657–X
ISSN: 0899–0166

First published in 1996

Greenwood Press, 88 Post Road West, Westport, CT 06881
An imprint of Greenwood Publishing Group, Inc.

Printed in the United States of America

The paper used in this book complies with the
Permanent Paper Standard issued by the National
Information Standards Organization (Z39.48–1984).

10 9 8 7 6 5 4 3 2 1

CONTENTS

PREFACE

I first became interested in the history of women in the military while working as History Bibliographer at Mugar Library, Boston University. I discovered a biography by an Army nurse who had served in the China-India-Burma Theater in World War II (see **198**). I knew nothing of the role of military women in World War II, and started reading everything I could find on women's service. Although I had served as an active duty Army officer from 1980 to 1984 and was an Army ROTC cadet at the time the Women's Army Corps was disestablished, my military schooling had not included anything about the history of women in the service. I decided to compile a bibliography on women in the United States military to aid researchers in finding materials on the topic.

There is no other bibliography available on women in the United States military. Most military bibliographies and bibliographies on women either completely ignore women's roles in the armed forces or mention them only briefly. Standard reference sources, such as general encyclopedias and biographical dictionaries, include few or no references to military women.

PURPOSE

This research guide and bibliography is intended to assist both the beginning and the more experienced researcher, or anyone interested in learning about military women, in finding and selecting materials. It provides, in a one volume reference, quick access to important research on military women. It addresses the issues of conducting research, including sources for archival materials, useful journal indexes and important journals, organizations pertaining to military women, addresses of World Wide Web pages, and an annotated bibliography.

CRITERIA FOR INCLUSION

This bibliography includes books, research reports, student papers from various senior service schools (such as the Army War College), technical reports, conference papers, theses and dissertations, archival materials, and government documents, as well as articles from scholarly journals. No articles from popular or news magazines, such as *Time* or *Newsweek*, or service magazines, such as *Airman* or *Soldiers*, are included. I have read all included materials, the majority of which were obtained through interlibrary loan. There are 857 entries. Most of the materials regarding women in the military have been published in the last twenty years (Figure 1).

The bibliography is meant to be comprehensive in the coverage of personal narratives and official histories, and selective of other monographs. Government documents included are primarily recent (within the past twenty years) reports from the Government Accounting Office, government sponsored research reports, or Congressional hearings. Archival materials included are representative of the types of resources which are available and major collections are identified. Monographs excluded were generally of poor quality, repetitive of other works, not of historical interest, or could not be obtained through interlibrary loan. Journal articles are a selective compilation of articles with a primary focus on some aspect of servicewomen. All items are in English.

Other types of materials excluded (with a few exceptions) are military regulations and manuals, videotapes and films, book chapters, juvenile literature, fiction, and newspaper articles. Psychological studies, such as research on women veterans and post-traumatic stress disorder, are included, while technical studies on differences between men and women in physiological capacities, injury susceptibility, anthropometry, etc., are not. These excluded technical studies represent a substantially different body of literature from the medical/technical field and would be better represented in a separate bibliography for a medical/technical user. Readers interested in pursuing research on these types of studies should consider using databases such as MEDLINE, a major medical database which is widely available both on CD-ROM and online, and the National Technical Information Service (NTIS), which is a

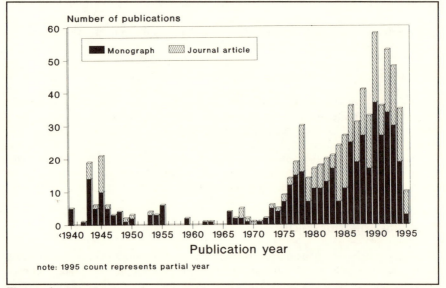

Figure 1. Distribution of monograph and journal article entries in this book by year of publication.

main source for the federal government's scientific and technical information.

The time period covered is from the establishment of the Army Nurse Corps in 1901, when women first officially became part of the United States military, to August 1995. It does not include materials about women who worked for the military before 1901, whether they served disguised as men or in some other role such as nurses or cooks, or women in the National Guard or Reserve. Women serving in or veterans of the Air Force, Army, Marine Corps and Navy are included, as well as women cadets at the service academies (but not women in ROTC). Women in the Coast Guard are included as well; although Coast Guard women officially serve under the Department of Transportation, they come under the control of the Navy in wartime. There is no coverage of women serving in the military of other countries.

ORGANIZATION AND FORMAT

Chapter 1 discusses ways to conduct research on military women. The subsequent chapters are arranged by subject: a chapter on the military in general, then on each service, as well as chapters dealing with issues faced by military women, such as women in combat, family and pregnancy issues, and veterans. Each chapter is prefaced by a short discussion of the subject. Subject chapters begin with entries listing important archival sources for materials on that particular chapter. For example, Chapter 8, Women Airforce Service Pilots, lists the location of the papers of Jacqueline Cochran (**505**) and large archival holdings for WASP papers (**506-510**). Appendix A lists major military archival sources. The user can turn to the subject chapter of interest or can locate topics using the table of contents or subject index.

Entries are arranged within chapters by subject, then alphabetically by author within subject. If appropriate, bibliographies are listed after archival sources, followed by general works, then specific subjects. Subjects are then chronologically arranged. Each entry includes an accession number, citation information, an annotation, and if applicable, the Superintendent of Documents (SuDocs) number, the Online Computer Library Center (OCLC) number, the international standard book number (ISBN), and in the case of documents available through Educational Resources Information Center (*ERIC*), the *ERIC* Document (ED) number. These numbers are included to facilitate obtaining items through interlibrary loan. Cross references are provided where necessary. I have tried to clarify citations by avoiding abbreviations, especially in journal titles. See page xvi for sample entries.

Appendices are provided as a ready reference source of several items, including archival resources, organizations for military women, a chronology of women's service, and addresses of military World Wide Web pages.

SOURCES CONSULTED

I consulted a wide variety of reference sources in preparing this guide, both electronic and print (Table 1). Many of these will be discussed in greater detail in Chapter 1.

Table 1. Sources Consulted

Online Public Access Catalogs

All were searched for relevant materials by subjects and titles. These catalogs were selected due to their very large holdings.

> *Library of Congress Information System (LOCIS)*
> *University of California/California State University (MELVYL)*
> *Harvard University (HOLLIS)*
> *Colorado Alliance of Research Libraries (CARL)*

Other Online Databases

> *Online Computer Library Center (OCLC)*
> *Research Libraries Information Network (RLIN)*

Journal Indexes

Both print and electronic indexes were consulted, including a complete run of each index to the most recent issue available at the time of writing.

> *Air University Library Index to Military Periodicals*
> *America: History and Life*
> *C.R.I.S.: The Combined Retrospective Index Set to Journals in*
>   *History, 1838-1974*
> *Cumulative Index to Military Literature*
> *Current Index to Military Literature* (now titled *Current Military*
>   *and Political Literature)*
> *ERIC*
> *General Science Index*
> *GPO Monthly Catalog*
> *Historical Abstracts*
> *Humanities Index*
> *Index to U.S. Government Periodicals*
> *International Index to Periodicals*
> *International Nursing Index*
> *MEDLINE*

Table 1. Sources Consulted

Journal Indexes (continued)

PAIS
PsycLIT
Social Sciences Index
Sociological Abstracts
UnCover
Women Studies Abstracts
Women's Studies Index

Bibliographies

*Military History of the United States: An Annotated
    Bibliography*
*A Selected and Annotated Bibliography of American Naval
    History*
*A Subject Bibliography of the Second World War: Books in
    English, 1939-1974*
*A Subject Bibliography of the Second World War: Books in
    English, 1975-1983*
United States Air Force History: An Annotated Bibliography
Women in American History: A Bibliography. Volumes I and II
*Writings on American History: A Subject Bibliography of
    Articles*

Theses and Dissertations

Comprehensive Dissertation Index: History
Dissertation Abstracts International
*Dissertations in History: An Index to Dissertations Completed in
    History Departments of United States and Canadian
    Universities*
Dissertations in History, June 1970-June 1980
Master's Theses in the Arts and Social Sciences

SAMPLE ENTRIES

The following examples illustrate how to interpret entries in this book.

Archives and Manuscripts[1]

400[2]   *Records of the War Department General and Special Staffs.*[3]   Record Group 165, National Archives.[4]
Contains a wealth of materials on the WAC, including recommendations for medals, overseas conditions, minorities, pregnancy, historical materials on the formation of the WAAC/WAC, and correspondence of the WAC Directors (formerly classified).[5]

Books

039   *Holm, Jeanne.*[6]   *Women in the Military: An Unfinished Revolution.*[7]
Revised edition. Novato, CA:[8] Presidio Press,[9] 1992.[10] 435p.[11] OCLC 26012907;[12] ISBN 0891414509.[13]
Major General Jeanne Holm served as the Director, WAF, from 1965-1973, and was the highest ranking woman to serve in the U.S. armed forces.   Covers key issues and events regarding women in the U.S. military from the Revolution through the Persian Gulf War, including family policy, the draft, combat, and service academies. Very widely cited, this is a "must read," and would be the choice for the reader looking for a one volume comprehensive book on women in the military. Indexed, bibliography.

Journal Articles

718   *Wilds, Nancy G.   "Sexual Harassment in the Military."*[14]   *Minerva*[15]
8(4):[16] 1-16,[17] Winter 1990.[18]
Sexual harassment continues to be a problem in the military, lowering unit cohesion, morale and productivity and increasing attrition rates, lost time, and human misery.   A detailed account of surveys taken to measure harassment suggests what women who are harassed should do, and discusses the question of whether or not men are sexually harassed.

---

[1]Type of material
[2]Accession number
[3]Collection name
[4]Collection location
[5]Annotation
[6]Author
[7]Title of work
[8]City/state of publication
[9]Publisher

[10]Year of publication
[11]Number of pages
[12]OCLC number for interlibrary loan
[13]International Standard Book Number
[14]Article title
[15]Journal title
[16]Volume (issue number) of journal
[17]Pages of article
[18]Date of publication

ACKNOWLEDGMENTS

This work could not have been completed without the efforts of librarians and staff of interlibrary loan departments across the United States. I would like to thank Rhoda Bilansky, Interlibrary Loan Supervisor, and her staff at Mugar Memorial Library, Boston University, where the majority of interlibrary loan materials were requested, and Patrick Cronk at the Fort Detrick Post Library for obtaining the last few works I needed to complete this book.

I appreciate the support of my friends and former colleagues at Mugar Library, Boston University, especially J. Christina Smith, for helping me with RLIN, checking OCLC numbers, and generally commiserating with me over the problems of writing a bibliography.

Thanks also to my mother, Karen J. Millan and stepfather, Monte McCrary, for spending part of their vacation xeroxing journal articles for me at the University of Maryland.

A special thanks to my husband, Lieutenant Colonel Karl E. Friedl, for his support and for typing and formatting the final manuscript.

ABBREVIATIONS AND ACRONYMS

AAF- Army Air Forces
ANC- Army Nurse Corps
ATA- Air Transport Auxiliary
CARL- Colorado Alliance of Research Libraries
DACOWITS- Defense Advisory Committee on Women in the Service
DCPC- Direct Combat Probability Code
DOD- Department of Defense
ED- ERIC Document
ERIC- Educational Resources Information Center
ETO- European Theater of Operations
EWITA- Evaluation of Women in the Army Study
GAO- Government Accounting Office
GPO- Government Printing Office
GRA&I- Government Reports Announcements & Index
ISBN- International Standard Book Number
LC- Library of Congress
LOCIS- Library of Congress Information System
MACV- Military Assistance Command, Vietnam
MCWR- Marine Corps Women's Reserve
MOS- Military Occupational Specialty
MTO- Mediterranean Theater of Operations
NNC- Navy Nurse Corps
NTIS- National Technical Information Service
NUC- National Union Catalog
n.p.- no place of publication/no publisher
OCLC- Online Computer Library Center
OCS- Officer Candidate School
POW- Prisoner of War
PTSD- Post-Traumatic Stress Disorder
RLIN- Research Libraries Information Network
ROTC- Reserve Officer Training Corps
SERE- Survival, Escape, Resistance, Evasion
SPAR- Semper Paratus Always Ready
SuDocs- Superintendent of Documents
USARV- United States Army, Vietnam

USMA- United States Military Academy
USNA- United States Naval Academy
URL- Unrestricted Line Officer
WAAC- Women's Army Auxiliary Corps
WAC- Women's Army Corps
WAF- Women in the Air Force
WAFC- Women's Armed Forces Corps (Vietnam)
WAFS- Women's Auxiliary Ferrying Service
WASP- Women Airforce Service Pilots
WAVES- Women Accepted For Voluntary Emergency Service
WFTD- Women's Flying Training Detachment
WIMSA- Women in Military Service for America
WITA- Women in the Army Study
WREI- Women's Research & Education Institute
Yeoman (F)- Yeoman (Female)

1

CONDUCTING RESEARCH

This chapter is primarily a guide to the important sources for information on military women, not to basic research methods. However, readers may want more information on library research and resources. There are several excellent research guides and handbooks available. A current guide which can be recommended for researchers of all skills is *The American Library Association Guide to Information Access: A Complete Research Handbook and Directory* [**001**], edited by Sandy Whiteley (New York: Random House, 1994). It is both a guide and directory to information sources in print and electronic form, including government information, online services, the internet, libraries, archives, general reference sources, and specialized subject information. It provides outstanding coverage of electronic sources. It would also be useful to consider a specialized guide to general sources in American history when researching military women such as *Handbook for Research in American History: A Guide to Bibliographies and Other Reference Works* [**002**], 2nd edition, revised, by Francis Paul Prucha (Lincoln, NE: University of Nebraska Press, 1994). This is a detailed guide to resources such as library catalogs, specialized bibliographies, history journals, book review indexes, online databases, oral history materials, and government documents. These two handbooks should answer many research questions, including how to search online catalogs, CD-ROMs, and other electronic databases, finding specialized dictionaries and encyclopedias, archival research, interlibrary loan, and using periodical and newspaper indexes.

BOOKS

Books on the subject of military women can be found in a number of ways. I used the online public access catalogs of several large research libraries, including the University of California (Melvyl), Harvard University (HOLLIS), and the libraries which are members of the Colorado Alliance of Research Libraries (CARL), as well as the Online Computer Library Center (OCLC) database, the Research Libraries Information Network (RLIN), the Library of Congress (LOCIS), the bibliographies of other books and journal articles on the subject, and specialized bibliographies (see Table 1).

Two of these databases, OCLC and RLIN, are not widely available to the public. The OCLC database was created to help libraries in cataloging materials and now contains records for over thirty million books, videotapes, manuscripts, periodicals, etc. from libraries in the United States and many foreign countries. It can be used to determine which library owns a particular work. Each item on OCLC is assigned a unique record number. I have included this OCLC number in citations for items I found in OCLC to facilitate locating records for interlibrary loan requests. OCLC is searched in a number of ways, including title, author, corporate author (such as a military service school or other institution), International Standard Book Number (ISBN), and OCLC number. Subject searching has recently become available through a menu driven service called FirstSearch. Additionally, FirstSearch allows searching of more than forty periodical indexes.

OCLC was one of the most valuable sources for this book. I had great success finding materials with the scan title search, by guessing the titles for books on military women, such as *Women in the Military*, then searching for books with that title. I also used OCLC to search for works by corporate authors and personal authors. For example, if I knew a researcher published items on military women, an author search on OCLC would frequently yield many other appropriate works by the same author. A number of unique materials were found this way.

OCLC was also useful for verifying citations. For example, if a book citation included only a title or an author, I searched OCLC by title or author to find the complete bibliographic citation.

RLIN is a database of the Research Libraries Group (RLG), that contains records for over fifty-six million items, such as books, videotapes, manuscripts, and photographs. One useful feature is the ability to search the *National Union Catalog of Manuscript Collections (NUC)* from 1987 to the present. A new menu-driven version, called Eureka, is available at member libraries.

The main drawbacks to OCLC and RLIN are that they are not available at all libraries or are not available for public use, and they are more difficult to use than online catalogs. With the advent of services such as FirstSearch and Eureka, this problem is partially resolved. New services are being added to both OCLC and RLIN so check with a librarian for updates. The extremely large holdings of these databases make them essential to the researcher.

As previously mentioned, I also searched the online public access catalogs of several large research libraries, all available through the internet or by direct dialing with a computer and modem. These were selected due to their large number of holdings. The primary way these catalogs were searched was by subject. However, subject headings for books on military women are problematic. The books I located often had too few subject headings or inappropriate ones. This is especially true for relatively obscure personal accounts of women's service which are often published by small presses and owned by few libraries. Some of the books found in OCLC had no subject headings at all. When searching for books by subject headings in online catalogs, I had the most success using the Library of Congress (LC) Subject Heading **United States--Armed Forces--Women.** However, I found books cataloged under a number of other LC subject headings (Table 2).

Table 2. Useful subject headings for retrieval of titles on women in the U.S. military.
United States--Armed Forces--Women Military Women Women in the Military Women Soldiers Women Sailors Women Marines Military Nursing United States. Air Force Nurse Corps United States. Army Nurse Corps United States. Navy Nurse Corps United States. Air Force--Women United States. Army--Women United States. Army. Women's Army Corps United States. Army. Women's Army Auxiliary Corps United States. Coast Guard--Women United States. Marine Corps--Women United States. Marine Corps Women's Reserve United States. Navy--Women United States. Naval Reserve. Women's Reserve Women's Air Service Pilots Women in Combat Women Veterans--United States Persian Gulf War, 1991--Participation, Female

If an online catalog has the capability of searching keywords in subjects, the search request **marine women** could be used instead of **United States. Marine Corps Women's Reserve** or **United States. Marine Corps--Women**. If keyword subject searching is not available, the subject heading may have to be typed exactly as it appears in the *Library of Congress Subject Headings.* Check the online catalog instructions or consult a librarian.

Another useful tool for finding books is keyword title searching. This is a good way not only for finding books on a topic, but of checking the appropriate subject heading. Keyword title searching enables the researcher to guess what words might be included in a title, then search for a title containing these. For example, a book about the Army Nurse Corps would likely have those words in the title, such as *History of the Army Nurse Corps.* A keyword title search for **Army Nurse Corps** could be done. Check the subject headings for the items found, then use these headings to do subject searches.

Books can be found by checking the bibliographies of known books and journal articles on the subject of military women. It is also useful to consult book review indexes, such as *Book Review Index*, *Book Review Digest*, or journal indexes which include book reviews, such as *America: History and Life*.

JOURNAL ARTICLES

Articles on military women can be found in a variety of journals, including history, psychology, sociology, military and medical, to name a few. The interdisciplinary nature of women's studies necessitates a search through a number of different indexes or subject bibliographies for relevant materials. There is no one source, print or electronic, which provides comprehensive coverage of the subject.

I searched many periodical indexes, both print and electronic, and several bibliographies, as listed in the **Sources Consulted** section of the preface. The advantages of using electronic sources, such as the *PsycLIT* CD-ROM versus the print *Psychological Abstracts*, are both speed and the ability to search many years of citations at a time. One of the disadvantages is, if the subject searched is very broad, such as *military women*, too many items may be retrieved which are not relevant. Most electronic databases have a thesaurus which lists appropriate subject headings and subheadings which help focus the search. It is helpful to consult the thesaurus when formulating a search, or to check with a librarian.

Periodical indexes list materials on military women under a number of different subject headings. Some, such as *America: History & Life* and *Sociological Abstracts*, have separate sections on the military which are short enough to be easily browsed. Often subject headings used in indexes conform to LC book subject headings. The most common subject heading I found used for items on military women was **Women** followed by a subheading such as *military.* The second most common heading was **United States--Armed Forces**, followed by a subheading such as *Army Nurse Corps*, or *women.* Indexes often are issued in cumulations, so many years may be searched at once.

The most useful indexes in locating journal articles for this bibliography were *America: History & Life, Air University Library Index to Military Periodicals, PsycLIT* and *ERIC.* While this bibliography excludes articles from popular magazines, many articles on military women have appeared in this literature, such as *Life, Newsweek, U.S. News and World Report*, etc. These magazines are indexed by *Readers' Guide to Periodical Literature*.

The major journal in women's military studies which should be consulted is *Minerva: Quarterly Report on Women and the Military. Minerva* publishes articles on all aspects of military women, as well as book reviews. A companion publication is *Minerva's Bulletin Board: The News Magazine on Women and the Military*, also issued quarterly. *Minerva's Bulletin Board* provides information on current events and other news items of interest to, or about women in the military. *Minerva* is indexed by *America: History & Life, Current Military and Political Literature, Historical Abstracts*, and *Women's Studies Index*.

Other military journals which have published a number of articles on women in the military are:

Armed Forces and Society
Journal of Military History (formerly *Military Affairs*)
Journal of Political and Military Sociology
Naval War College Review
Parameters, Journal of the US Army War College
Proceedings: U.S. Naval Institute

The services publish several professional or informational magazines and newspapers for their members, some of which are available via the World Wide Web (see Appendix D). While these are outside the scope of this bibliography, they may be of interest to researchers. Many of these are indexed by *Index to U.S. Government Periodicals.* Some of the more popular of these are:

> *Air Force Times*
> *Airman* (Air Force)
> *All Hands* (Navy)
> *Army Times*
> *Marine Corps Gazette*
> *Navy Times* (Marine Corps, Navy and Coast Guard)
> *On Watch* (Marine Corps, Navy and Coast Guard)
> *Soldiers* (Army)

GOVERNMENT DOCUMENTS

Federal government documents are an excellent, if often overlooked, source of information. They include congressional hearings, public laws, technical reports, and statistics. Locating these documents can be more difficult than locating other sources of materials, not only due to their numbers, but because there is no one central agency controlling their publication and distribution. The federal government has designated some libraries as depositories for documents which can be accessed by the general public. Many other libraries purchase documents, which are usually cataloged as monographs and are listed in the library catalog. Both research guides previously mentioned, the *American Library Association Guide to Information Access* [**001**] and *Handbook for Research in American.History* [**002**], include useful information on accessing documents. A specialized guide to government information recommended for researchers is *Tapping the Government Grapevine: The User-Friendly Guide to U.S. Government Information Sources* [**003**], 2nd edition, by Judith Schiek Robinson (Phoenix, AZ: Oryx Press, 1993). This book explains how to find and use government information sources, including electronic databases, archives, scientific information, regulations, legislative and executive branch information, statistics, and depository libraries. It also details the use of bibliographies and indexes to government information.

There are several widely available indexes and lists of federal documents. A good place to start is the *Monthly Catalog of United States Government Publications* [**004**], which is available in print and on CD-ROM as GPO. The *Monthly Catalog* is the most comprehensive list of federal publications, but even it does not include all government publications. It has several indexes, including subject and title. Scientific and technical documents are collected and indexed by the National Technical Information Service (NTIS). NTIS is indexed in print by *Government Reports Announcements & Index (GRA&I)* [**005**] and is available electronically as NTIS. There are specialized indexes for finding other types of publications, including legislative and executive branch information, regulations, statistics, etc. Detailed information on using these indexes is available in *Tapping the Government Grapevine* [**003**].

I found the majority of government documents included in this book by subject searching online catalogs and GPO for items on military women and from citations in other works. For example, the online catalogs of the University of California/California State University system (Melvyl) and Harvard University (HOLLIS) contain records for many documents.

Copies of documents may be obtained in a variety of ways. Access is often available through a visit to a depository library or through interlibrary loan. There are several large vendors of government information. Documents sold by the Government Printing Office are listed in the *GPO Sales Publications Reference File (PRF)* [**006**], a microfiche file available at many libraries. The GPO operates government bookstores in several large cities, where some documents may be purchased or ordered. NTIS documents are also available for purchase. Some issuing agencies will provide copies of documents, such as the General Accounting Office, which distributes one free copy of reports upon individual request. Check the *Monthly Catalog* [**004**] or *GRA&I* [**005**] for current telephone numbers and addresses. Both the GPO and GAO maintain World Wide Web sites where documents may be ordered (see Appendix D).

Another source for locating government documents on military women which should be consulted is *United States Government Documents on Women, 1800-1990: A Comprehensive Bibliography. Volume 1: Social Issues; Volume 2: Labor* [**007**], by Mary Ellen Huls (Westport, CT: Greenwood Press, 1993). This work describes nearly 7,000 documents representing most of the published reports of agencies, commissions, and Congress on women or on topics directly affecting women's health and welfare. Volume 2, Chapter 10, "Military Nursing and Health Care Providers," and Chapter 11, "Women in the Armed Forces" are an excellent source of government documents concerning women in the nursing services and regular military branches.

MANUSCRIPT COLLECTIONS AND ARCHIVES

Personal papers, photographs, uniforms, oral histories, equipment, and manuscripts relating to military women are only a few of the items which are maintained in libraries, museums and archives. These items can be of great interest to the researcher. The problem is in locating these collections which are not always described in library catalogs. There are several resources available to help find these collections. The *National Union Catalog of Manuscript Collections (NUC)* [**008**] is prepared by the Library of Congress and gives the name of manuscript collections, locations, years covered, and a brief description. The *NUC* is indexed by name, place, subject, and occupation in a separate publication. There are two compilation indexes available: *Index to Personal Names in the National Union Catalog of Manuscript Collections: 1959-1984* [**009**] and *Index to Subjects and Names in the National Union Catalog of Manuscript Collections: 1959-1984* [**010**]. These may be searched much more quickly than the indexes issued by the Library of Congress. The print version of the *NUC* was discontinued in 1993, but is available online from 1987 to the present through the RLIN database. *American Women and the U.S. Armed Forces: A Guide to the Records of Military Agencies in the National Archives Relating to American Women* [**011**], Charlotte Palmer Seeley, compiler; revised by Virginia C. Purdy and Robert Gruber (Washington, DC: National Archives and Records Administration, 1992), describes the records of Federal military agencies in the National Archives and records in the Presidential Libraries that relate to American women. It is arranged numerically by group record number. This is an essential guide which should be consulted for further information about the National Archives holdings listed in individual chapters of this book. The National Archives has a World Wide Web page which provides information on conducting archival research (see Appendix D). *Directory of Archives and Manuscript Repositories in the United States* **[012]**, 2nd edition, by the National Historical Publications and Records Commission (Phoenix, AZ: Oryx Press, 1988) is a guide to archives and repositories rather than individual collections and is useful for identifying potential sources for materials. *Subject Collections: A Guide to Special Book Collections and Subject Emphases As Reported by University, College, Public, and Special Libraries and Museums in the United States and Canada* **[013]**, by Lee Ash and William G. Miller (New Providence, NJ: R.R. Bowker, 1993) lists collections arranged by subject. This includes entries for Women in the Military, and Women in Aeronautics. *Women's History Sources: A Guide to Archives and Manuscript Collections in the United States* **[014]**, 2 volumes, Andrea Hinding, editor (NY: Bowker, 1979), is a compilation of collections from a nationwide survey done between 1975-1979 of 11,000 archives and repositories for collections of unpublished works on the history of women. It describes 18,026 collections in 1,586 repositories, and is arranged geographically. There is a separate name, subject, and geographic index, and many entries for military women are included.

There are also directories of oral history collections. Two of the better known are *Directory of Oral History Collections* **[015]** by Allen Smith (Phoenix: Oryx Press, 1988) and *Oral History Collections* **[016]**, by Alan M. Meckler and Ruth McMullin, (New York: Bowker, 1975).

Electronic sources are available to locate archival materials. RLIN is an excellent source of manuscripts and archives and, as previously mentioned, includes the *National Union Catalog of Manuscript Collections* **[008]** from 1987 to present. Many libraries and archives also list these collections on OCLC. Other good sources are online catalogs. Harvard's HOLLIS is an especially important and useful online catalog as it lists the manuscript holdings of the Arthur and Elizabeth Schlesinger Library on the History of Women in America at Radcliffe College. The Schlesinger Library holds a number of materials on military women, including manuscripts and personal papers. Many of these materials are also available or indexed on the World Wide Web (see Appendix D).

Many small collections are not listed in these guides. State and local historical societies can help in locating other archival materials. Manuscripts, personal papers, and other primary source materials are often held by museums as well. Directories such as *Directory of Historical Organizations in the United States and Canada* and *The Official Museum Directory* can help in locating historical societies and museums. A specialized directory to military museums is also available, *U.S. Military Museums, Historic Sites, & Exhibits,* 2nd edition **[017]**, by Bryce D. Thompson (Falls Church, VA: Military Living Publications, 1992). This provides information on museums of all the U.S. services located in the United States and overseas. It includes types of items on display, visitor information, hours, phone numbers and addresses. Large military archival sources and major museums are listed in Appendix A, *Archival Resources.*

SUGGESTIONS FOR FURTHER RESEARCH

Women have been part of the United States Military for nearly one hundred years, yet there are relatively few scholarly works or studies on these women or memoirs written by them, especially compared to the abundance of such materials available on servicemen.

The individual services have not all documented women's roles. The Army has published two excellent official histories of the Women's Army Corps, *The Women's Army Corps* [**408**], by Mattie E. Treadwell, as part of the series titled *United States Army in World War II: Special Studies*, and *The Women's Army Corps, 1945-1978* [**469**], by Bettie Morden. The Army has not published any further official histories of its women. Service of Marine Corps women is documented in *Women Marines in World War I* [**380**], by Linda L. Hewitt, *Marine Corps Women's Reserve in World War II* [**383**], by Pat Meid and *A History of the Women Marines, 1946-1977* [**392**], by Mary V. Stremlow. One official published history of the Army Nurse Corps during World War I is available: *The Medical Department of the U.S. Army in the World War: Volume XIII. Part 2: The Army Nurse Corps* [**125**], by Julia Stimson, the Superintendent of the Corps. The Coast Guard documented womens' World War II service in *The Coast Guard at War, Volume XX, Women's Reserve* [**372**]. There have been no official comprehensive histories yet published on women in the Air Force, the Navy, the Nursing Corps, or the Army and Marine Corps after 1978. There are also no published biographies of any of the Directors of the women's services.

There are only a small number of published books by women who served in the military (Table 3). I found four accounts about women who served primarily during World War I (see **134, 137, 141, 284**), one from the Korean War era (see **488**), three from the Vietnam War (see **231-232, 263**), one from the 1970s (see **321**), two from the Persian Gulf War (see **234, 813**) and two from women who attended the U.S. Military Academy (see **596-597**). Memoirs by women who served during World War II are more numerous, and their numbers are growing. To my surprise, I found no personal accounts by women who served after World War II, with the exception of those above. Nothing has been published by nurses who served in the Korean War, or women who served in Vietnam, with the exception of three nurses. Where are the accounts of the women who have participated in so many military "firsts", such as the first military pilots, the first women at the Air Force, Coast Guard and Naval Academies, the first women generals, the first woman to command a Coast Guard ship, the first women assigned to Air Force missile crews?

Women's writings about their military service can greatly enhance our understanding of their role in the armed forces. More women's experiences need to be recorded, either through oral histories or written accounts. Many of the personal narratives in this bibliography were written for a popular, rather than scholarly audience, and are not always useful for historical purposes. For example, dates of service and unit assignments are often omitted and it is not unusual for a writer to include more detail about her social life than her military experiences. Many have been published by small presses or are self-published, and while interesting, are not always well written or edited. Some outstanding exceptions, which could be used as a guide for other women documenting their service, are *One Woman's Army: A Black Officer Remembers the WAC*, by Charity Adams Earley (see **411**), *Lady in the Navy: A Personal Reminiscence*, by Joy Bright Hancock (see **314**), *Home before Morning: The Story of an Army Nurse in Vietnam*, by Linda Van Devanter (see **232**) and *In the Men's House: An Inside Account of Life in the Army by One of West Point's First Female Cadets*, by Carol Barkalow (see **596**).

Table 3. Personal Memoirs/Biographies of Individual Women.								
Service/Era		WWI	WWII	50s	Viet	70s	PG	Total
Army	Nurses	3	18		2		1	24
	Others		25	1		*2	1	29
Navy	Nurses		1		1			2
	Others	1	6			1		8
Marines			3					3
WASP			5					5
Total		4	58	1	3	3	2	71

*U.S. Military Academy
abbreviations: WWI = World War I; WWII = World War II; 50s = 1950s; Viet = Vietnam War; 70s = 1970s; PG = Persian Gulf War

2

WOMEN IN THE MILITARY

Women have served with the United States armed forces since colonial times. Tales abound of women, some disguised as men, who took up arms to defend their country. Some of the better known of these from the American Revolution are Mary Ludwig Hays, or "Molly Pitcher," and Deborah Samson, who fought under the name of "Robert Shirtliffe." Women's roles during the Civil War have been well documented. Not only did they serve as nurses under the direction of Clara Barton, but in 1864, Dr. Mary Walker received a commission as a doctor in the Union Army and was later awarded the Congressional Medal of Honor. It is estimated that several hundred women actually served as soldiers while assuming male identities.

Women played an important role during the Spanish-American War. Organized by Dr. Anita Newcomb McGee, over 1,500 women served in the U.S. and overseas as nurses. Their important contributions were recognized in 1901, with the establishment of the Army Nurse Corps, followed by the Navy Nurse Corps in 1908. Both corps were auxiliaries of their services and members did not receive benefits equal to men.

It was not until World War I that women received full status as members of the military. In 1917, the Navy became the first of the services to recruit women, with almost 12,000 eventually serving as Yeomen (F). The Marine Corps followed, enlisting 305 women shortly before the end of the war. The Yeomen (F) and Marine Reservists (F) were discharged after the war with the same military benefits as men.

World War II brought manpower shortages so severe that the services were forced to consider filling some positions with women. In 1942, the Army began to accept women in the newly formed Women's Army Auxiliary Corps (WAAC) to serve with, but not in, the Army. The WAAC's status as an auxiliary caused problems from the start. The women did not receive the same pay as men, did not have the same ranks (for example, a WAAC Second Lieutenant was called a "Third Auxiliary"), and were not entitled to full benefits. This was remedied in 1943, when the WAAC was replaced by the Women's Army Corps (WAC). The other services also began recruiting women in 1942. The Navy's women were WAVES (Women Accepted for Voluntary Emergency Service), the Coast Guard women were known as SPARs (Semper Paratus Always Ready), and the Marine women were simply women Marines. By the end of the war, nearly 350,000 women had served.

Another group of women served the military as civilians in World War II, receiving recognition as military veterans in 1977. These were the Women Airforce Service Pilots (WASP). The WASP ferried planes from factories to airfields in the United States and worked in other aviation jobs as well, such as training male pilots, towing targets, and test flying.

After the war, efforts were made to ensure women a place in the peacetime military. In 1947, the Army-Navy Nurse Act (Public Law 36-80C) made the corps a permanent part of their services. In 1949, nurses from the Army Air Forces formed the Air Force Nurse Corps. Women earned a place in the regular military in 1948, with the passage of the Women's Armed Services Integration Act (Public Law 625). While women were now assured of a right to serve, Public Law 625 severely restricted their numbers. A two percent ceiling was placed on the proportion of women in the regular establishment of each service and allowed as the highest rank only one full colonel or Navy captain. It laid down restrictions on types of duty assignments, specifying that in the Navy and Air Force, women could not be assigned to aircraft while the aircraft was engaged in combat missions, nor could they serve on vessels of the Navy except on hospital ships and Navy transports. Only the Army retained their women in a separate corps, the WAC.

Women's military participation in the years following World War II was limited. At the start of hostilities in the Korean War, there were only 22,000 women on active duty, including nurses. While only a few women on special assignment, other than medical personnel, actually served in Korea, all the services increased their efforts to recruit women. However, none of the services were able to meet their recruiting goals. In 1951, then Secretary of Defense George Marshall, formed a committee of fifty prominent women, to study ways in which recruiting goals could be met. The committee, named the Defense Advisory Committee on Women in the Service (DACOWITS), suggested a combined recruitment campaign to increase numbers. Ultimately, even this effort was unsuccessful. At its height, the number of women serving in the Korean War years reached just under 49,000.

By 1965, the number of women on active duty had dropped to 30,600, despite the military build up during the Vietnam War. Estimates of the number of women sent to Vietnam vary from 6,000-12,000. While the majority of these were nurses, 700 WAC, thirty-six women Marines, nine Navy officers and between 500-600 Air Force women are estimated to have served in Vietnam.

During this time period, roles for women in the military were slowly shrinking. Emphasis was placed less on military skills, such as firing a rifle or field training, and more on traditionally female skills, such as clerical work. One bright spot of the time was the passage of Public Law 90-130, which reduced the career restrictions on women by, among other things, lifting the two percent ceiling on regular line officers and enlisted strengths and removing the barrier to promotion to general officer.

The 1970s produced a surge in the numbers of women in military service, which can be credited, in part, to the end of the draft and the expected passage of the Equal Rights Amendment. Opportunities opened up for women in each service. The first women since the WASP in World War II were trained as pilots, and women were assigned to some noncombatant Navy ships. The Army disestablished the WAC in 1978 and opened up fourteen new career fields for enlisted women and eight for officers. Women officers were now able to serve in Field Artillery and Air Defense Artillery branches. They were accepted into the Reserve Officer Training Corps (ROTC), the major source of commissioned officers, and in 1976, the first group of women entered the service academies.

Changes in other policies also benefitted women. In 1973, as a result of a Supreme Court ruling, women were now entitled to the same payments for dependents as men. Women were also no longer automatically discharged for pregnancy or parenthood.

By 1980, women in the military had grown to over eight percent of the total force. The decade saw many significant events for military women. The first group of women graduated from the service academies and entered active duty, 170 women participated in the 1983 invasion of Grenada, and the number of women assigned to Navy ships grew from 2,000 in 1981 to nearly 8,000 in 1990. Jobs open to women reached fifty-two percent in the Army, fifty-nine percent in the Navy, twenty percent in the Marine Corps, ninety-seven percent in the Air Force, and one hundred percent in the Coast Guard.

Women played a vital role in the success of the first large-scale military operation since the Vietnam War, the Persian Gulf War in 1991. It was the largest ever deployment of military women. Depending on the source, from 27,066 to over 40,000 military women served in the gulf. Eleven Army women were killed and two were taken as prisoners of war.

Women's service in the Gulf was widely reported and renewed debate about issues surrounding women in the military, including pregnancy and parenthood, dual service couples, and women in combat. Congressional hearings were held on family issues, but the services successfully resisted efforts to change deployment policies for parents.

Nearly all legal restrictions against women in combat were lifted by Congress in the early 1990s. In 1993, then Secretary of Defense Les Aspin, ordered the services to drop restrictions on women flying combat missions, and in 1994, the Navy opened assignments to women aboard combatant ships. By mid-1995, women were serving as part of mixed sex crews on Navy combat ships and women pilots were flying combat aircraft.

Women currently account for twelve percent of the total military force. It remains to be seen what effect, if any, the downsizing of the military will have on these numbers.

This chapter contains general materials written about military women or items concerning women in more than one service. Materials about women in specific services are covered in the subject chapters. The universal reference materials **[001-017]** can be found in Chapter 1.

ARCHIVES AND MANUSCRIPTS

018 *McCann: Women in Uniform. 1938-1944.* United States Army Military History Institute, Carlisle Barracks, PA.
Scrapbooks of clippings and government recruiting and information brochures concerning women in the armed forces during World War II. Includes information on WACs, WAVES, WAFs, SPARs, Army Nurse Corps and Marine Corps Women's Reserve.

019 ***United States. Defense Advisory Committee on Women in the Services. Records, 1951-1959.*** Schlesinger Library, Radcliffe College, Cambridge, MA.
Contains minutes, reports, directives, recommendations, speeches, publicity materials, photos, etc.

020 ***Women in the American Military Oral History Project. Interviews, 1984-1985.*** Schlesinger Library, Radcliffe College, Cambridge, MA.
A collection of oral history interview tapes and transcripts conducted by Dorothy and Carl J. Schneider for their book *Sound Off: American Military Women Speak Out* (see **047**).

BIBLIOGRAPHIES

021 *Campbell, D'Ann.* **"Women in Uniform: The World War II Experiment."** *Military Affairs* 4(3): 137-139, July 1987.
A narrative bibliography of important works on women in the military during World War II. States that it covers almost all of the useful material published in English on this era. Includes excellent recommendations for further research on military women.

022 *Gibish, Jane E.* **Women in the Armed Forces: Selected References.** Maxwell Air Force Base, AL: Air University Library, 1986. 84p. OCLC 13695094.
Includes items held at the Air University Library, such as books, conference proceedings, journal articles, government documents, and student papers dealing with women in the military. No annotations.

023 *Haas, Mary E.* **"An Annotated List of Resources on Women and Wartime."** *Social Education* 58(2): 101-103, February 1994.
An annotated bibliography of teaching materials, videotapes, and books containing first hand accounts and histories of wartime experiences.

024 *Harrell, Karen Fair.* **Women in the Armed Forces: A Bibliography, 1970-1980.** Monticello, IL: Vance Bibliographies, 1980. 11p. OCLC 6410461.
No indication is given of criteria for inclusion. Includes journal articles and a few books and government documents. No annotations or index.

025 *Hunter, Edna J., Sharon J. Rose and J. Bradley Hamlin.* **"Women in the Military: An Annotated Bibliography."** *Armed Forces and Society* 4(4): 695-716, August 1978.
An annotated bibliography with forty-three entries for papers, book chapters, books, and journal articles on women in the military. Only includes items dealing specifically with women on active duty.

026 *Miller, Lester L., Jr.* **Women in Service: A Bibliography of Periodical Articles.** Fort Sill, OK: U.S. Army Field Artillery School Library, 1983. 14p. OCLC 9445380.

Lists articles in magazines such as *Army*, *Air Force Magazine*, etc. held at the library of the U.S. Army Field Artillery School. Arranged by service, then chronologically. Not evaluative. No index.

027 *Peets, Eleanor E.* **USAF History of Women in the Armed Forces: A Selected Bibliography.** Maxwell Air Force Base, AL: Historical Reference Branch, Albert F. Simpson Historical Research Center, 1976. 18p. OCLC 12151436.
Annotated bibliography of references available at the Albert F. Simpson Center Library dealing with women in the armed forces. Arranged by type of reference (books, documents, historical studies, oral history interviews, etc.), then chronologically. Includes ninety-four items. Partially indexes the collection at the Research Center.

028 *Pentagon Library.* **Women in the Military.** Washington, DC: The Library, 1983. 20p.
Lists books, general and legal periodical articles, and congressional materials on women in the U.S. military. Most items from the years 1970 to 1983, but some published earlier. Updated in 1987 (see **029**).

029 *Pentagon Library.* **Women in the Military: A Selective Bibliography.** Washington, DC: The Library, 1987. 40p. OCLC 16930705.
A selective listing of books, articles and Congressional materials on women in the military which are available for loan from the Pentagon Library. Arranged by document type, than alphabetically by author. No annotations or index. Revises a 1983 bibliography (see **028**).

030 *Simpson, Diana B.* **Women in the Armed Forces: Selected References.** Maxwell Air Force Base, AL: Air University Library, 1993. 44p. OCLC 27778562.
A list of selected book holdings, government documents, and periodical articles held at the Air University Library. A few entries have very brief annotations.

031 *Wagner, Christine.* **"Women and the U.S. Military: Invisible Soldier and Veteran: An Annotated Bibliography."** *Feminist Teacher* 5(3): 34-39, Spring 1991.
A short bibliography geared towards teachers. Divided into two parts, Women and the Military and Women and Vietnam. Includes newspaper articles, books, and journal and magazine articles.

GENERAL WORKS

032 *Assistant Secretary of Defense.* **Military Women in the Department of Defense.** Annual. Washington, DC: Assistant Secretary of Defense (Force Management and Personnel), 1983-. SuDocs D1.2:W84/4/vol.
A yearly publication compiling statistics on women in the military. Good source for statistics, including jobs held by women, levels of attrition, numbers on active duty, reenlistment rates, etc.

033   *Assistant Secretary of Defense.* **Report Task Force on Women in the Military.** Washington, DC: Assistant Secretary of Defense, 1988. 34p. Results of a task force created by the Secretary of Defense in response to concerns raised by DACOWITS about the full integration of women in the armed forces. Addresses three primary topics: attitudes and treatment of women in the military and their impact on the morale and quality of life, consistency in application of combat exclusion statutes and policies, and the manner in which force management policies may adversely affect women's career development.

034   *Becraft, Carolyn.* **Women in the Military: 1980-1990.** Washington, DC: Women's Research and Education Institute, 1990. 10p. OCLC 22327351.
An overview of women in the military from 1980-1990. Good statistical source for numbers of active duty personnel in each service, broken down by sex and race, as well as percentage of jobs in each service open to women. Also includes a discussion of combat exclusion laws.

035   *Chorak, Carolyn S.* **Marching to a Different Drummer: Military Women in American Popular Magazines, 1975-1985.** Thesis (M.A.)--California State University, Northridge, 1986. 355p. OCLC 13749909.
Examines ninety-eight articles written about women in the military from popular American magazines from 1975 to 1985. Each article is analyzed in detail. Found that news magazines provided the most coverage and coverage in all magazines emphasized stories about women officers and women working in non-traditional jobs. Well written and interesting project. Author suggests more women known for research and knowledge of military women should write these articles.

036   *Collier, Ellen C.* **Women in the Armed Forces.** Washington, DC: Library of Congress, Congressional Research Service, 1981. 22p. OCLC 8048426.
An issue brief discussing national security and the role of women in the armed forces. Good, basic discussion of issues, such as expanding women's roles, women in combat, and women and the draft. Includes some statistics as well as a summary of legislation regarding women in the services from 1975-1980. Lists reference sources.

037   *Devilbiss, Margaret Conrad.* **Women and Military Service: A History, Analysis, and Overview of Key Issues.** Maxwell Air Force Base, AL: Air University Press, 1990. 86p. OCLC 22869239.
A short report which explores questions concerning the development of policies regarding women in the military. A good, fairly current, summary of the historical role of servicewomen. Covers key issues, such as family, numbers of women serving, training, combat, minority women, and the draft.

038   *Devilbiss, Margaret Conrad.* **Women in the Armed Forces**. New Haven, CT: M.C. Devilbiss, 1981. 19p. OCLC 16258822.
Paper presented at the Fifth Berkshire Conference on the History of

Women, June 1981. A good, although brief, summary of women's participation in the U.S. military since the Revolutionary War. Suggests the need for further research in women's military history.

039 *Holm, Jeanne.* **Women in the Military: An Unfinished Revolution.** Revised edition. Novato, CA: Presidio Press, 1992. 435p. OCLC 26012907; ISBN 0891414509.
Major General Jeanne Holm served as the Director, WAF, from 1965-1973, and was the highest ranking woman to serve in the U.S. armed forces. Covers key issues and events regarding women in the U.S. military from the Revolution through the Persian Gulf War, including family policy, the draft, combat, and service academies. Very widely cited, this is a "must read," and would be the choice for the reader looking for a one volume comprehensive book on women in the military. Indexed, bibliography.

040 *Hunter, Edna J. and Carol B. Million.* **"Women in a Changing Military."** *Proceedings: U.S. Naval Institute* 103(7): 50-58, July 1977.
Provides a summary of women's roles in the military since World War I, demographics on military women, their status in the 1970s military, occupations open to them, problems, and male attitudes towards them.

041 *Johnson, Jesse J., editor.* **Black Women in the Armed Forces, 1942-1974: A Pictorial History.** Hampton, VA: Johnson, 1974. 110p. OCLC 1659367; ISBN 0915044110.
Organized by chapters on black women in the Army, Air Force, Navy, Marine Corps, nursing corps and training. Very disorganized, primarily a photograph collection. Many photographs have nothing to do with the book. No index.

042 *Levin, Michael.* **"Women As Soldiers-The Record So Far."** *Public Interest* #76: 31-44, Summer 1984.
Discusses changes facing military women in the 1970s and 1980s. During this time, more jobs were opened, the service academies began accepting women, and there was an expansion of the numbers of women in the service. Describes problems with women, including lack of physical strength, pregnancy, and morale. Author believes civilians have had too much influence on military policy as the point of the military is to fight, and women can't.

043 *Luckett, Perry D.* **"Military Women in Contemporary Film, Television, and Media."** *Minerva* 7(2): 1-15, Summer 1989.
Discusses military women in contemporary media, where they are usually stereotyped. Analysis of military women in *Mash*, the films *Private Benjamin* and *Stripes*, and others.

044 *Maisels, Amanda and Patricia M. Gormley.* **Women in the Military: Where They Stand.** Washington, DC: Women's Research and Education Institute, 1994. 20p.
A current summary of the status of women in the military. Gives

information on minority women, education levels, proportion of job positions open to women by service, etc. Also includes information by service of numbers of women serving and significant events from 1984-1994.

045   *Moore, Brenda L.   "African-American Women in the U.S. Military."*
Armed Forces and Society 17(3): 363-384, Spring 1991.
Used data from the Department of Defense's 1985 Survey of Officer and Enlisted Personnel and the 1988 and 1989 Population Representation in the Military Services Reports to analyze the participation of African-American women in the armed forces. Provides many statistics on Afro-American women, such as military occupations, educational level, numbers of officers and enlisted, etc. Concludes the rapid increase in enlistment of minority women is due to the decline of eligible men, high rates of minority unemployment, and expanded opportunities in the military for women and minorities.

046   *Odom, Geraldine.   The Military Woman: A Leisure Profile.* Thesis (M.R.A.)--Georgia Southern University, 1990. 45p. OCLC 23031904.
Survey conducted to determine if there are significant differences in the leisure motivation and leisure satisfaction of specific segments of servicewomen stationed at Moody Air Force Base, Georgia. The most popular leisure pursuits were watching television, reading, listening to the radio, and going to the movies. Recommends the Morale, Welfare and Recreation Division should provide more leisure activities for women.

047   *Schneider, Dorothy and Carl J. Schneider.   Sound Off!   American Military Women Speak Out.* Revised edition. New York: Paragon House, 1992. 300p. OCLC 2541452; ISBN 1557785058.
Written from interviews with over 300 women of all ranks in the military, conducted at sixteen stateside military installations. The women discuss stereotypes, sexual harassment, jobs, families, promotions, combat issues, etc. Well done. This revised edition contains a chapter on the Persian Gulf War. Oral history tapes and transcripts for this book are held at the Schlesinger Library, Radcliffe College (see **020**).

048   *Segal, David R. and H. Wallace Sinaiko, editors.   Life in the Rank and File: Enlisted Men and Women in the Armed Forces of the United States, Australia, Canada, and the United Kingdom.* Washington, DC: Pergammon-Brassey's International Defense Publishers, 1986. 283p. OCLC 12134757; ISBN 0080323871.
Includes many chapters on women in the U.S. military, including women Marines, women serving overseas, and the debate over women soldiers.

049   *Segal, Mady Wechsler and Amanda Faith Hansen.   "Value Rationales in Policy Debates on Women in the Military: A Content Analysis of Congressional Testimony, 1941-1985."* Social Science Quarterly 73(2): 296-309, June 1992.
Catalogs and analyzes policy positions taken by speakers before the House and Senate, along with the rationales for these positions, and

explores how these positions and arguments changed over time. Found most of the testimony and debate was in the 1940s and 1980s, and sixty-nine percent of the speakers were men. Other findings were that all of the military effectiveness value positions taken in the 1940s were positive on expanded military roles for women, while in the 1980s, thirty-seven percent of these statements were negative.

050 *Segal, Mady Wechsler.* ***"Women in the Military: Research and Policy Issues."*** *Youth & Society* 10(2): 101-126, December 1978.
Excellent discussion of research conducted on women in the military (as of the late 1970s), which the author states has been policy oriented, descriptive, controlled by the military, and primarily attitudinal.   Also provides a brief history of women in the military and a discussion of the major issues involved in policy decisions regarding the future of women's roles.

051 *Stiehm, Judith.* **Arms and the Enlisted Woman.** Philadelphia: Temple University Press, 1989. 331p. OCLC 17386094; ISBN 0877225656.
An overview of the issues facing enlisted women. Discusses policy and the military's bias against women.

052 *Stiehm, Judith Hicks.* **"The Generations of U.S. Enlisted Women."** *Signs: Journal of Women in Culture and Society* 11(11): 155-175, Autumn 1985.
Uses cohort analysis as an approach to understanding seven distinct groups of military women who entered the service between 1952 and 1976. Contrasts the way cohort members have been affected by rapid changes in military policy between 1948 and 1980. Concludes rapid military changes have led to differences between female cohorts not seen in male cohorts and made the kind of statistical projections applied to men inapplicable to women.

053 *Thomas, Patricia J.* **"Women in the Military; America and the British Commonwealth; Historical Similarities."** *Armed Forces and Society* 4(4): 623-646, August 1978.
A review of women's roles in the military, both in the United States and British Commonwealth. Detailed discussion of the formation of the women's services and their roles since World War I.

054 *Wekesser, Carol and Matthew Polesetsky, editors.* **Women in the Military.** San Diego, CA: Greenhaven Press, 1991. 192p. OCLC 24173805; ISBN 0899085792.
Collection of book excerpts and reprinted journal and newspaper articles which present pro and con views regarding women in the military. Topics include women's roles, women in combat, and discrimination. Good for recent materials, including women in the Persian Gulf War. Has a general bibliography and list of organizations to contact for further information.

WORLD WAR I

055   *Schneider, Carl J. and Dorothy Schneider.* **"American Women in World War I."** *Social Education* 58(2): 83-85, February 1994.
Good summary of the role of women serving during World War I, including Red Cross nurses and Army nurses serving overseas, as well as Yeomen (F) and women Marines.

056   *Schneider, Dorothy and Carl J. Schneider.* **Into the Breach: American Women Overseas in World War I.** New York: Viking, 1991. 368p. OCLC 22707733; ISBN 0670839361.
Records the participation of American women who served abroad during World War I. Includes information about Army nurses and the "Hello Girls", who worked for the U.S. Army Signal Corps in France as telephone operators. Photographs, bibliography and index.

057   *Sillia, Helene M.* **Lest We Forget... A History of Women's Overseas Service League.** n.p: The League, 1978. 318p. OCLC 6486146.
A history of the Women's Overseas Service League, which was founded by women who served overseas during World War I. Has personal accounts by Army and Navy nurses.

WORLD WAR II

058   *Alsmeyer, Marie Bennett.* **Those Unseen Unheard Arkansas Women: WAC, WAVES, Women Marines of World War II.** Conway, AR: Marie Alsmeyer, 1988. 31p. OCLC 26646954.
Very disorganized collection of short anecdotes from women serving during World War II who were from Arkansas or who trained in that state. Written from interviews with the author.

059   *Burstein, Herbert.* **Women in War: A Complete Guide to Service in the Armed Forces and War Industries.** New York: Service Publishing Company, 1943. 166p. OCLC 2570804.
An information book for women interested in joining one of the military services or getting defense jobs. Reproduces application forms for the Women's Army Auxiliary Corps and the WAVES, and lists requirements for joining the various services. Some photographs.

060   *Campbell, D'Ann.* **"Servicewomen of World War II."** *Armed Forces and Society* 16(2): 251-270, Winter 1990.
Studied women veterans of World War II using new questionnaires and old surveys to discover the true experience of their military service during the war. Includes statistics and descriptions of the backgrounds of women recruits, their education and motivation for service, as well as what they gained.

061   *Lissey, Jeannette F. and Edith Harvey, compilers.* **Prepare for the Official Tests for WAACS, WAVES, SPARS, and Marines: A Complete**

Guide and Instruction Book for Women in Military Service. New York: Capitol Publishing Company, 1943. 196p. OCLC 5242958.
Lists requirements for women interested in enlisting in one of the women's services (in 1943). Gives requirements for enlistment, and describes training, jobs available, sample entrance tests, etc. Some photographs.

062 *Litoff, Judy Barrett and David C. Smith.* **We're in This War Too: World War II Letters from American Women in Uniform.** New York: Oxford University Press, 1994. 272p. OCLC 28890537; ISBN 0195075048.
A collection of edited letters written by U.S. servicewomen, as well as a few Red Cross workers. Each letter is introduced with general historical information as well as a brief biography of the writer. Includes photographs, an index and a list of books for further reading.

063 *Power, James R.* **Brave Women and Their Wartime Decorations.** New York: Vantage Press, 1959. 97p. OCLC 2567010.
Provides a short overview of women in the military in the U.S, as well as other countries. Gives lists of awards awarded to women nurses in World War I, World War II and Korea, as well as awards for SPARs, women Marines and WAAC/WAC in World War II. No awards are listed for WAVES and no names of individual awardees are included.

064 *Ross, Mary Steele.* **American Women in Uniform.** Garden City, NY: Garden City Publishing Company, 1943. 72p. OCLC 3512789.
Book of illustrations of uniforms for women in all branches of the military during World War II, including civilian workers. Good source of uniform illustrations (see **217**).

065 *Schloz, Lois J.* **"The Logistical Challenges of Integrating Women into the Military."** *Air Force Journal of Logistics* 16(2): 5-7, Spring 1992.
Provides information about the logistics problems encountered when women were first integrated into the military during World War II. Discusses housing, health care, recruiting, uniforms, and jobs held by women.

066 *Sherman, Janann.* **"'They Either Need These Women or They Do Not': Margaret Chase Smith and the Fight for Regular Status for Women in the Military."** *Journal of Military History* 54(1): 47-78, January 1990.
At the end of World War II, Representative Margaret Chase Smith was instrumental in the passage of the Women's Armed Services Integration Act. A detailed article about Smith's actions in promoting and eventually passing legislation which made women a permanent part of the services.

067 *Wadge, D. Collett.* **Women in Uniform.** London, Sampson Low, Marston & Company, LTD., 1946. 386p. OCLC 1508821.
Written shortly after the end of World War II, includes information about all the English speaking women's services, including those in the U.S. Gives basic facts about each service as well as some statistics. Valuable for the many photographs.

068   *Weatherford, Doris.* **American Women and World War II.** New York: Facts on File, 1990. 338p. OCLC 20852849; ISBN 0816020388.
Interesting account of the roles played by American women during World War II. The first chapters deal with military women, including nurses, WAACs, WAVES, and women Marines. Good information on the problems faced by black servicewomen. Indexed with photographs.

PERSIAN GULF WAR

069   *Becraft, Carolyn.* **Women in the U.S. Armed Services: The War in the Persian Gulf.** Washington, DC: Women's Research and Education Institute, 1991. 4p. OCLC 27446352.
An excellent summary of women's role in the Gulf War. Gives total number of women deployed by service, as well as the total number in each service. Highlights women's jobs in the war.

070   *Becraft, Carolyn.* **"Women in the U.S. Armed Services: The War in the Persian Gulf."** *Women & Criminal Justice* 4(1): 155-163, 1992.
A reprint of the author's report written for the Women's Research and Education Institute (see **069**).

071   *Hurrell, Rose Marie and John H. Lukens.* **"Attitudes toward Women in the Military during the Persian Gulf War."** *Perceptual and Motor Skills* 78(1): 99-104, February 1994.
Describes the development of a scale to measure public attitudes toward women in the military and reports its use with a sample of ninety-seven college women surveyed during the Persian Gulf War. Found that those surveyed tended to have attitudes endorsing equivalent capabilities of men and women to function in the military.

072   *United States. General Accounting Office.* **Operation Desert Storm: Race and Gender Comparison of Deployed Forces with All Active Duty Forces.** GAO/NSIAD-92-111FS. Washington, DC: GAO, 1992. 62p. SuDocs GA 1.13:NSIAD-92-111FS; OCLC 26220297.
Provides statistical information on the composition of active duty troops deployed to Operation Desert Shield/Desert Storm with that of active duty military personnel for each service by rank, race, gender and combat/noncombat position. Women represented six percent of the deployed personnel. Good source for statistics.

073   *United States. General Accounting Office.* **Women in the Military: Deployment in the Persian Gulf.** GAO/NSIAD-93-93. Washington, DC: The Office, 1993. 58p. SuDocs GA 1.13:NSIAD-93-93.
Addresses the women's roles and performance, their ability to endure deployment conditions, their effect on unit cohesion, and on a unit's ability to deploy. Found women performed well, and cohesion in mixed gender units was generally effective. Informative discussion of issues. Includes many statistics.

ASSIGNMENTS AND UTILIZATION

For materials regarding the assignment of women to combat positions, see **Chapter 13, Women in Combat**.

074 *Anderson, Barbara Gallatin.* **A Pilot Report on Women's Assessment of Their Military Careers.** Research Triangle Park, NC: Army Research Office, 1988. 21p. OCLC 20973269.
Twenty-four women from the Army, Air Force, and Navy were interviewed in this exploratory research project. The goal was to design and test an intensive interview form that would provide the basis for a reconstruction of the career histories of women in the military. Found that women want more opportunities for mentoring, believe that they can have a successful career, and that women's status will improve when combat jobs open to them.

075 *Aspin, Les.* **Manning the Military: The Female Factor.** Washington DC: L. Aspin, 1984. 15p. OCLC 12340163.
Suggests that due to the low numbers of qualified male recruits available, it will be necessary to expand the pool of recruits by greater utilization of women. This would reduce pressure on manpower resources. Includes discussion of objections to utilizing more servicewomen.

076 *Binkin, Martin and Shirley J. Bach.* **Women and the Military.** Washington, DC: The Brookings Institute, 1977. 134p. OCLC 3089696; ISBN 0815709668.
Results of a two year study of women in the military. Authors estimate that about one third of all military jobs could be filled by women without causing significant problems. Traces the evolution of women in the armed forces. Widely cited, although dated.

077 *Brown, Robert P.* **The Utilization of Women by the Military.** Newport, RI: Naval War College, 1987. 32p. OCLC 17637104.
The author, an Army major, discusses how the services utilize women. Concludes that the services need to expand women's roles in the future.

078 *Landrum, Cecile.* **"Policy Dimensions of an Integrated Force."** *Armed Forces and Society* 4(4): 689-694, August 1978.
Discusses the limitations, problems, and unresolved dilemmas in the utilization of women in the U.S. military. Addresses issues surrounding women's service, such as women in combat, job assignments, marriage and family issues.

079 *Rogers, Deborah L.* **"The Force Drawdown and Its Impact on Women in the Military."** *Minerva* 10(1): 1-13, Spring 1992.
A discussion of what a smaller military force will mean for women. Gives statistics on separations, both voluntary and involuntary, and positions available to women in the services. States the Department of Defense is trying to maintain the present percentage of women serving.

080 *Thomas, Patricia J.* **Role of Women in the Military: Australia, Canada, the United Kingdom and the United States.** San Diego, CA: Navy Personnel Research and Development Center, 1978. 66p. OCLC 4162016.
A research report detailing the enlistment, attrition/retention, attitudes, interpersonal factors, and utilization and job performance of women in the armed forces of various countries, including the U.S. Presents a historical overview of women's service in each country.

081 *United States. General Accounting Office.* **Women in the Military: Career Progression Not a Current Problem but Concerns Remain.** GAO/NSIAD-89-21-210BR. Washington, DC: GAO, 1989. 36p. OCLC 20444864.
Studied whether or not impediments exist to women's career progression in the military. Interviewed enlisted women and officers and reviewed assignment and promotion policies. Concluded women were promoted at a similar rate to men.

HEALTH

082 *Henley, Mozettia H.* **Women's Drinking in the U.S. Armed Forces: Sociodemographic, Contextual Factors and Alcohol Consumption.** Thesis (Ph.D.)--University of California, San Francisco, 1991. 145p. OCLC 26373216.
Studied the level of alcohol consumption among women in the armed forces, as there have been no studies previously conducted on women's drinking in the military. Found that the risk of a woman becoming a heavy drinker was increased if she worked in a predominantly male job.

083 *Hoiberg, Anne.* **"Health Status of Women in the U.S. Military."** *Health Psychology* 3(3): 273-287, 1984.
Focuses on major health related issues, pregnancy, physical injuries and capabilities, and stress-related disorders. The most frequent reason for hospitalization was for pregnancy related conditions. Women recruits had the highest rates of injury related hospitalizations and women assigned to nontraditional jobs had higher injury rates than those working in traditional jobs.

RECRUITMENT, ENLISTMENT, TRAINING, AND RETENTION

084 *Arbogast, Kate Avery.* **The Procurement of Women for the Armed Forces: An Analysis of Occupational Choice.** Thesis (Ph.D.)--George Washington University, 1974. 266p. OCLC 23932728.
Written for a degree in economics, looks at recruitment from an economic point of view. Author concludes that the services have no problem in attaining recruiting goals, so conduct no research analyzing the female labor pool. Emphasis on Navy enlisted women.

085 *Hosek, James R. and Christine E. Peterson.* **Serving Her Country: An Analysis of Women's Enlistment.** Santa Monica, CA: Rand Corporation, 1990. 67p. OCLC 20894718; ISBN 083301031X.
Authors are concerned with defining the appropriate recruiting market segment, the role of educational expectations and the effect of family background and employment on women's enlistment. Found that men and women enlist for similar reasons, so recruiting techniques for men should work for women.

086 *Schaffter, Dorothy.* **What Comes of Training Women for War.** Washington, DC: American Council on Education, 1948. 223p. OCLC 1448049.
A study commissioned by the Commission on Implications of Armed Services Educational Programs, to explore the training of women in the Army, Air Force, Navy, Marines, Coast Guard, and WASP during World War II. Good discussion of jobs held by women and the types of training they received.

087 *Stewart, James B. and Juanita M. Firestone.* **"Looking For A Few Good Men: Predicting Patterns of Retention, Promotion, and Accession of Minority and Women Officers."** *The American Journal of Economics and Sociology* 51(4): 435-458, October 1992.
Examines the extent to which differences exist across race/ethnicity, sex, and service group in rates of retention and promotion of military officers. Results indicated that while retention rates for minorities appear high, there will be little change in the number of higher ranking minority servicemembers if current recruitment and promotion practices continue. Suggests programs to increase numbers of women and minorities in the officer corps should focus on recruitment rather than retention.

088 *United States. General Accounting Office.* **Women in the Military: Attrition and Retention.** Washington, DC: GPO, 1990. GAO/NSIAD-90-87-87BR. 145p. SuDocs GA1.13:NSIAD-90-87BR; OCLC 22621139.
Covers fiscal years 1980-1988, on attrition and retention rates for active duty men and women in each service, Found that while the basic pattern of attrition was essentially similar for both men and women, the overall attrition rate for enlisted women was 48.6% versus 44.1% for men. Primarily a collection of charts, tables, and statistics.

3

NURSES

Women have worked as nurses for the armed forces since the founding of the nation, when they were hired by George Washington to nurse disabled soldiers during the Revolutionary War. Their contributions during the Civil War have been well documented. Under the direction of Dorothea Dix, a corps of nurses was recruited and trained to serve as civilians with the Union Army. Despite their heroic efforts, the military did not recognize the essential role of the women nurses and they were disbanded after the war.

During the Spanish-American War, the Army was unable to recruit enough men to serve in the medical field and was forced to employ women. Headed by Dr. Anita Newcomb McGee, 1,500 civilian female nurses served between 1898-1901, both in the U.S. and overseas. Their contributions were rewarded in 1901, with the establishment of the Army Nurse Corps (ANC), followed in 1908 with the Navy Nurse Corps (NNC).

Both the Army and Navy Nurse Corps functioned as auxiliaries of their respective services. This meant that nurses had no official military rank, military benefits, or equal pay with men. While the number of nurses in each corps was small (400 in the ANC and 460 in the NNC at the beginning of World War I), they formed a nucleus of skilled military nurses which could be expanded in time of war.

World War I proved the wisdom of maintaining a military nursing corps. By the war's end, more than 10,000 nurses had served overseas, winning awards from the Distinguished Service Cross to foreign medals such as the French Croix de Guerre.

In World War II, the nurses again served bravely. Navy nurses worked on hospital ships at sea, the first flight nurses were trained (see **154-166**), nurses were captured as prisoners of war (see **203-214, 257-261**) and served closer to the front lines than ever before. In 1944, the government finally made the nurses full members of the military, granting them officer's commissions, equal pay, and retirement benefits. Despite the service of 59,000 Army nurses and 11,000 Navy nurses, nursing shortages were so critical that legislation was proposed to draft nurses. However, the end of the war in Europe relieved the shortage and a draft was not necessary. After the war, The Army-Navy Nurse Act, passed in 1947, established the nursing corps as a permanent staff corps of the two services. In 1949, the newly formed Air Force established the Air

Force Nurse Corps.

The next test of military nurses would be in Asia. During the Korean War, between 500-600 Army nurses served in the war zone. In the Vietnam War, between 5,000 and 6,000 nurses and medical specialists served in the combat area, working in field hospitals, aboard hospital ships and in mobile surgical units. The most recent wartime service of Army, Air Force and Navy nurses was during the Persian Gulf War in 1991 (see **103, 234**).

This chapter is arranged by service, Air Force Nurse Corps, Army Nurse Corps, and Navy Nurse Corps, and then chronologically by time period. Although there have been no official comprehensive histories published for any of the service's nursing corps, the official history of the Army Nurse Corps in World War I (see **125**) is available, as well as general histories about specific time periods for the other Corps.

GENERAL WORKS

089   *American Journal of Nursing*. 1901-present.
Excellent source of information about military nursing, especially during World War I and World War II. Includes letters from military nurses, photographs, lists awards received, assignments, promotions, statistics, etc. Essential for researchers of military nursing.

090   *Gurney, Cindy. "Military Nursing: 211 Years of Commitment to the American Soldier."* NSNA/Imprint 34(5): 36-41, February/March 1987.
Describes the role of military nurses from the Revolutionary War to Vietnam. Highlights significant events in the Army, Navy, and Air Force Nurse Corps. Photos.

091   *Kalisch, Philip A. and Margaret Scobey. "Female Nurses in American Wars: Helplessness Suspended for the Duration."* Armed Forces and Society 9(2): 215-244, Winter 1983.
Good summary of the role of female military nurses, from civilians serving during the Spanish American War, to military nursing in World Wars I and II, including nurse prisoners of war.

General Works - World War I

092   *Fitzgerald, Alice. "To Nurses Preparing for Active Duty."* American Journal of Nursing 18(3): 188-191, March 1918.
Advises nurses preparing to enter military service that they need to possess endurance and tact, as well as patience and the willingness to give up many personal comforts.

General Works - World War I - Rank for Nurses

093   *Greeley, Helen Hoy. "Rank for Nurses."* American Journal of Nursing 19(11): 840-853, November 1919.

Author was a member of the National Committee to Secure Rank for Nurses. Article advocates rank for nurses as well as women serving in prominent positions in the service, such as on the staff of the Surgeon General of the United States. An excellent detailed presentation of the problems caused by treating the women as inferior members of the service and proposed solutions.

094 *"Rank for Nurses: What Some Doctors Say about It."* *American Journal of Nursing* 20(4): 302-306, April 1920.
Contains excerpts from letters written by medical officers who served in World War I, as to the need for rank for nurses. All present positive views.

095 *"Some Quotations from the Hearings before the Subcommittee of the Committee on Military Affairs, United States Senate."* *American Journal of Nursing* 20(1): 30-38, January 1920.
Reprint of testimony from a Senate hearing regarding rank for military nurses. Not having rank caused problems for military nurses, especially with their authority over enlisted men. Nurses' testimony reveals difficulties with obtaining transportation, pay, even leave.

096 *The World War and the Army Nurse.* Washington, DC: National Committee to Secure Military Rank for Army Nurses, 1918. 48p. OCLC 19684212.
Discusses the need for rank for Army nurses. Nurses had authority above all noncommissioned officers, but below West Point cadets. However, their authority was not defined and they were not ranked as officers. Also discusses legislation to give nurses rank and the various arguments for and against doing so.

General Works - World War II

097 *"ANC and NNC on the Job."* *American Journal of Nursing* 44(11): 1056-1057, November 1944.
Two pages of photographs of members of the Army Nurse Corps and Navy Nurse Corps serving overseas.

098 *"Christmas, Christmas, Everywhere."* *American Journal of Nursing* 44(12): 1112-1115, December 1944.
Short stories from different locations (New Zealand, Panama, Africa) on how Army and Navy nurses spent Christmas. Photographs.

099 *Kalisch, Philip A. and Beatrice J. Kalisch. "The Women's Draft: An Analysis of the Controversy over the Nurses' Selective Service Bill of 1945." Nursing Research* 22(5): 402-413, September/October 1973.
An excellent, detailed discussion of how a shortage of military nurses during World War II caused a draft of nurses to be considered. Provides information about admission standards for nurses, views of professional associations, congressional actions, and questions raised by the

controversy over the nurse draft. Includes statistics regarding nurses on active duty between 1938 and 1945 and the strength of the Army Nurse Corps from 1939 to 1946.

100   *"Military Honors to Nurses."* American Journal of Nursing 45(10): 852-856, October 1945.
Extensive list of awards earned by military nurses during World War II.

101   *"The Nurses' Contribution to American Victory: Facts and Figures from Pearl Harbor to V-J Day."* American Journal of Nursing 45(9): 683-686, September 1945.
The source for facts and figures from Pearl Harbor to V-J Day on military nurses. Includes awards, citations, salaries, etc.

General Works - Vietnam

102   *Alkana, Linda Kelly.* *"Women Warriors, Women Healers: American Military Nurses in Vietnam."* The Valley Forge Journal 4(4): 352-361, 1989.
Describes the Vietnam nurse through oral histories. Most nurses who have discussed their experiences were from working class or lower middle class families where they were expected to work before marriage. Nursing was seen as an acceptable occupation. These nurses were critical of the Army for not letting them know what to expect in Vietnam.

General Works - Desert Shield/Desert Storm

103   *"Military Nurses Rally for Operation Desert Shield."* American Journal of Nursing 90(10): 7, 11, October 1990.
A brief article about nurses in the Army, Navy and Air Force being sent to Saudi Arabia during Desert Shield in 1990.

AIR FORCE NURSE CORPS

Archives and Manuscripts

104   *Albert F. Simpson Historical Research Center.* Office of Air Force History, Maxwell AFB, AL.
Collection includes reports about Air Force nurses, rosters, the nurse procurement program, and an oral history interview.

105   *Records of Headquarters, United States Air Force Air Staff.* Record Group 341, National Archives.
Contains administrative correspondence of the Air Force Nurse Corps, also personnel actions, reports, training, etc.

106 ***United States Air Force Office of Air Force Nurse History***. Bolling Air Force Base, Washington, DC.
Serves as a depository for photographs, records, correspondence and historical memorabilia of the Air Force Nurse Corps.

Air Force Nurse Corps - General Works

107 *Haritos, Dolores J.* **"The United States Air Force Nurse Corps Documents Its History."** *Journal of Nursing History* 1(1): 19-29, November 1985.
Author was the Nurse Corps Historian. Explores the role and commitment of military nurses and how these contributions are being documented. Discusses how the Air Force Nurse Corps is documenting it's history, by collecting photographs, records, correspondence, historical memorabilia and oral histories.

108 *Villareal, Roland.* **Work Role Satisfaction and Its Relationship to Retention of Air Force Nurse Corps Officers.** Thesis (M.S.)--Southern Illinois University, 1990. 72p. OCLC 23093220.
The author, a member of the Air Force Nurse Corps, questioned Air Force nurses during their initial active duty tour to identify which factors and/or motivators were perceived to influence their decision to stay in the Air Force. Of interest to recruiters.

Air Force Nurse Corps - World War II

For works about nurses who served with the Army Air Forces during World War II (before the establishment of the Air Force), see **Army Nurse Corps-World War II-Flight Nurse (154-166).**

Air Force Nurse Corps - Korean War

109 *Albert, Janice.* **"Air Evacuation from Korea--A Typical Flight."** *Military Surgeon* 112(4): 256-259, April 1953.
Describes a typical air evacuation flight experienced by an Air Force flight nurse to Korea to pick up wounded, including preparations, the evacuation flight, loading patients, and patient care in the air.

Air Force Nurse Corps - Vietnam War

110 *Marshall, Kathryn.* **In the Combat Zone: An Oral History of American Women in Vietnam, 1966-1975.** Boston, MA: Little, Brown & Company, 1987. 270p. OCLC 13859647; ISBN 0316547077.
Keith Walker did it first and better (see **233**). Marshall includes interviews of three Air Force nurses, six Army nurses, one WAC and ten civilian women. Although she interviews three of the same women as

Walker (Christie, Mishkel, and Adams), she doesn't acknowledge his book in her bibliography. Each interview includes a brief biography of the subject.

111 *Norman, Elizabeth M. Dempsey.* **Nurses in War: A Study of Female Military Nurses Who Served in Vietnam during the War Years, 1965-1973.** Thesis (Ph.D.)--New York University, 1986. 172p. OCLC 15125463.
Fifty women who served in Vietnam in the Army, Navy, and Air Force Nurse Corps were interviewed about their war experiences and the effects of these experiences on their lives. It was found that two main factors, branch of service and the specific years served in Vietnam influenced their experiences. Documents post-traumatic stress disorder in some of the nurses. Expanded into a published book (see **112**).

112 *Norman, Elizabeth M.* **Women at War: The Story of Fifty Military Nurses Who Served in Vietnam.** Philadelphia: University of Pennsylvania Press, 1990. 211p. OCLC 21332836; ISBN 0812282493.
Based on the author's dissertation (see **111**). Describes military nurse's experiences. Includes excerpts from interviews, where nurses recount their war service, homecomings and years after the war, including struggles with post-traumatic stress disorder.

113 *O'Neill, Jacquelyn S.* **An Exploration of the Process of Coping As Experienced by Nurses Who Served in the Vietnam War.** Thesis (Ph.D.)--University of Texas at Austin, 1990. 202p. OCLC 24401796.
Survey of twelve women who served in Vietnam, ten Army nurses and two Air Force nurses. Found they coped with the stress of their jobs in two different ways, using an engagement coping response or an avoidance coping response. The younger women tended to use the avoidance coping response. Includes many excerpts from the author's interviews.

ARMY NURSE CORPS

Archives and Manuscripts

114 *Nursing Archives, Special Collections.* Mugar Library, Boston University. Boston, MA.
Contains the personal papers, correspondence, photos, and biographical papers of Florence A. Blanchfield, Superintendent of the Army Nurse Corps (ANC) during World War II (see **153**). Also holds papers of other members of the ANC, including Frances Y. Slanger, the first American nurse killed in Europe during World War II (see **167**).

115 *Oral History Interviews.* U.S. Army Center of Military History. Washington, DC.
Owns a copy of an unpublished history of the Army Nurse Corps, by

Pauline Maxwell. Also holds over 300 interviews with nurses who served in World War I, World War II, the Korean War, Vietnam War, and Somalia.

116 ***Records of the Office of the Surgeon General (Army).*** Record Group 112, National Archives.
Many records concerning official correspondence, nurses' letters, training, assignments, awards, clothing, the historical files of the Army Nurse Corps (ANC) from 1900-1947, newspaper clippings and photographs.

117 ***World War I Survey: Army Nurse Corps. Records, 1918-1919.*** United States Army Military History Institute, Carlisle Barracks, PA.
Contains correspondence, questionnaires, scrapbooks and official records concerning the Army Nurse Corps during World War I.

Army Nurse Corps - General Works

118 *Byrne, Rosemary Adeline.* **Women, War and Nursing: The Army Nurse Corps, 1901-1952.** Thesis (M.A.)--Arizona State University, 1986. 288p. OCLC 15797604.
A brief narrative history of the Army Nurse Corps. Includes a chapter on the struggle for black nurses to enter the Corps and a discussion of the Draft Nurses Bill. The most interesting part is the appendix, which contains the transcripts of interviews with eight Army Nurse Crops veterans of World War II.

119 *Kalisch, Philip A.* **"How Army Nurses Became Officers."** *Nursing Research* 25(3): 164-177, May/June 1976.
An excellent, detailed analysis of the World War I experiences of Army nurses, dramatizing their need for rank and illustrates the struggle for legislation to provide rank for Army nurses. Includes information about the nurses' uniforms, status of nurses, and congressional actions (see **093-096**).

120 *Piemonte, Robert V. and Cindy Gurney, editors.* **Highlights in the History of the Army Nurse Corps.** Washington, DC: United States Army Center of Military History, 1987. 94p. SuDocs D114.2:N93/987; OCLC 16642253.
A chronology of the Army Nurse Corps which emphasizes significant legislature and other factors which have aided the Corps. Starts in June 1775 and ends in July 1980. Includes an appendix of Superintendents and Chiefs of the Army Nurse Corps and a list of memorials to Army nurses.

121 *Roberts, Mary M.* **The Army Nurse Corps, Yesterday and Today.** Washington, DC: United States Army Nurse Corps, 1955(?). 47p. OCLC 9596535.
An informational pamphlet, published by the Army Nurse Corps. Includes

the history of the Corps, up to 1945, as well as a description of career opportunities. Includes some photographs.

122 *Shields, Elizabeth A.* ***A History of the Army Nurse Corps (Female): 1901-1937.*** Thesis (Ed.D.)--Teacher's College, Columbia University, 1980. 232p. OCLC 14885269.
Traces the development of the Army Nurse Corps from the first use of professional nurses in the Spanish American War to 1937, when Major Julia Stimson resigned as the Superintendent of the Corps. The author makes heavy use of primary source documents, including the Army Nurse Corps records in the National Archives and the Historical Unit of the U.S. Army Medical Department. She also consulted the personal papers of Julia Stimson. Interesting and well written. Contains several appendices.

123 *Stimson, Julia Catherine.* ***History and Manual of the Army Nurse Corps.*** Carlisle Barracks, PA: Medical Field Service School, 1937. 115p. OCLC 5986315.
Gives Army Nurse Corps members a detailed history of the Corps (to 1937) and its regulations and answers general questions about the ANC. Lists the types of positions held by nurses, places where they were stationed, pay schedules, requirements for appointment, etc.

124 *United States. Army Nurse Corps.* ***Tradition and Destiny of the U.S. Army Nurse Corps.*** Washington, DC: n.p., 1949. 48p. OCLC 7649046.
An information booklet containing a very basic history of the Army Nurse Corps and information on career opportunities in the Corps.

Army Nurse Corps - World War I

125 *Crane, Arthur G. and Julia C. Stimson.* ***The Medical Department of the U.S. Army in the World War. Volume XIII.*** Washington, DC: GPO, 1927. 998p. SuDocs W44.19:13; OCLC 3879785.
Part 2 of this volume, "The Army Nurse Corps" is the official history of Army nurses in World War I, written by Julia Stimson, the Superintendent of the Corps. Discusses training, assignments, pay, uniforms, etc. Gives the numbers of nurses serving overseas and the locations of hospitals, as well as casualty lists for 1917-1919 by month, of the nurses serving with the American Expeditionary Forces.

126 *Foster, Dorothy.* ***"Nurses, Join Now!"*** *American Journal of Nursing* 18(8): 610-612, August 1918.
An appeal for women to join the Army Nurse Corps and serve overseas. The author writes of her service as an Army nurse with the Harvard Hospital Unit in France and states any nurse who does not serve will regret it in years to come.

127 *Johnson, Katherine Burger.* **Called to Serve: American Nurses Go to War, 1914-1918.** Thesis (M.A.)--University of Louisville, 1993. 150p. Discusses the role of the over 10,000 American women who served overseas as nurses and nurse's aides during World War I through their letters, diaries, memoirs, unit histories, and official reports.

128 *Stimson, Julia C.* **"Nurses Overseas."** *American Journal of Nursing* 20(1): 24-38, 1920.
Author was the Superintendent of the Army Nurse Corps (see **141**). She had extensive experience serving overseas and writes of the difficulties faced by nurses overseas. These included problems with transportation, nurses working at jobs for which they were not suited, and personality clashes between nurses and corpsmen. Also writes of her support of rank for nurses (see **093-096**).

129 *Ziegler, Susan L.* **In Uncle Sam's Service: American Women Workers with the American Expeditionary Force, 1917-1919.** Thesis (Ph.D.)--New York University, 1991. 366p.
Examines why the U.S. government engaged women for war work overseas and why so many women volunteered. Discusses Army nurses, analyzing their service. Estimates 10,000 Army nurses served overseas.

Army Nurse Corps - World War I - Personal Narratives

130 *Allison, Grace E.* **"Some Experiences in Active Service--France. Part I."** *American Journal of Nursing* 19(4): 268-272, April 1919.
Written by the chief nurse of Army Base Hospital 4, mobilized in April 1917. The hospital was sent overseas on the Cunard Liner, *Ordunna*, landing in England. After spending five days in London, where hospital personnel attended a reception at Buckingham Palace, the unit was sent to France. Continued by **131-133**.

131 *Allison, Grace E.* **"Some Experiences in Active Service--France. Part II."** *American Journal of Nursing* 19(5): 354-359, May 1919.
Continues **130**. Good description of the Base Hospital, nurse's quarters, problems with supplies (for example, had a severe shortage of fuel), patient treatment, etc. See **132-133**.

132 *Allison, Grace E.* **"Some Experiences in Active Service--France. Part III."** *American Journal of Nursing* 19(6): 430-434, June 1919.
Continues **131**. In Part III, the author discusses how the patient was treated, starting with the First Aid Dressing Stations, just back of the front, then was sent by ambulance to the nearest emergency hospital, called Casualty Clearing Stations. These were located four to ten miles from the front. From there, patients were transferred to Base hospitals by railroad, called ambulance trains. Interesting description of treating patients who had been gassed. See **130-131, 133**.

133   *Allison, Grace E.* **"Some Experiences in Active Service--France. Part IV."** *American Journal of Nursing* 19(7): 513-517, July 1919.
Part four of a four part article (see **130-132**). Part four describes air raid attacks and the establishment of a mobile unit sent to serve nearer the front which included twenty nurses. Allison also provides insight as to why the nurses needed rank, as hospital orderlies often would not obey the nurses.

134   *Anonymous.* **"Mademoiselle Miss"; Letters from an American Girl Serving with the Rank of Lieutenant in a French Army Hospital at the Front.** Boston: W.A. Butterfield, 1916. 102p. OCLC 1192388.
Author was the daughter of an ex-Medical Director of the U.S. Navy. She was in France at the outbreak of World War I, and received a nurse's diploma in the French Red Cross. She was given the rank of lieutenant and served in a French army hospital near the trenches of the Marne in September 1915. Book is a compilation of the letters she wrote while serving on an operating ward. Has a few photographs.

135   *Bigelow, Glenna Lindsley.* **"Ellis Island from Three Points of View. Part III."** *American Journal of Nursing* 18(8): 616-623, August 1918.
Last of a three part article (see **138-139**). Describes living in a dormitory, being fitted in boots and uniforms, shopping for supplies to take overseas, and receiving supplies. Photographs of nurses in uniform.

136   *Coleman, Laura E.* **"Experiences of the Justice Hospital Group, Base Hospital 51."** *American Journal of Nursing* 19(12): 931-939, December 1919.
Author was the chief nurse of Base Hospital 51, an Army hospital assigned to France in September 1918. Interesting and detailed descriptions of service overseas.

137   *Evert, Gertrude S.* **My 28 Years As an Army Nurse.** New York: Exposition Press, 1959. 84p. OCLC 3096233.
The author, along with her sister, joined the Army Nurse Corps near the end of World War I. Describes her travels and assignments in the United States and overseas. During World War II, she was stationed in Massachusetts, where she retired in 1945. Note that it took her twenty years to be promoted from second to first lieutenant. Brief, but contains many small details about Army life.

138   *Graham, Flora A.* **"Ellis Island from Three Points of View. Part I."** *American Journal of Nursing* 18(8): 613-614, August 1918.
A brief account of waiting at Ellis Island to sail for Europe by an Army nurse assigned to Base Hospital 33 (see **135, 139**).

139   *Haviland, Jean.* **"Ellis Island from Three Points of View. Part II."** *American Journal of Nursing* 18(8): 614-615, August 1918.
Part II of a three part article about nurses waiting at Ellis Island to sail for Europe. Reports her reception at arrival and outfitting in Army uniform (see **135, 138**).

140   *McMahon, Katherine B.* **"A War Nurse in the Fighting Fields of Europe."** *American Journal of Nursing* 18(8): 603-610, August 1918. Written by an Army nurse member of the Harvard Unit, which sailed from New York in June 1915 to Europe and was stationed in France. The hospital treated soldiers from the western front and many of the injuries are described, from chemical casualties to amputees. Photographs.

141   *Stimson, Julia Catherine.* **Finding Themselves: The Letters of an American Army Chief Nurse in a British Hospital in France.** New York: MacMillan Company, 1927. 231p. OCLC 1309780. Stimson was the Superintendent of the Army Nurse Corps from 1919-1937 (see **128**). Collection of letters she wrote to her family while serving as a nurse in France during World War I. Gives interesting details of nursing during the war as well as of serving overseas. The author also wrote the official history of the ANC during World War I (see **125**).

142   *Williamson, Mayme E.* **"Inside a Camp Window."** *American Journal of Nursing* 18(8): 643-648, August 1918. Author was an Army nurse from California who thought she was being sent to France, but ended up assigned to the base hospital at Camp Meade, MD. Briefly talks about her nursing duties and asks other nurses to join the service. Photographs of nurses.

Army Nurse Corps - World War II

143   **"Army Nurses on the Fighting Fronts."** *American Journal of Nursing* 43(12): 1078-1079, December 1943. A two page collection of photographs of Army nurses serving overseas, including nurses in India, Australia, New Guinea, and working in Italy.

144   **"Army Nursing: Negro Nurses."** *American Journal of Nursing* 42(12): 1386-1387, December 1942. Two pages of photographs of black nurses in the Army Nurse Corps. The nurses are identified by name and duty station.

145   *Aynes, Edith A.* **"The Hospital Ship Acadia."** *American Journal of Nursing* 44(2): 98-100, February 1944. Describes nursing patients on a ship. *Acadia* was the first U.S. Army hospital ship to be operated under the Hague Convention. Photographs of unloading patients and nurses.

146   *Bellafaire, Judith A.* **The Army Nurse Corps: A Commemoration of World War II Service.** Washington, DC: United States Army Center of Military History, 1993(?). 32p. SuDocs D114.2:N93/2. A brochure describing the highlights of the Army Nurse Corps in World War II. Discusses Army Nurse Corps operations in the Pacific, Europe, and the China-Burma-India Theater; recruitment and training; black nurses, flight nurses, and nurse prisoners of war. Good summary of Army nurses' World War II service. Some photographs.

147 *Flikke, Julia (Otteson).* **Nurses in Action**. Philadelphia: J.B. Lippincott Company, 1943. 239p. OCLC 1170964.
Written by the Superintendent of the Army Nurse Corps for the purpose of providing information on the Corps and to try and recruit nurses. Provides a history of the Corps, information on becoming an Army nurse, etc. Includes excerpts from letters written by Army nurses stationed all over the world during World War II.

148 *Frid, Rhoda E.* **"Training on Bivouac."** *American Journal of Nursing* 43(8): 734-736, August 1943.
First Lieutenant Frid describes how her unit, the 27th Evacuation Hospital, prepared for overseas service. They trained for six months, running a 750 bed hospital in tents. Includes photographs.

149 **"More Awards to Army Nurses."** *American Journal of Nursing* 45(3): 238-239, March 1945.
List of awards to Army Nurse Corps members during World War II.

150 **"Six Army Nurses Lost on the Comfort."** *American Journal of Nursing* 45(7): 576, July 1945.
Lists names of six Army nurses killed on the United States Army Hospital Ship *Comfort* (see **151**). Also provides casualty totals for Army nurses.

151 *Thuma, Marion E.* **"'Anchors Aweigh,' ANC."** *American Journal of Nursing* 44(9): 830-831, September 1944.
Story of the USS *Comfort*, an Army hospital ship, and the thirty-seven Army nurses assigned to her. Six Army nurses were later killed while serving on the *Comfort* (see **150**).

Army Nurse Corps - World War II - General - Personal Narratives

152 *Aynes, Edith A.* **From Nightingale to Eagle: An Army Nurse's History.** Englewood Cliffs, NJ: Prentice-Hall, 1973. 318p. OCLC 532221; ISBN 0133322629.
The author was an active duty nurse in the Army Nurse Corps before, during, and after World War II. Served primarily as a nurse-anesthesiologist. An interesting and detailed book about both her service and the activities of the ANC. Includes some photographs and is indexed. Widely cited.

153 *Bombard, Charles F., Wynona M. Bice-Stephens and Karen L. Ferguson.* **"The Soldier's Nurse: Colonel Florence A. Blanchfield."** *Minerva* 6(4): 43-49, Winter 1988.
A short biography of Florence Blanchfield, who was Chief of the Army Nurse Corps from 1943-1947 (see **114**).

Army Nurse Corps - World War II - Flight Nurses

154 *"Army Nurse Wins Air Medal."* American Journal of Nursing 43(5): 443-444, May 1943.
On 26 March 1943, the first Air Medal awarded to a woman was given to Lieutenant Elsie S. Ott, an Air Evacuation Nurse of the First Troop Carrier Command (see **158**).

155 *Barger, Judith.* **Coping with War: An Oral History of United States Army Flight Nurses Who Flew with the Army Air Forces in World War II.** Thesis (Ph.D.)--University of Texas at Austin, 1986. 223p. OCLC 23147202.
The author conducted a study to determine how women assigned as flight nurses with the Army Air Forces during World War II coped with situations they perceived as taxing or exceeding their resources. Interviewed twenty-five flight nurses and includes many excerpts from these interviews. Found that the women perceived their wartime service as a challenge and made the best of the stressful war situation. Extensive references. Well done.

156 *Barger, Judith.* **"Origin of Flight Nursing in the United States Army Air Forces."** Aviation, Space & Environmental Medicine 50(11): 1176-1178, November 1979.
Brief article tracing the origin of flight nursing in the Army Air Force from 1937 to 1942.

157 *Barger, Judith.* **"Rivalry for the Sky: A Prelude to the Development of the Flight Nurse Program in the US Army Air Forces."** Aviation, Space & Environmental Medicine 56(1): 73-78, January 1985.
History of the rivalry between the Aerial Nurse Corps of America and the American Red Cross concerning flight nursing from 1937 to 1942, before the start of the flight nurse program in the Army Air Forces.

158 *Barger, Judith.* **"U.S. Army Air Forces Flight Nurses: Training and Pioneer Flight."** Aviation, Space & Environmental Medicine 51(4): 414-416, April 1980.
Short history of the training of the first Army flight nurses, at Bowman Field, KY. Also tells the story of Lieutenant Elsie S. Ott, who was the first Army nurse to participate in an air evacuation flight (see **154**).

159 *Berendsen, Dorothy M.* **The Way It Was: An Air Force Nurse's Story.** New York: Carlton Press, 1988. 80p. OCLC 19997978; ISBN 0806231998.
A short, but worthwhile account of the author's service as a flight nurse during World War II with the Army Air Force and after the war, as a nurse in the newly formed Air Force. During the war she worked as a chief nurse in England and France, evacuating patients from field hospitals to hospitals in the rear.

160   *Link, May Mills and Hubert A. Coleman.* **Medical Support of the Army Air Forces in World War II.** Washington, DC: GPO, 1955. 1027p. OCLC 25267093.
Chapter V, Air Evacuation Mission, discusses the flight nurse. Gives a short history of flight nursing and describes flight nurse training.

161   *Rice, Dorothy M.* **"Flight to Kirawagi."** *American Journal of Nursing* 45(1): 10-11, January 1945.
The author, a flight nurse assigned to New Guinea, tells the story of an air evacuation mission from Nadzab to Kirawagi, a native village. There they picked up an Air Corps member who had survived a plane crash and was being cared for by local natives.

162   *Robertson, Patsy Hensley.* **Flight Nurses: Pioneers in Aviation-Military Medicine, 1942-1945.** Thesis (M.A.)--Auburn University, 1986. 138p. OCLC 15477507.
A history of the development of flight nursing. Describes the training and life of the flight nurse. Includes stories of the "Balkan Nurses" who were on a flight which crashed in Albania during World War II and also Reba Whittle, captured by the Germans (see **203, 209**).

163   *Skinner, Robert E.* **"The U.S. Flight Nurse: A Supplementary Bibliography."** *Aviation, Space & Environmental Medicine* 54(8): 735-737, August 1983.
Supplements **164**, adding fifty more entries.

164   *Skinner, Robert E.* **"The U.S. Flight Nurse: An Annotated Historical Bibliography."** *Aviation, Space & Environmental Medicine* 52(11): 707-712, November 1981.
Summary of the origin of flight nursing, with an annotated bibliography. Brief annotations for 136 book and journal article entries (see **163**).

165   *Stroup, Leora B.* **"Aero-Medical Nursing and Therapeutics."** *American Journal of Nursing* 44(6): 575-577, June 1944.
Presents requirements for becoming a flight nurse. Includes detailed information on aircraft and the effects of altitude on injuries.

166   *White, Ruth Y.* **"Army Nurses - In the Air."** *American Journal of Nursing* 43(4): 342-344, April 1943.
Details instruction for the first class of air evacuation nurses at Bowman Field, KY. Describes their duties, uniforms, physical requirements, etc.

Army Nurse Corps - World War II - European Theater

167   **"An Army Nurse Writes an Editorial."** *American Journal of Nursing* 45(1): 1, January 1945.
Reprint of a widely quoted letter to *Stars and Stripes* on 21 October 1944 by Army Nurse Corps Second Lieutenant Frances Slanger. She was killed by a German shell the same day, becoming the first American

nurse to die in action in the European Theater. Slanger's papers are held in the Nursing Archive, Boston University (see **114**).

168 *Blanchfield, Florence A.* **"Report from the ETO and the MTO."** *American Journal of Nursing* 45(6): 427-430, June 1945.
Colonel Blanchfield was the Superintendent of the Army Nurse Corps (see **153**). She writes of conditions facing nurses in the European Theater and Mediterranean Theater and describes the types of hospitals where nurses were assigned.

169 *Blythe, LeGette.* **38th EVAC: The Story of the Men and Women Who Served in World War II with the 38th Evacuation Hospital in North Africa and Italy.** Charlotte, NC: Heritage Printers, 1966. 261p. OCLC 3502512.
A yearbook type history of the 38th Evac Hospital. Interesting for the photographs of life in an overseas Army hospital.

170 *Clayton, Frederick.* **"An Evacuation Unit Serves under Fire."** *American Journal of Nursing* 44(5): 453-455, May 1944.
Report on an Evacuation Unit which landed at Anzio Beach on D-day + 3. The nurses arrived on a convoy attacked fourteen times by dive bombers.

171 *Clayton, Frederick.* **"Front-Line Surgical Nurses."** *American Journal of Nursing* 44(3): 234-235, March 1944.
Story of Army surgical nurses working in advanced field hospitals near the front in Italy. Includes two photographs of nurses.

172 *Covi, Ruth Eleanor.* **"Surgery in a Station Hospital Overseas."** *American Journal of Nursing* 44(12): 1141-1143, December 1944.
Describes the ingenious equipment used by the nurses at the author's hospital in Africa.

173 *Cree, Edna M.* **"Health of the Army Nurse Corps in the ETO."** *American Journal of Nursing* 45(11): 915-916, November 1945.
Provides hospital admission rates for Army Nurse Corps and WACs for the European Theater of Operations (ETO). Notes a total of twenty-eight deaths occurred, one due to direct enemy action.

174 **"D-Day Found Army Nurses Prepared."** *American Journal of Nursing* 44(8): 728, August 1944.
Brief account of how Army nurses prepared for D-Day. They had special training in dealing with injuries, learned how to care for equipment under field conditions, took intense physical training, etc.

175 *Humphrey, Yvonne E.* **"On Shipboard with German Prisoners."** *American Journal of Nursing* 43(9): 821-822, September 1943.
The author, a second lieutenant in the Army Nurse Corps, was the only woman aboard a ship which brought back American wounded and German prisoners from North Africa. Gives her impressions of German officers and enlisted men.

176 *Jose, Mary.* **"Hi, Angels."** *American Journal of Nursing* 45(4): 267-270, April 1945.
Article written by a war correspondent about the nurses and the soldiers they treated in the 103rd Evacuation Hospital in Bastogne, France.

177 *Moline, Anna Lisa.* **"U.S. Army Nurses in Russia."** *American Journal of Nursing* 45(11): 904-906, November 1945.
Story of the nurses assigned to a hospital unit in Russia. Good description of bombing of the hospital. Photographs.

178 *Paxton, Vincoe M.* **"ANC Reinforcements Land in France."** *American Journal of Nursing* 45(1): 13-16, January 1945.
The story of how a group of Army nurses stationed in England were sent to forward hospitals in France shortly after D-Day. Interesting descriptions of the French countryside after the invasion.

179 *White, Ruth Y.* **"At Anzio Beachead."** *American Journal of Nursing* 44(4): 370-371, April 1944.
Brief article about landing at Anzio. Includes the names of Army nurses killed as a result of enemy action at Anzio.

Army Nurse Corps - World War II - European Theater - Personal Narratives

180 *Archard, Theresa.* **G.I. Nightingale: The Story of an American Army Nurse.** New York: W.W. Norton & Company, Inc., 1945. 187p. OCLC 396392.
The author joined the Army Nurse Corps in 1941. She arrived in North Africa on D Day, and served as a chief nurse in various mobile surgical hospitals, some very near the front. In July 1943, she was sent to Sicily, then was medically evacuated back to the States with malaria. A colleague of Ruth Haskell (see **183**), she later served at Ft. McCoy, Wisconsin.

181 *Buchanan, Margaret S.* **Reminiscing: An Account of the 300th Army General Hospital in WWII.** Dickson, TN: M.S. Buchanan, 1988. 174p. OCLC 20391237; ISBN 18732065.
Author served as an operating room nurse in the 30th Army General Hospital. She joined the Army Nurse Corps in September 1942, and was sent with her unit to Bizerte, Tunisia, then to Italy. Writes in detail about patient care, service life, daily life, and travel. Includes references and photographs. One of the better accounts.

182 *Franklin, Ann.* **"An Army Nurse at Dachau."** *American Journal of Nursing* 45(11): 901-903, November 1945.
Author was assigned to the 116th Evac Hospital at Dachau, where she nursed political prisoners liberated from a concentration camp. Describes in detail the horror of finding dead bodies stacked like wood on the floor and in freight cars.

183 *Haskell, Ruth G.* **Helmets and Lipstick.** New York: G.P. Putnam's Sons, 1944. 207p. OCLC 1727489.
The author was divorced with a ten year old son, whom she left with her parents when she was deployed to North Africa. She served with various medical units until she injured her back and was evacuated back to the States. Worth reading for the description of crossing the Atlantic in a convoy to England and then to North Africa, where her unit landed on the beach under hostile fire. No dates are given and there is no mention of how long the author spent in the service. The author was a colleague of Theresa Archard (see **180**).

184 *Hovis, Gretchen L.* **"The 50th General Hospital: A Memoir of World War II."** *Minerva* 7(3): 47-61, Fall 1994.
Author was a physical therapist who served in the 50th General Hospital during World War II. Arrived in England in January 1944, and later landed on Utah Beach on 17 July 1944, then set up the hospital in France. Interesting descriptions of training and service in Europe.

185 *Kielar, Eugenia M.* **Thank You, Uncle Sam: Letters of a World War II Army Nurse from North Africa and Italy.** Bryn Mawr, PA: Dorrance, 1987. 220p. OCLC 17638685; ISBN 0805930825.
Another collection of letters written by an Army nurse who served in North Africa and Italy. Spends a lot of time describing her social life and problems with men. Has some good descriptions of what it was like serving as a nurse overseas.

186 *Lutz, Alma, editor.* **With Love, Jane: Letters from American Women on the War Fronts.** New York: John Day Company, 1945. 199p. OCLC 3684001.
A collection of heavily edited letters from WACs and Army nurses, as well as a few Red Cross workers and civilians, who served overseas in World War II. The writers are briefly identified with short biographies.

187 *Paxton, Vincoe M.* **"With Field Hospital Nurses in Germany."** *American Journal of Nursing* 45(2): 131-133, February 1945.
The author's story of her experiences as an Army nurse in a field hospital in Germany. The hospital was moved into Germany immediately behind the first combat troops which entered the country. Good depiction of the exhausting work under difficult conditions.

188 *Peto, Marjorie.* **Women Were Not Expected: An Informal Story of the Nurses of the 2nd General Hospital in the ETO.** West Englewood, NJ: The Author, 1947. 159p. OCLC 2024251.
The author was an Army nurse who was sent to Europe in June 1942 as part of one of the first medical units to arrive from the U.S. She served in England until July 1944, when her unit moved to France. Includes interesting details of Army life and the typical problems encountered when serving overseas; poor uniforms, problems with housing, etc. Also includes a list of women who served with the 2nd General Hospital.

189   *Sforza, Eula Awbrey.* **A Nurse Remembers.** Wheaton, IL: E.A. Sforza, 1991. 233p. OCLC 25054051.
Author joined the ANC in 1942 and was sent overseas with the 12th Field Hospital in October 1943. Eventually served in England, France, Germany, and Belgium. Good descriptions of wartime nursing under hazardous conditions. After marriage, she became pregnant and was sent back to the U.S. Includes a list of 12th Field Hospital personnel, copies of orders and various monthly reports. Many large photographs.

190   *Tayloe, Roberta Love.* **Combat Nurse: A Journal of World War II.** Santa Barbara, CA: Fithian Press, 1988. 110p. OCLC 16950564; ISBN 0936784482.
The author joined the Army Nurse Corps in April 1942 and was sent overseas with the Roosevelt Hospital Unit (9th Evac) from New York City In September 1942. The unit landed in North Africa, setting up near Oran. In September 1943, the unit moved to Italy. Not a lot of details about military life, the book contains more information about the author's social life and travel.

191   *Wandrey, June.* **Bedpan Commando: The Story of a Combat Nurse during World War II.** Second edition. Elmore, OH: Elmore Publishing Company, 1991. 234p. OCLC 28102918; ISBN 0962555509.
Author sent overseas to a field hospital in March 1943. Served in Oran, Sicily, Italy, France and in Germany, where she worked with prisoners in a displaced persons camp. Primarily a collection of letters and diary entries, not very detailed. Photographs.

Army Nurse Corps - World War II - Pacific and Asian Theaters

192   *"Army Nurses at Leyte."* *American Journal of Nursing* 45(1): 44, January 1945.
Brief account of the first contingent of Army nurses to return to the Philippines since the fall of Corregidor. They arrived at Leyte shortly after the initial landing by U.S. forces when the Japanese were conducting air raids both day and night.

193   *Bianchi, Linda Noreen.* **United States Army Nurses in the China-Burma-India Theater of World War II, 1942-1945.** Thesis (Ph.D.)-- University of Illinois at Chicago, Health Sciences Center, 1990. 325p. OCLC 23744805.
The author's mother was an Army nurse who served in the China-Burma-India Theater during World War II. Many primary sources are used, including archival materials, letters, diaries, and interviews with twenty-five theater nurses. Discusses nurse's jobs, their daily lives, administration, socialization, etc.

194   *Gress, Agnes D.* **"The 14th Evac on the Ledo Road."** *American Journal of Nursing* 45(9): 704-706, September 1945.
Author served as a lieutenant with the 14th Evacuation Hospital in India.

Describes the hospital where hundreds of Chinese battle casualties were treated. Worked under poor conditions with scarce fresh food and inadequate equipment.

195 *Hohf, Josephine.* **"Somewhere in Australia."** *American Journal of Nursing* 45(1): 42-43, January 1945.
The author describes recreational facilities in Australia where she served for two years as an Army nurse before her unit was sent to New Guinea. Includes several photographs of nurses at play.

196 *Jose, Mary.* **"Army Nurses Return from the Pacific."** *American Journal of Nursing* 45(10): 810, October 1945.
Describes the first contingent of Army nurses returning to the U.S., most veterans of more than three years of nursing in the Pacific.

197 *Parker, T.C.* **"Thirteen Women in a Submarine."** *Proceedings: U.S. Naval Institute* 76(7): 717-721, July 1950.
The author served on the USS *Spearfish*, the submarine which evacuated eleven Army nurses, one Navy nurse and one civilian woman from Corregidor on 3 May 1942 (see **199, 200, 202**). Good account of life on a submarine.

Army Nurse Corps - World War II - Pacific and Asian Theaters - Personal Narratives

198 *Hardison, Irene.* **A Nightingale in the Jungle.** Philadelphia: Dorrance and Company, 1954. 133p. OCLC 3178135.
Hardison was a nurse at Cedars of Lebanon Hospital in Hollywood, CA at the start of World War II. Joined the ANC and served in the China-Burma-India Theater from 1943 until March 1945, primarily as a nurse anesthesiologist. The book cover states that the book is "both a factual and fictional account." The author concentrates more on describing her social activities than nursing, but the book is still useful for the descriptions of life in the jungle during the war.

199 *Jopling, Lucy Wilson.* **Warrior in White.** San Antonio, TX: Watercress Press, 1990. 133p. OCLC 25118439; ISBN 0934955182.
Author was an Army nurse serving in the Philippines in October 1941, when the Japanese invaded. After the invasion, she worked in the Malita Tunnel until she was evacuated by submarine to Australia on 3 May 1942 (see **197, 200, 202**). Later became a flight nurse and was assigned to New Hebrides and Guadalcanal. Married a former POW after the war. Includes many photographs and lists nurses who served in Bataan and Corregidor.

200 *McKay, Hortense E.* **Jungle Angel: Bataan Remembered.** Brainerd, MN: Bang Printing Company, 1988. 104p. OCLC 19072302; ISBN 0961789417.
An account of the service of Hortense McKay, an Army nurse, written

by a friend.   Was stationed in Manila when it was bombed by the Japanese on 8 December 1941.   Served in the Malita Tunnel Hospital on Corregidor, until she was evacuated by submarine, the USS *Spearfish*, to Australia (see **197, 199, 202**).   Excellent descriptions of the terrible living conditions on Bataan.   Photographs.

201   *Ratledge, Abbie C.*   **Angels in Khaki.**   San Antonio, TX: Naylor Company, 1975.   182p.   OCLC 1144720; ISBN 0811105547.
The author served with the Army Nurse Corps in the South Pacific from March 1944 until the end of the war.   She was assigned to New Guinea and was later sent to Biak and the Philippines.   Valuable for the "unromantic" view presented of service in the South Pacific.

202   *Redmond, Juanita.* **I Served on Bataan.** Philadelphia: Lippincott, 1943. 167p.   OCLC 1655031.
Redmond was serving as an Army Nurse in the Philippines at the outbreak of World War II.   She and a number of other nurses, as well as doctors and corpsmen, were ordered to Bataan, and then to Corregidor after the fall of Bataan.   When Corregidor was invaded, she escaped with several other nurses by submarine to Australia and then to the United States (see **197, 199, 200**).   The nurses, doctors, and corpsmen left behind were taken prisoner by the Japanese and were still in captivity when this book was written.   Excellent descriptions of wartime nursing. Widely cited.

Army Nurse Corps - World War II - Prisoners of War

For other materials on prisoners of war, see ***257-261, 792-794****.*

203   **"Army and Navy Nurses Tell Us."** *American Journal of Nursing* 45(4): 318, April 1945.
A short notice that Second Lieutenant Reba Z. Whittle, the first Army nurse to be taken prisoner in the European Theater when her plane was shot down while she worked as a flight nurse, was released after four months in captivity (see **162, 209**).

204   **"Army Nurses Released from Manila Prison Camp."** *American Journal of Nursing* 45(3): 238, March 1945.
A list of sixty-six Army nurses released from San Tomas Prison Camp on 4 February 1945.

205   *Clarke, Alice R.*   **"An Army Nurse Returns to the Philippines."** *American Journal of Nursing* 45(3): 77-78, March 1945.
Brief account of Lieutenant Mabel Robertson Mear's attempt to escape from Mindanao with her British husband, and her capture by a Japanese patrol. They later escaped, and Lieutenant Mear rejoined the Army Nurse Corps.

206   *Clarke, Alice R.* **"Thirty-Seven Months As Prisoners-of-War."** *American Journal of Nursing* 45(5): 342-345, May 1945.
Lengthy story of the sixty-six Army nurses interned in the Philippines, describing their capture and life in prison camp. The nurses had been serving in various army hospitals in the Philippines when the Japanese invaded. They were transferred to Bataan in December 1941, and later to Corregidor. Includes several photographs of the nurses.

207   *Davis, Dorothy.* **"I Nursed at Santo Tomas, Manila."** *American Journal of Nursing* 44(1): 29-30, January 1944.
Author was a civilian nurse working for the Army Nurse Corps in the Sternberg General Hospital in Manila. She applied to join the Army Nurse Corps shortly before the fall of Manila, and was then interned with military nurses and other civilians in Santo Tomas. She describes nursing in the camp and provides the first information available on the nurses who had been left on Corregidor. She was repatriated with about sixty civilian nurses and 1,500 American and Canadian citizens from internment camps in China and Manila, returning to the U.S. on the *Grisholm.*

208   *Frank, Mary E.V.* **"Army and Navy Nurses Held As Prisoners of War during World War II."** *Minerva* 6(2): 82-88, Summer 1988.
In 1941, the Army and Navy Nurse Corps had 105 nurses assigned to the Philippines and Guam. A short, but interesting account of the nurses who were taken prisoner by the Japanese.

209   *Frank, Mary E.V.* **The Forgotten POW: Second Lieutenant Reba Z. Whittle, AN.** Carlisle Barracks, PA: United States Army War College, 1990. 42p. OCLC 22250306.
Second Lieutenant Reba Whittle was captured by the Germans when the flight on which she was serving as the flight nurse was shot down on 27 September 1944. She became the only American nurse captured by the Germans. During her captivity she kept a diary, on which this paper is based. She was repatriated in January 1945 (see **162, 203**).

210   **"The Heroic Nurses of Bataan and Corregidor."** *American Journal of Nursing* 42(8): 896-898, August 1942.
Describes awards ceremonies for fifteen Army nurses who had served at Bataan and Corregidor and had successfully escaped before capture by the Japanese. Lists names of the nurses honored and includes a photograph of an awards ceremony.

211   *Kalisch, Philip A. and Beatrice J. Kalisch.* **"Nurses under Fire: The World War II Experience of Nurses on Bataan and Corregidor."** *Nursing Research* 25(6): 406-429, November/December 1976.
An excellent, detailed account of what happened to the more than 100 Army and Navy nurses assigned to units in the Philippines in December, 1941. Many excerpts from nurses' accounts, maps, photographs, etc. are included. Discusses their work before their capture, life in the camps, and their liberation.

212   *Manning, Michele.* **Angels of Mercy and Life Amid Scenes of Conflict and Death: The Combat Experience and Imprisonment of American Military Nurses in the Philippines, 1941-1945.** Quantico, VA: Marine Corps Command and Staff College, 1985. 90p. OCLC 16379002.
The author, a major in the Marine Corps, presents an excellent account of Army and Navy Nurses who were imprisoned in the Philippines during World War II. A good source for information about servicewomen who were held as prisoners of war and internees.

213   *Norman, Elizabeth M. and Sharon Eifried.* **"How Did They All Survive? An Analysis of the American Nurses' Experiences in Japanese Prisoner-of-War Camps."** *Nursing History Review* 3: 105-127, 1995.
Story of the military nurses stationed in the Philippines who became Japanese prisoners of war in 1942. Describes how the Army and Navy nurses lived, the organization of the camps, the strains of life in confinement, problems with obtaining food and supplies, and their return home. Interesting and well written.

214   *Williams, Denny.* **To the Angels.** Presidio of San Francisco, CA: Denson Press, 1985. 225p. OCLC 12314084; ISBN 0961418818.
The author was a former Army nurse living in Manila with her civilian husband when the Japanese invaded the Philippines. When her husband joined the Army, she went to work at Sternberg Hospital, a military facility. She later fled to Bataan and then Corregidor, where she was captured along with other personnel and was interned at a prison camp at the University of Santo Thomas. At some point she rejoined the Army Nurse Corps, although when this happened isn't made clear. In the prison camp she served with other military nurses until the camp was liberated in September 1944. Excellent details of the Philippines and life in the camp.

Army Nurse Corps - World War II - Uniforms

215   *Burns, Robert W.* **History and Development of the Field Jacket Wool OD; and, Nurses and WAC Uniforms in the European Theater.** Maryland (?): n.p., 1945. 32p. OCLC 27117238.
A two part history of uniform development. Part two, titled "History of Nurses and WAC Uniforms in the European Theater, 1942-1945" describes problems with the uniforms. These included incorrect fit, wrong fabric, distribution problems, and scarcity of small sizes.

216   **"A New Wardrobe for the ANC."** *American Journal of Nursing* 43(3): 240-241, March 1943.
Descriptions and many photographs of various uniforms for the Army Nurse Corps.

217   *Petersen, George A., compiler.* **American Women at War in World War II, Volume I: Clothing, Insignia, and Equipment of the US Army WACs and Nurses, American Red Cross, USO, AWVS, Civil Defense and**

Related Wartime Womans Organizations. Springfield, VA: George A. Petersen, 1985. 29p. OCLC 13305946.
A reprint of the Army Service Forces Quartermaster Supply Catalog 3-2, *List of Items for Troop Issue: Wacs' and Nurses' Clothing and Equipment* (October 1943 and May 1946), Army Regulations 600-36 and 600-37, covering the prescribed service uniforms for women, and the book *American Women in Uniform* by Mary Steele Ross (see **064**). Has many photographs and descriptions of the components of uniforms as well as equipment.

218   *Risch, Erna.* **A Wardrobe for the Women of the Army.** Washington, DC: Historical Section, General Administrative Services Division, Office of the Quartermaster General, 1945. 156p. SuDocs W77.36:12; OCLC 14957608.
Traces the development of uniforms and their manufacture for the WAAC, WAC and the Army Nurse Corps. Includes many photographs and sketches. Indexed.

219   *Ross, Mary Steele.* **American Women in Uniform.** Garden City, NY: Garden City Publishing Company, 1943. 72p.
See **064**.

220   *United States. Army Service Forces. Quartermaster Corps.* **Quartermaster Supply Catalog. WACS' and Nurses Clothing and Equipment.** Washington, DC: Headquarters, Army Service Forces, 1943. 25p. OCLC 20313570.
A supply catalog for ordering WAC and nurses's uniforms and equipment. There are photographs of all equipment. Reprinted in Petersen (see **217**).

Army Nurse Corps - Korean War

221   *Aynes, Edith A.* **"Hospital Trains in Korea."** *American Journal of Nursing* 52(2): 166-167, February 1952.
Describes the life of Army nurses serving on hospital trains in Korea, which transported patients from the north to both bring patients to hospitals in Pusan, and from an airstrip near Pusan into hospitals in the city. Includes details about patient care, supplying the trains, living conditions for the nurses, and experiences of some of the train nurses. Photographs.

222   **"Korean Assignment."** *American Journal of Nursing* 53(6): 678-679, June 1953.
A two page display of photographs of Army nurse Lieutenant Mary Daly, who was serving in Korea. Shows her bunk, washing up, on duty, washing her clothes, and touring Seoul.

223 *"With the Army Nurse Corps in Korea."* American Journal of Nursing 51(6): 387, June 1951.
Describes the mobile army surgical hospitals, to which wounded soldiers were sent directly from the battlefield, first tried out under combat conditions in Korea. Article written from an interview with Army nurse Captain Margaret G. Blake, member of the 8055th MASH. She details procedures for caring for MASH patients.

224 *"With the First MASH."* American Journal of Nursing 51(6): 386, June 1951.
Presents several photographs of the thirteen Army nurses in the first mobile army surgical unit serving in Korea. Shows them standing in line for the mess hall, washing clothes in a helmet, putting on make-up, and filling oil stoves.

Army Nurse Corps - Vietnam War

See **Chapter 14, Veterans** *for materials about nurses as Vietnam veterans and post-traumatic stress disorder.*

225 *Neel, Spurgeon H.* **Medical Support of the U.S. Army in Vietnam, 1965-1970.** Washington, DC: Department of the Army, 1973. 196p. OCLC 692975.
Documents the Army medical service in Vietnam. Chapter XII, "Corps Services" discusses the Nursing Services (pages 142-146), noting that sixty percent of the Army nurses sent to Vietnam had less than six months of active duty service and lacked experience in combat nursing. Pages 158-161 describe the work of the Army Specialist Corps, which included some women. Statistics are provided on injuries, patient evacuations, etc, and also includes maps of medical facilities in Vietnam. Many photographs and an index.

Army Nurse Corps - Vietnam War - Personal Narratives

226 *Freedman, Dan, editor.* **Nurses in Vietnam: The Forgotten Veterans.** Austin, TX: Texas Monthly Press, 1987. 164p. OCLC 15015677; ISBN 087719047X.
A collection of personal narratives of nine nurses who served in Vietnam. Discusses their jobs, attitudes towards the war, and coping with the problems caused by their service. Includes photographs.

227 *Marshall, Kathryn.* **In the Combat Zone: An Oral History of American Women in Vietnam, 1966-1975.** Boston, MA: Little, Brown & Company, 1987. 270p.
See **110**.

228 *Norman, Elizabeth M. Dempsey.* **Nurses in War: A Study of Female Military Nurses Who Served in Vietnam during the War Years, 1965-**

1973. Thesis (Ph.D.)--New York University, 1986. 172p.
See **111**.

229 *Norman, Elizabeth M.* **Women at War: The Story of Fifty Military Nurses Who Served in Vietnam.** Philadelphia: University of Pennsylvania Press, 1990. 211p.
See **112**.

230 *O'Neill, Jacquelyn S.* **An Exploration of the Process of Coping As Experienced by Nurses Who Served in the Vietnam War.** Thesis (Ph.D.)--University of Texas at Austin, 1990. 202p.
See **113**.

231 *Smith, Winnie.* **American Daughter Gone to War: On the Front Lines with an Army Nurse in Vietnam.** New York: William Morrow and Company, Inc., 1992. 352p. OCLC 24430893; ISBN 0688111882.
The author was assigned to Vietnam in 1966, where she served with the Third Field Hospital in Saigon and the 24th Evac Hospital in Long Binh. A moving, well-written account of the author's struggles to deal with the war, both during her service and after her return to "real life", where she suffered from post-traumatic stress disorder. Some photographs.

232 *Van Devanter, Lynda with Christopher Morgan.* **Home before Morning: The Story of an Army Nurse in Vietnam.** New York: Beaufort Books, 1983. 382p. OCLC 8930181; ISBN 0825301327.
A classic, not only of women's wartime experiences, but of Vietnam War literature. Van Devanter was sent to the 71st Evacuation Hospital in Pleiku Province in June 1969. A wrenching story of wartime nursing, the author's battle with post-traumatic stress disorder, and her involvement with veterans' groups. Widely available in many printings and frequently cited. A must read.

233 *Walker, Keith.* **A Piece of My Heart: The Stories of 26 American Women Who Served in Vietnam.** Novato, CA: Presidio Press, 1986. 350p. OCLC 12586925; ISBN 0891412417.
Interviewed fourteen Army nurses, one Navy nurse, two Army WACs and nine women who served in a civilian capacity. A brief introduction to each interview tells the date/time of the interview, the woman's current occupation, and the dates and place of her Vietnam service, as well as a photograph. Includes other photographs and an appendix of statistics on American women who served in Vietnam. Well done.

Army Nurse Corps - Persian Gulf War

234 *Kassner, Elizabeth.* **Desert Storm Journal: A Nurse's Story.** Lincoln, MA: Cottage Press, 1993. 96p. OCLC 28375892; ISBN 1882063198.
Kassner, an Army nurse, was sent to Saudi Arabia in January 1991, with the 31st Combat Support Hospital in preparation for Operation Desert Storm. This is her diary, kept during the time she served in Saudi Arabia

(January-April 1991). Each chapter is prefaced with a summary of the progress of the war. Good descriptions of life in the desert, waiting for the start of the ground war. Her unit ended up treating mostly Iraqi casualties.

NAVY NURSE CORPS

Archives and Manuscripts

235   *Records of the Bureau of Medicine and Surgery.* Record Group 52, National Archives.
Includes *Records Relating to the History of the Navy Nurse Corps, 1908-1975*, prints and transparencies of Navy Nurse Corps uniforms from 1908-1970, records of legislation pertaining to the Corps, official correspondence, and letters.

Navy Nurse Corps - General Works

236   *Fitzgerald, Helen M.* **A History of the United States Navy Nurse Corps from 1934 to the Present.** Thesis (M.S.)--Ohio State University, 1968. 166p. OCLC 8655760.
A narrative of the history of the Navy Nurse Corps from 1934 to the mid 1960s. Covers uniforms, training, recruiting, POWs etc.

237   *Hickey, Dermott Vincent.* **The First Ladies in the Navy: A History of the Navy Nurse Corps, 1908-1939.** Thesis (M.A.)--Columbian College of the George Washington University, 1963. 172p. OCLC 6582696.
A history of the Navy Nurse Corps from its founding in 1908 to 1939. Discusses the requirements for joining the service, working overseas, World War I activities of the Corps, etc. Has appendices of pay and allowances, a chronology, and laws relating to the Corps.

Navy Nurse Corps - World War I

238   *Braun, Frederica.* **"Duty and Diversion in Guam."** *American Journal of Nursing* 18(8): 650-653, August 1918.
Report of Navy nurses at the Naval Hospital in Guam. Their duties included treating tropical diseases and training native women as midwives. Some unusual injuries and diseases were seen, such as fish bites, fractures from falls from coconut trees, and yaws. Photographs of the hospital and nurses.

239   *Neil, Elizabeth Wells.* **"The Experiences of An Ex-Navy Nurse on Recruiting Duty."** *American Journal of Nursing* 18(8): 625-626, August 1918.
Discusses the author's experiences as a recruiter for the Navy Nurse Corps and why many nurses were hesitant to join. Found it

disheartening that those best qualified were waiting for better pay or rank for nurses before joining. Photograph of the barracks is included.

240 *Trippett, Josephine.* **"Sketch of a Naval Emergency Hospital."** *American Journal of Nursing* 18(8): 683-687, August 1918.
A Navy nurse describes life at Naval Hospital No. 3, Pelham Bay Training Station, NY. Tells of nursing duties, the nurses' quarters, shopping in New York City and watching sailors being shipped overseas. Photographs of members of the hospital staff and the operating room.

Navy Nurse Corps - World War II

241 *Cooper, Page.* **Navy Nurse.** New York: McGraw-Hill Book Company, Inc., 1946. 226p. OCLC 1399586.
Not a history of Navy nurses, rather the story of life as a Navy nurse while serving in different locations during World War II. Some of the stories tell of Navy nurses on the hospital ships *Solace*, *Relief*, and *Rescue*, of nurses serving in Samoa who were captured by the Japanese, and nurses serving in the Pacific, Europe, Africa, and the United States. A good overview of the types of assignments held by Navy nurses during the war (see **244-245, 250**).

242 *Dewitt, Gill.* **The First Navy Flight Nurse on a Pacific Battlefield: A Picture Story of a Flight to Iwo Jima.** Fredericksburg, TX: Admiral Nimitz Foundation, 1983. 28p. OCLC 27647444.
A scrapbook type publication containing photographs of Ensign Jane Kendiegh, a flight nurse sent to help evacuate the wounded from Iwo Jima. Very little text.

243 *Dunbar, Ruth B.* **"Return to the Philippines."** *American Journal of Nurses* 45(12): 1015-1018, December 1945.
Story of Navy nurses serving at a hospital in the Philippines who treated 149 survivors of the *Indianapolis*. More detailed than most. Includes photographs.

244 *"Navy Nurses on the U.S.S. Solace."* *American Journal of Nursing* 41(10): 1173-1175, October 1941.
Presents the new hospital ship *Solace* and the nurses serving on her. Includes several photographs (see **241, 244, 250**).

245 *Newcomb, Ellsworth.* **Brave Nurses: True Stories of Heroism.** New York: Appleton-Century Company, 1945. 177p. OCLC 1474774.
Has no foreword or explanatory material. Each chapter is the story of bravery by a nurse or group of nurses serving in World War II. Includes the story of the Navy hospital ship USS *Solace* which was at Pearl Harbor when it was bombed, a Navy nurse rescued from Corregidor, and various others. Includes photographs (see **241, 244, 250**).

246 *O'Toole, Sarah.* **"They Pioneered on Tinian."** *American Journal of Nursing* 45(12): 1013-1015, December 1945.
Account of Navy nurses who worked on Tinian, the first white women ever seen on the island. Describes hospital facilities.

247 *Staats, Mary H.* **"Navy Nurses in the Solomons."** *American Journal of Nursing* 45(7): 534, July 1945.
Describes daily life for 127 Navy nurses stationed in the Solomon Islands. Discusses how the climate affected nursing procedures, malaria control methods, and recreation.

248 *Tomblin, Barbara B.* **"Beyond Paradise: The US Navy Nurse Corps in the Pacific in World War II (Part One)."** *Minerva* 11(2): 33-53, Summer 1993.
Part one of the experiences of Navy nurses assigned to Hawaii, the Philippines, Guam, and other areas of the Pacific during World War II (see **249**). Accounts of prison camps, service on hospital ships, and base hospitals are included.

249 *Tomblin, Barbara B.* **"Beyond Paradise: The US Navy Nurse Corps in the Pacific in World War II (Part Two)."** *Minerva* 11(3-4): 37-56, Fall/Winter 1993.
Part two of the experiences of Navy nurses in the Pacific during World War II (see **248**). Many interesting details of wartime nursing, including work on hospital ships and Navy flight nursing.

250 *White, Ruth Young.* **"The Solace Plies the Tasman and Coral Seas."** *American Journal of Nursing* 44(6): 552-554, June 1944.
An interview with Navy Lieutenant Catherine Shaw, a nurse who served for a year in the psychiatric ward of the *Solace* (see **241, 244-245**).

Navy Nurse Corps - World War II - Personal Narratives

251 *Desmarais, Mary Virginia.* **"Navy Nursing on D-Day Plus 4."** *American Journal of Nursing* 45(1): 12, January 1945.
Ensign Desmarais describes treating casualties on D-Day plus four, who were brought to England from France after receiving basic first aid for injuries.

252 *Glines, Edna Lee.* **Heads in the Sand.** Los Angeles, CA: Authors Unlimited, 1990. 83p. OCLC 24027039; ISBN 1556660413.
Written by her sister, this is the story of Polly Glines, a nurse who entered the Navy after the bombing of Pearl Harbor. She served as a nurse on the hospital ship USS *Benevolence.* Polly's ship was in the vicinity of the Bikini Atoll during testing of the atomic bomb. A little over a year later, she developed breast cancer, and died in 1949. While this book covers a serious subject, the poor writing detracts from the story.

253   *Goudreau, Alice Aurora.* **"Nursing at an Advance Naval Base Hospital: During the Iwo Jima Campaign."** *American Journal of Nursing* 45(11): 884-886, November 1945.
Lieutenant Goudreau of the Navy Nurse Corps worked at the U.S. Naval Base Hospital 18 on Guam during the invasion of Iwo Jima, when nurses worked 14-16 hours a day. Describes the "unbelievable" number of men admitted suffering from war neuroses. Some photographs.

254   *Hayes, Teresa M.* **"It Was Hot on the Island."** *American Journal of Nursing* 44(11): 1058-1059, November 1944.
Short story of the author's service at a Navy hospital in the South Pacific, where she worked in the orthopedic ward.

255   *Shaw, Catherine.* **"We Traveled by Transport."** *American Journal of Nursing* 43(11): 1022-1024, November 1943.
A Navy nurse describes travel on a transport ship to duty in the South Pacific.

256   *St. Peter, Olivine B.* **"In the Southwest Pacific: The Marianas."** *American Journal of Nursing* 45(12): 1012-1013, December 1945.
Author served as a nurse in a hospital on Guam during the Battle of Iwo Jima. Describes the types of battle wounds, including flash burns, head and eye injuries etc.

Navy Nurse Corps - World War II - Prisoners of War

*For other materials on prisoners of war, see **203-214, 792-794**.*

257   *Evans, Jessie Fant.* **"Release from Los Banos."** *American Journal of Nursing* 45(6): 462-463, June 1945.
Story of the eleven Navy nurses who were released on 25 February 1945, from the Los Banos Prison Camp, after being imprisoned for over thirty-seven months. Includes several photographs of the nurses.

258   *Jackson, Leona.* **"I Was on Guam."** *American Journal of Nursing* 42(11): 1244-1246, November 1942.
A Navy nurse discusses her duties at a Naval hospital in Guam. Shortly after September 1941, the island was occupied by the Japanese, and the nurses, patients and other medical personnel were sent to a prison camp in Japan in January 1942. In March the author was sent with four other nurses to a detention house in Kobe and in June 1942, they were sent back to the U.S. in a prisoner exchange.

259   *Manning, Michele.* **Angels of Mercy and Life Amid Scenes of Conflict and Death: The Combat Experience and Imprisonment of American Military Nurses in the Philippines, 1941-1945.** Quantico, VA: Marine Corps Command and Staff College, 1985. 90p.
See **212**.

260 *"Navy Nurses Released."* American Journal of Nursing 45(4): 315, April 1945.
Lists eleven Navy nurses released from Los Banos.

261 *Norman, Elizabeth M. and Sharon Eifried.* ***"How Did They All Survive? An Analysis of American Nurses' Experiences in Japanese Prisoner-of-War Camps."*** *Nursing History Review* 3: 105-127, 1995.
See **213**.

Navy Nurse Corps - Korean War

262 *Harrington, Eleanor.* ***"Aboard a Hospital Ship."*** American Journal of Nursing 53(5): 584-586, May 1953.
A Navy nurse details life and patient treatment on the USS *Haven*, a hospital ship that accommodated 795 patients and numerous medical staff, including thirty nurses. The ship was stationed at Pusan, Korea, where nursing care for troops of the United Nations Forces was provided. Includes some photographs.

Navy Nurse Corps - Vietnam War

263 *Hovis, Bobbi.* ***Station Hospital Saigon: A Navy Nurse in Vietnam, 1963-1964.*** Annapolis, MD: Naval Institute Press, 1992. 167p. OCLC 25009507; ISBN 1557503761.
Hovis was the first Navy nurse to volunteer for duty in Vietnam. She served from September 1963-October 1964 at the U.S. Naval Station Hospital, Saigon, the first Navy hospital in South Vietnam. Interesting details about life in Saigon in the earlier years of the war, including a description of the overthrow of the Diem government. Contains more information about her travels than military nursing.

264 *Norman, Eilzabeth M. Dempsey.* ***Nurses in War: A Study of Female Military Nurses Who Served in Vietnam during the War Years, 1965-1973.*** Thesis (Ph.D.)--New York University, 1986. 172p.
See **111.**

265 *Norman, Elizabeth M.* ***Women at War: The Story of Fifty Military Nurses Who Served in Vietnam.*** Philadelphia: University of Pennsylvania Press, 1990. 211p.
See **112.**

266 *Walker, Keith.* ***A Piece of My Heart: The Stories of 26 American Women Who Served in Vietnam.*** Novato, CA: Presidio Press, 1986. 350p.
See **233**.

4

NAVY AND COAST GUARD

The Navy was the first service to accept women as full members with the establishment of the Yeomen (F) during World War I. Faced with a manpower shortage, the Secretary of the Navy, Josephus Daniels, considered using women to fill the many duties required to keep the fleet afloat. After examining the Naval Act of 1916 authorizing a buildup of Naval forces, Daniels concluded "It does not say ...anywhere that a yeoman must be a man." On 19 March 1917, commandants of all Naval districts were notified to enroll women and on 21 March, Loretta Perfectus Walsh became the first of nearly 12,000 women to enlist in the Naval Reserve during World War I (see **288**). The Yeomen (F) worked in a variety of positions; as clerks, switchboard operators, translators, fingerprint experts, in Naval Intelligence, and as recruiters, among others. The women did the same work and received the same pay as men of equal rank. At the end of the war, the women were placed in an inactive status until the completion of their enlistments. The passage of the Naval Reserve Act of 1925, which limited enrollment in the Naval reserve to male citizens only, ensured that women would not be allowed to continue their service.

The Army led the other services in enrolling women during World War II, with the formation of the Women's Army Auxiliary Corps (WAAC) in May 1942. In July 1942, the Navy followed, with the passage of Public Law 689, establishing the Navy Women's Reserve. The women would be known as WAVES, Women Accepted For Voluntary Emergency Service and unlike the WAAC, the WAVES would actually serve with the Navy, not as an auxiliary. This helped prevent many of the problems later faced by the WAAC regarding legal status, benefits, etc. The woman chosen as the first Director of the WAVES was Mildred McAfee, who had been serving as the President of Wellesley College at the time of her appointment. In November 1942, the Coast Guard Women's Reserve, known as the SPAR (Semper Paratus Always Ready), was formed, under the direction of Dorothy Stratton, who was already on active duty as a WAVE lieutenant (see **363**). She recruited volunteers from women undergoing WAVE officer training to form the nucleus of the SPAR officer corps.

By the summer of 1945, there were almost 8,400 WAVE officers and more than 73,000 enlisted women on active duty, nearly two percent of the total Navy force. Among their many duties, WAVES performed about eighty percent of the administrative and supervisory work of the Navy's mail service for the fleet and activities outside of the United States, over 1,000 worked as WAVE Link trainer instructors teaching instrument flying to men, and others served as codebreakers in Washington, DC. Almost 10,000 women joined the Coast Guard and were assigned to a variety of positions, including yeoman, radioman, pharmacist's mate, parachute rigger, and storekeeper.

The Coast Guard completely disbanded the SPAR by 1946, and except for a few women who were recalled during the Korean War, did not begin to recruit women again until 1974. The post-war years saw an enormous drop in the numbers of women serving in the Navy. After the passage of the Women's Armed Services Integration Act in 1948, the Navy planned on maintaining a small number of women on active duty, about 500 officers and 6,000 enlisted personnel, which could be expanded quickly in time of need.

The numbers of Navy women on active duty during the Korean War grew to nearly 9,000. The women generally performed the same types of duties as in World War II. After the war, numbers of women serving dropped and never came close to the two percent ceiling imposed by Congress. During the Vietnam War, only nine women officers and no enlisted Navy women served in Vietnam.

The 1970s saw an expansion of women's roles in the Navy. Admiral Elmo Zumwalt, the Chief of Naval Operations, issued a series of messages (called Z-grams) to the Navy setting new policies and guidelines. One of these, Z-gram 116, "Equal Rights and Opportunities for Women in the Navy", established a task force to examine all laws, regulations, and policies which had to be changed to eliminate any disadvantages to women resulting from legal or attitudinal restrictions. This led to several extremely important changes for women, including opening the Naval ROTC program to women, assigning women as commanders of units ashore, and under a pilot program, a small number of officer and enlisted women were assigned to the crew of a noncombatant ship, the USS *Sanctuary*. Other changes authorized enlisted women limited entry to all ratings, women could be considered for promotion to rear admiral, and women would be selected to study at the joint-service colleges. The changes caused by Z-Gram 116 would have far reaching consequences for Navy women in the 1980s and 1990s.

In the 1970s, the Coast Guard again began recruiting women, and in 1978, the Commandant of the Coast Guard made the decision that there would be no restriction based on sex in the use of its personnel. Women have served aboard Coast Guard ships since 1977, and by the end of the 1980s, Coast Guard vessels with mixed sex crews were common, with women in command of all types of craft. By the 1990s, the number of job positions open to Coast Guard women was 100 percent.

The Navy has had more difficult problems than the Coast Guard in opening jobs to women, especially jobs at sea. However, there has been a steady expansion of the number of women assigned to ships, and with the November 1993 repeal of the legislation on assigning women to combat ships, more women will be serving at sea. In April 1993, Secretary of Defense Les Aspin ordered the services to drop restrictions against women serving as combat aviators, and the Navy was the first service to do so. In April 1995, the USS *Eisenhower* returned to port, completing a six month deployment to the Mediterranean and the Persian Gulf, becoming the first combat vessel to carry a crew of men and women and the first aircraft carrier to launch women naval aviators on a combat mission.

This chapter is divided into two parts, Navy and Coast Guard. While the Coast Guard is under the Department of Transportation, in the event of war, operational control would transfer to the Department of the Navy. The small numbers of materials included on the Coast Guard did not merit a separate chapter, so they are included here.

NAVY

ARCHIVES AND MANUSCRIPTS

267 ***Records of the Bureau of Naval Personnel.*** Record Group 24, National Archives.
The Bureau Of Naval Personnel is responsible for the recruitment, assignment, and separation of naval personnel, including the Yeomen (F), the Navy Nurse Corps, and the WAVES. Contains records pertaining to the enlistment of women in World War I, and records from the office of the Director of the WAVES. The WAVES records include enlistment, training, discipline, and discharge and document policy decisions. Also includes special Navy regulations pertaining only to WAVES.

268 ***Reynard, Elizabeth. Papers, 1932-1962 (inclusive).*** Schlesinger Library, Radcliffe College, Cambridge, MA.
Correspondence, articles, reports, newsletters, manuals, photos, clippings, and other records reflecting Reynard's career in the Navy, including her assignment at the WAVES training School at Hunter College. Reynard was instrumental in the formation of the WAVES. Also includes information about WAVES personnel and organization regulations.

269 ***United States Naval Historical Center.*** Washington, DC.
Owns bound copies of oral history interviews (see **270**), records of the Assistant Chief for Women, Bureau of Naval Personnel, a two volume administrative history of the Women's Reserve, and a history of the Naval Reserve Midshipman's School, among other items.

270 ***United States Naval Institute Oral History Collection.*** Annapolis, MD.
Holds oral history interviews of several prominent members of the WAVES and Navy women, including Captain Joy Bright Hancock (see **312, 314**), and Captain Jean Palmer. There is an index on cards covering various topics in the oral history transcripts, which is held at the Naval Institute, the Naval Historical Center in Washington, DC (see **269**), and the Nimitz Library at the Naval Academy. Each of these three repositories also holds copies of the bound transcripts. A catalog of transcripts is available from the Naval Institute.

271 **WAVES: United States Naval Training School (WR)**. Lehman College, Bronx, NY.
Hunter College (now Lehman College) operated as the Navy's boot camp for enlisted WAVES from 1943-1945. Collection includes memorabilia of former WAVES, photographs, slides, articles, microfiche Naval reports and Naval history materials (see **302**).

BIBLIOGRAPHIES

272 *Thomas, Patricia J.* **Annotated Bibliography of Publications on Women in the Navy.**   San Diego, CA: Navy Personnel Research and Development Center, 1995. 23p.
An annotated bibliography of about fifty reports, journal articles, and book chapters published at the Navy Personnel Research and Development Center on military women in the Navy. Publication dates range from May 1976 to December 1994.

273 *United States.   Bureau of Naval Personnel.* **Bibliography of WAVE Utilization Reports, April 1953**. Washington, DC: Bureau of Naval Personnel, 1953. 9p. OCLC 12645011.
Bibliography of reports conducted to study the WAVES. Originally was a restricted document. Includes summaries of recommended utilization of enlisted women in the Naval Reserve.

274 *White, Anthony G.* **U.S. Servicewomen--Sea Duty Debate: A Selected Bibliography.** Monticello, IL: Vance Bibliographies, 1986. 4p. OCLC 14158679.
A very brief bibliography citing articles from military journals and popular magazines. Arranged alphabetically by author. No annotations.

GENERAL WORKS

275 *Dunne, Martha Suzanne.* **"Leading Women into the 21st Century."** *Proceedings: U.S. Naval Institute* 121(7): 60-62, July 1995.
The author, a Navy lieutenant, discusses ways Navy leaders should deal with the integration of women into combat ships and squadrons. Analyzes problems of fraternization, special treatment of women, and communications between men and women. Suggests leaders should eliminate gender bias, trust their subordinates, hold personnel to high standards, listen to troops, and enforce fraternization rules.

276 *Ebbert, Jean and Marie-Beth Hall.* **Crossed Currents: Navy Women from WWI to Tailhook.** Washington, DC: Brassey's, 1993. 321p. OCLC 27011064; ISBN 0028810228.
The only comprehensive history available on women in the U.S. Navy that covers the period from the founding of the Navy Nurse Corps to the present day. Very current, discusses the general history of Navy women, issues of women serving at sea, sexual harassment, women in

aviation, the Persian Gulf War, Tailhook, etc. Includes some photographs. Indexed.

277 *Fletcher, Jean W., Joyce S. McMahon and Aline O. Quester. **"Tradition, Technology, and the Changing Roles of Women in the Navy."*** *Minerva* 11(3/4): 57-85, Fall/Winter 1993.
Reviews traditions which have fostered the exclusion of women from the military and explores how technological change and the nature of modern warfare will affect the tradition of exclusion. Technological change reduces the number of jobs requiring physical strength, which has been favorable to women. Good discussion of issues surrounding women's roles in the Navy.

278 *Johnston, Mary Ann. **The Role of Women in the Modern Navy: Issues and Attitudes.*** Thesis (M.P.P.)--University of Central Florida, Orlando, 1981. 239p. OCLC 802118.
An examination of the historical and current status of women in the military as well as an assessment of individual and institutional attitudes towards military women. 330 military personnel (ninety percent Navy), sixty percent men and forty percent women, were surveyed on their attitudes towards women. Includes a good summary of the issues of increased utilization of women in the military. Suggests statutory barriers to women on combat ships be lifted.

279 *Sadler, Georgia Clark. **"Women in the Sea Services, 1972-1982."*** *Proceedings: U.S. Naval Institute* 109(5): 140-155, May 1983.
Discusses changes in the Navy, Marine Corps, and Coast Guard for women from 1972 to 1982. Provides many statistics, such as numbers of women, attrition rates, occupations, and reenlistment rates. Also discusses changes in policy and law and provides a chronology of important events from 1972-1982.

280 *United States. Navy Department. Office of Information. **WAVES of the U.S. Navy.*** Washington, DC: The Office, 1955. OCLC 12382847.
A pamphlet designed to assist Navy Information Officers in providing information about the WAVES. It includes a short history, requirements for officer commissions and enlistments, and a description of the uniforms. It also includes a speech about the WAVES for use on television or radio interviews.

281 *United States. Office of the Chief of Naval Operations. **Navy Study Group's Report on Progress of Women in the Navy.*** Washington, DC: Department of the Navy, 1987. Not paged. OCLC 18827870.
The members of the study group visited ships, squadrons, and shore commands and conducted interviews with over 2,500 Naval personnel. Their recommendations includes a redefinition of the Navy's combat mission, that more women must enter nontraditional ratings or their increasing percentage of Navy strength will adversely affect male sea/shore rotation, and that women officer's career patterns are not clearly defined.

282   *United States. Office of the Chief of Naval Operations, Navy Women's Study Group.* **An Update Report on the Progress of Women in the Navy.** Washington, DC: Chief of Naval Operations, 1991. 1 volume. OCLC 23666304.
The conclusions of a comprehensive study to examine current Naval policy regarding women and to provide recommendations that would lead to improved assimilation of women and expansion of their opportunities. Information was gathered in briefings, interviews, and surveys. Covers pregnancy, career advancement, sexual harassment, fraternization, single parents, assignments, housing, etc. Includes many statistics.

283   *WAVES National.* **Navy Women, 1908-1988: A Pictorial History.** Calif?: WAVES National, 1990. 319p. OCLC 22335311.
Divided into four sections: a brief history of Navy women, photographs, tributes and memorials, and autobiographies. The photographs include notes about the subject.

WORLD WAR I

284   *Butler, Henry F. (Mrs.)* **I Was a Yeoman (F).** Washington, DC: Naval Historical Foundation, 1967. 14p. OCLC 5850376.
Brief memoir of how the author came to join the Navy as a Yeoman (F) during World War I. Provides a short description of her job and the effects of the influenza epidemic of 1918.

285   *Dessez, Eunice Cecelia.* **The First Enlisted Women, 1917-1918.** Philadelphia: Dorrance & Company, 1955. 93p. OCLC 1724542.
Not a personal narrative, although the author served as a Yeoman (F) in World War I. Gives basic information about women serving as Yeomen (F) during World War I. Details enlistment procedures, physical exams, training (conducted at night to indoctrinate the women into "the Navy way"), promotions, uniforms and demobilization. Includes a very detailed description of uniforms, as well as a copy of a discharge certificate.

286   *Godson, Susan H.* **"Womanpower in World War I."** *Proceedings: U.S. Naval Institute* 110(12): 60-64, December 1984.
Short, but informative summary of how the Yeomen (F) of World War I were formed, requirements for service, their training, jobs held, etc.

287   *Guthrie, Lou MacPherson.* **"I Was a Yeomanette."** *Proceedings: U.S. Naval Institute* 110(12): 57-64, December 1984.
Author was working for the Bureau of War Risk Insurance in Washington, DC during World War I, when she enlisted in the Navy. Discusses her job in accounting and life as a Yeoman (F).

288   *Walsh, James J.* **America's Forgotten Heroine.** Washington, DC: Navy Department Library, 1992. 20p. OCLC 26937189.
A brief paper telling the story of Loretta Walsh, the first woman to enlist in the Navy during World War I. No bibliography or index.

WORLD WAR II

General Works

289   *Akers, Regina T.* **"Female Naval Reservists during World War II: A Historiographical Essay."** *Minerva* 8(2): 55-61, Summer 1990.
Describes some of the major published and unpublished studies written about the WAVES who served during World War II. Includes information about sources available in Navy archives. Good brief summary of some of the important publications regarding WAVES.

290   *Alsmeyer, Marie Bennett, compiler.* **Old Waves Tales. Navy Women: Memories of World War II.** Conway, AR: HAMBA Books, 1982. 48p. OCLC 8948878; ISBN 0960615210.
A short compilation of one paragraph anecdotes from WAVES who served during World War II. A list of contributors is included, but individual entries are not attributed.

291   *Armas, Maria T.* **"Women at War."** *Naval History* 8(2): 10-14, March/April 1994.
Summary of the formation of the WAVES in World War II, including information pertaining to enlistment standards, conduct rules, recruitment efforts, training and job assignments, and demobilization. Includes some photographs.

292   *Barsis, Max.* **They're All Yours, Uncle Sam!** New York: Stephen Days, 1943. 103p. OCLC 1728289.
A cartoon story of two women, one who joins the WAC and the other who joins the WAVES.

293   *Byerly, Dorothea J.* **Up Came a Ripple.** East Orange, NJ: Greenwood Press, 1945. Not paged. OCLC 26465270.
The story of a WAVE, from enlistment to training, to first assignment to discharge, told through cartoons. The author served as a WAVE during World War II.

294   *Godson, Susan H.* **"The WAVES in World War II."** *Proceedings: U.S. Naval Institute* 107(12): 46-51, December 1981.
Story of the formation of the WAVES and their recruitment, training, uniforms, training, uniforms, personnel policies, jobs, etc. A good, brief summary. Photographs.

295   *Harris, Mary Virginia.* **Guide Right: A Handbook of Etiquette and Customs for Members of the Women's Reserve of the United States Naval Reserve and the United States Coast Guard Reserve.** New York: MacMillan Company, 1944. 105p. OCLC 1822915.
A manual for women in the Navy and Coast Guard during World War II explaining Navy customs and etiquette. Provides guidance on saluting, uniforms, marriage between different ranks, etc.

296   *Hart, Eleanor and Harriet Welling. **While So Serving.** New York: R.W. Kelly Publishing Corporation, 1947. 87p. OCLC 1570748.*
A collection of full page photographs of WAVES performing various duties during World War II. There are no annotations or identifications of the subjects or their activities. Most are official U.S. Navy photographs.

297   *Hayes, Jean McGrath. **Women in the Navy, 1942-1948.** Thesis (M.A.)-- University of Houston, Clear Lake, 1988. 102p. OCLC 21465359.*
Brief history of the Women's Naval Reserve of World War II. Includes discussions of legislation which established the WAVES. Describes training, schooling, housing, and jobs. Statistics regarding women who served are included.

298   *Heckathorn, Mary E. **"The Navy WAVES the Rules."** Proceedings: U.S. Naval Institute 69(486): 1082-1085, August 1943.*
Describes the types of jobs held by WAVES and their training.

299   *McAfee, Mildred H. **"Women in the Services."** Academy of Political Science Proceedings 20(3): 225-230, May 1943.*
Discusses women's role in the Navy and men's surprise at their effectiveness. States that due to the small numbers of women in the service, they have a greater influence than men of comparable rank and that some men have a problem accepting that women receive equal pay.

300   *McAfee, Mildred H. **"Women's Reserves."** Annals of the American Academy of Political and Social Science 227: 152-155, May 1943.*
Written by the Director of the WAVES during World War II, clarifies the position of the Navy regarding WAVES benefits. Primarily discusses dependent's benefits, benefits for death and disability and medical care.

301   *McLaughlin, Florence C. **"Down to the Sea in Slips."** The Western Pennsylvania Historical Magazine 51(4): 377-387, October 1968.*
Story of recruiting WAVES from the Pittsburgh, Pennsylvania office during World War II. Written primarily from the notebooks of one of the recruiters, Lieutenant Wanda McLaughlin. Some photographs.

302   *Munch, Janet Butler. **"Making Waves in the Bronx: The Story of the U.S. Naval Training School (WR) at Hunter College."** The Bronx County Historical Society Journal 30(1): 1-15, Spring 1993.*
Interesting description of how Hunter College was transformed from a college to a training school for WAVES. Discusses all aspects of WAVE training including food preparation, uniforms, classroom instruction, drill, and physical training (see **271**).

303   *Ross, Nancy Wilson. **The WAVES, the Story of the Girls in Blue.** New York: Henry Holt and Company, 1943. 214p. OCLC 2866353.*
A propaganda type book written during the war to instruct potential recruits on life as a WAVE. Gives short anecdotes about life as a WAVE, including training, barracks life, etc. The appendix specifies requirements

for both officers and enlisted women and information about where and how to apply to the WAVES. Includes photographs and index.

304 *Van Voris, Jacqueline.* **Quiet Victory: The WAVES in World War II.** Northampton, MA: W.H. Van Voris, 1969. 159p. OCLC 6885106.
Study of the role of the WAVES in World War II. Includes a calendar of WAVE history and a list of rates open to enlisted WAVES. A microfilm copy of this manuscript is held at the Navy Department Library.

305 *WAVES National Corporation.* **Now Let Us Sing.** Sacramento, CA: The Corporation, 1950. 19p. OCLC 11758136.
The words to fifty-eight WAVES songs from World War II. No music or annotations are provided.

306 *Woodruff, J.L.* **"WAVE Training."** *Proceedings: U.S. Naval Institute* 71(504): 151-155, February 1945.
Presents the training conducted at the U.S. Naval Reserve Midshipmen's School at Smith College, where women officers were instructed.

World War II - Personal Narratives

307 *Alsmeyer, Marie Bennett.* **The Way of the Waves: Women in the Navy.** Conway, AR: Conway Books, 1981. 186p. OCLC 7673750; ISBN 0960615202.
An account of the author's service as a Pharmacist's Mate in the WAVES. She was stationed in the San Francisco area. Confusing due to the author's habit of switching between present and past tense in the same sentence.

308 *Angel, Joan.* **Angel of the Navy: The Story of a WAVE.** New York: Hastings House, 1943. 200p. OCLC 1815177.
Written before the end of the war, this is a mild propaganda piece emphasizing the fun of being a WAVE. Author enlisted in October 1942, and attended boot camp at the Iowa State Teacher's College in Cedar Falls, Iowa. Good description of the five week training course and her first assignment as a Pharmacist's Mate at the U.S. Naval Hospital in Bethesda, MD. Concludes with helpful advice for potential recruits, such as what clothes to bring to basic training and tips for dating male officers.

309 *Bistline, Beverly as told to Sam Hanson.* **"A Navy WAVE in War and Peace."** *Rendezvous: Idaho State University of Arts and Letters* 22(2): 29-31, 1987.
Author enlisted in 1944 and attended boot camp at Hunter College, then yeoman training at Iowa State Teachers' College. Served in Washington, DC doing secretarial work. Later served with the Naval Air Transport Service at Moffett Field in California.

310 *Butler, Elizabeth Allen.* **Navy Waves.** Charlottesville, VA: Wayside Press, Inc., 1988. 133p. OCLC 19092263.
Disorganized, but still an interesting account of the author's experiences as a WAVE during World War II. A librarian when she enlisted in 1943, she worked in Washington, DC in Naval communications and was later transferred to Bainbridge Island, WA. Contains many photographs, as well as a map of her WAVE quarters in DC and a weekly mess hall menu. Includes a bibliography.

311 *Gildersleeve, Virginia Crocheron.* **Many a Good Crusade: Memoirs of Virginia Crocheron Gildersleeve.** New York, Arno Press, 1980. 434p. OCLC 6015508; ISBN 040512841X.
Author was the Chairman of the Advisory Council for the establishment of the WAVES, the Women's Reserve of the Navy during World War II. While this is primarily her autobiography, she does devote several chapters to her role in chairing the council, which set up training centers, selected uniforms, established training procedures, etc.

312 *Godson, Susan H.* **"Capt. Joy Bright Hancock: Builder of the Co-Ed Navy."** *The Retired Officer* 15-17, December 1982.
Story of Joy Bright Hancock, a former Director of the WAVES (see **314**). She served as a Yeoman (F) in World War I, then worked in Naval Aviation where she was instrumental in convincing the Navy to establish the WAVES. During World War II, she served as the WAVE representative to the Navy Bureau of Aeronautics.

313 *Gunter, Helen Clifford.* **Navy WAVE: Memories of World War II.** Fort Bragg, CA: Cypress House Press, 1992. 147p. OCLC 25831715; ISBN 1879384167.
A junior high school teacher in Long Beach when she enlisted in the WAVES, the author trained at Mt. Holyoke College in February 1943, and was commissioned a Lieutenant. She worked on Navy films at the Photoscience Laboratory, Naval Air Station, Potomac River Naval Command. Gives good details of life as a woman Naval officer.

314 *Hancock, Joy Bright.* **Lady in the Navy: A Personal Reminiscence.** Annapolis, MD: Naval Institute Press, 1972. 289p. OCLC 482129; ISBN 0870213369.
The authoritative source for the history of the WAVES, as well as an excellent and entertaining account of the author's service as a Yeoman (F) during World War I, and as a WAVE. Joy Hancock was working as a civilian in Naval aviation at the outbreak of World War II, and was instrumental in getting Naval aviation to accept women for service. After the war she served as a Director of the WAVES. Includes many photographs, as well as appendixes with a chronology of the WAVES, officer and enlisted billets held by women, etc. Widely cited. Indexed.

315 *Stoddard, Eleanor.* **"Shore Duty: September 1942-April 1945. The Story of Frances Prindle Taft, Officer in the WAVES, World War II."** *Minerva* 5(1): 88-125, Spring 1987.

Transcript of an oral history interview with Taft. She attended officer training at Smith College, then stayed at Smith to teach new WAVE officer candidates. Discusses her training, uniforms, etc.

316 *Wingo, Josette Dermody.* **Mother Was a Gunner's Mate: World War II in the Waves.** Annapolis, MD: Naval Institute Press, 1994. 234p. OCLC 30109740; ISBN 1557509247.
Author joined the WAVES in 1944, trained at Hunter College, and served at Treasure Island, California, where she worked helping to train sailors in the Armed Guards to shoot antiaircraft guns. One of the better accounts. Photographs.

World War II - Uniforms

317 *Ross, Mary Steele.* **American Women in Uniform.** Garden City, NY: Garden City Publishing Company, 1943. 72p.
See **064**.

318 *United States. Bureau of Naval Personnel.* **Uniform Regulations, Women's Reserve, United States Naval Reserve 1943. Officers and Enlisted Women of the Women's Reserve.** Washington, DC: The Bureau, 1943. 31p. OCLC 9982439.
Regulation governing the wearing of the Naval uniform for officers and enlisted women of the Women's Reserve. No illustrations. Dated 20 March 1943, includes a list of uniform items for Navy women.

POST WORLD WAR II

319 *Elder, Robert Ellsworth.* **History of Demobilization of the United States Navy Women's Reserve, 1945-46.** Thesis (Ph.D.)--University of Chicago, 1947. 260p. OCLC 10750571.
Author was a Lieutenant (jg) assigned as a staff historian for the Bureau of Naval Personnel. Discusses the administrative problems involved in and traces the history of the demobilization of the Women's Reserve. Evaluates how well the WAVE demobilization program was run. Very detailed with an extensive bibliography.

320 *Rogers, Robert A., III.* **"These Boots Wear Skirts."** *Proceedings: U.S. Naval Institute* 75(9): 1022-1027, September 1949.
Story of the first class of women recruits to attend recruit training after the passage of the Women's Armed Services Integration Act. Describes physical characteristics of recruits, education, results of aptitude tests, how training was conducted, clothing, etc.

1970s - PERSONAL NARRATIVES

321   *Johnson, LouAnne. **Making Waves: A Woman in This Man's Navy.*** New York: St. Martin's Press, 1986.   233p.   OCLC 13902886; ISBN 0312508131.
Account of the author's Naval service, which appears to be at least partly fictional. Does not indicate her dates of service, but it seems to have taken place in the early to mid 1970s. Many descriptions of sexual harassment.

ENLISTED WOMEN

322   *Durning, Kathleen P.* **"Attitudes of Enlisted Women and Men toward the Navy."** *Armed Forces and Society* 9(1): 20-32, Fall 1982.
Used a Navy human management survey conducted in 1978 of over 20,000 enlisted men and women. Showed that as women moved up in rank, they were less positive about the Navy than were men. Mid-level women also had a lower level of satisfaction with their supervisors than did men.

323   *Hamel, Cheryl J., Janet Thompson, D. Robert Copeland and Herschel Hughes, Jr.* **Analysis of Recruit Training Practices Related to the Military Performance of Enlisted Navy Women.** Orlando, FL: Naval Training Analysis and Evaluation Group, 1983. 67p. ED 239073.
Identified aspects of training for male and female recruits at the Navy's Recruit Training Command which might lead to differential performance in the fleet.   The researchers wanted to change training to minimize male-female training differences and enhance female performance. Includes many recommendations for changes in training.

324   *Hinsdale, Kirsten, Barbara Collier, and J. David Johnson.* **Navy Enlisted Women in Traditional and Nontraditional Jobs.** Albion, MI: Validated Instruction Associates, 1978. 29p. OCLC 6419028.
133 Navy E-4 and E-5 women were interviewed to compare those working in traditional jobs with those in nontraditional jobs. The two groups had few differences in satisfaction, productivity, reenlistment intention, or attitudes towards women in the Navy. Women in traditional jobs described themselves as more feminine than women in nontraditional jobs.

325   *Hoiberg, Anne.* **"Women in the Navy: Morale and Attrition."** *Armed Forces and Society* 4(4): 659-671, August 1978.
Results of a questionnaire to measure male and female perceptions of the basic course Navy school and fleet experiences, compare biological, aptitude and personality characteristics. Also examines the performance of men and women in a Navy school and their subsequent performance in the fleet.   Found more women than men were satisfied with their occupational specialties, school assignments, and being in the Navy.

326 *Hoiberg, Anne and Jack F. White.* **Health Status of Women in the Armed Forces.** San Diego, CA: Naval Health Research Center, 1989. 24p. OCLC 25680174.
Examines the health status and attrition rates of three five year cohorts of Navy women who enlisted between 1973 and 1987. Found that pregnancy was the leading reason for hospitalization and the most frequent reasons for premature separation were pregnancy/parenthood and unsuitability.

327 *Hoiberg, Anne and Jack F. White.* **"Health Status of Women in the Armed Forces."** *Armed Forces and Society* 18(4): 514-533, Summer 1990.
Results of a study to assess the health status of enlisted women in the Navy and to determine whether or not women's illness, injury, and career patterns have changed over the fifteen year period since the advent of the all-volunteer force. Found hospitalization rates for pregnancy-related conditions have increased, and have decreased for psychiatric disorders, respiratory diseases, and accidental injury rates.

328 *Lurie, Philip M.* **Two-Term Survival of Female Personnel.** Alexandria, VA: Naval Studies Group, Center for Naval Analysis, 1982. 53p. OCLC 9749902.
A study of survival rates for female Navy recruits, estimated through eight years of service. Found that women with a high school diploma survived three to four months longer than those with a General Education Degree.

329 *Olson, Marsha S. and Patricia J. Thomas.* **Preenlistment Drug Experiences of Navy Women and Men: A Comparison.** San Diego, CA: Navy Personnel Research and Development Center, 1978. 35p. ED 165021.
The Navy's Drug Experiences Questionnaire was administered to 519 women in June 1976. Results were compared to a 1975 survey of males. Demonstrated similar male and female pre-service drug experiences.

330 *Pope, Louis T.* **Male and Female Performance in Ten Traditionally Male Navy Ratings.** San Diego, CA: Navy Personnel Research and Development Center, 1982. 27p. OCLC 22367203.
Performance of enlisted men and women working in ten traditionally male ratings in the Navy was studied to determine the attitudes of women towards their jobs and the attitudes of men and women towards mixed sex work groups. Peer ratings showed the overall performance of women was not significantly different from men, however more men than women felt that women did not perform as well as men.

331 *Thomas, Judith Ann.* **Women's Recruit Training in the United States Navy: A Study of the "Rites of Passage."** Thesis (M.A.)--California State University, Sacramento, 1972. 132p. OCLC 12896145.
The author investigated Naval recruit training for women, by interviewing

women at the U.S. Naval Station, Treasure Island, who had recently completed recruit training (January and February 1972). A description of basic training and how the military teaches individuals to function as part of a group.

332 Thomas, Patricia J. **Utilization of Enlisted Women in the Military.** San Diego, CA: Navy Personnel Research and Development Center, 1976. 23p. OCLC 2988139.
Reviews the status of American military women from an historical perspective, to determine what effect recent policy changes have had on their utilization, with an emphasis on Navy women. Found that due to combat exclusion laws, Navy women cannot participate fully in their units, even in peacetime.

333 Thomas, Patricia J. and Kathleen P. Durning. **"The Young Navy Woman: Her Work and Role Orientation."** Youth & Society 10(2): 135-159, December 1978.
Study to identify the factors that influenced young women to enlist in the Navy and to determine whether young men entering the Navy differed on these factors. Also studied the sex role attitudes held by junior enlisted Navy women. Found that young men and women entering the Navy came from similar backgrounds and men and women enlisted for similar reasons.

334 Thomas, Patricia J., Marilyn J. Monda, Shelly H. Mills, and Julie A. Mathis. **Navy Women in Traditional and Nontraditional Jobs: A Comparison of Satisfaction, Attrition, and Reenlistment.** San Diego, CA: Navy Personnel Research and Development Center, 1992. 41p. OCLC 9002699; ED 219575.
Examined the effects of gender appropriateness of job assignments and mix of men and women in a work group upon the attitudes and behavior of Navy women. Followed about 1,000 men and 1,000 women who joined the Navy in 1975. Found it didn't matter to women whether they were in a traditional or nontraditional job. Had no effect on attrition, job satisfaction, advancement, or reenlistment.

OFFICERS

335 Collins, Helen. **"Women in Naval Aviation: From Plane Captains to Pilots."** Naval Aviation News 8-18, July 1977.
Story of women in Naval aviation, from WAVES who worked for the Bureau of Aeronautics during World War II, to women serving as naval flight surgeons and pilots. Many photographs.

336 Davis, Barbara J. and A. Renee Gutierrez. **Gender Induced Differences in Naval Fitness Reports.** Monterey, CA: Naval Postgraduate School, 1991. 71p. OCLC 25836463.
Duplicated a 1983 study by the Naval Research and Development Center reviewing the possible differences in the narrative portions of Naval

Fitness Reports. The original study found significant differences in the average numbers of descriptors used in FitReps written about women versus men. This study found no differences.

337 *Johnson, Dean Frazier, Carolyn McConnell Wells and Robert Brekenridge.* **"Implications for Aging Service As a Female Naval Officer."** *Minerva* 7(1): 15-46, Spring 1986.
Compared 241 female ex-Naval officers to a group of ninety-six women who were their peers during World War II. Examined the psychological and social factors to assess the impact of Naval service on women's careers and their adjustment to aging.

338 *Leblanc, Lynne Marie.* **The Influence of Naval Training and Experience on the Life Choices of Women Officers.** Thesis (Ph.D.)--Northern Illinois University, 1992. 211p.
Designed to describe and interpret Navy officer training, work experience, and lifestyle of women commissioned in the Navy in the 1970s and 1980s. Used a case study method of twelve women officers. Found the women's military training and experience influenced the women's decisions to remain in the Navy, their choice of Navy technical specialties, occupational and career choices after leaving the Navy, choice of friends, and self-image.

339 *Lewis, Chrystal A.* **"Becoming a Naval Aviator."** *Proceedings: U.S. Naval Institute* 112(10): 104-107, October 1986.
A first hand account of Naval flight training at Pensacola, Florida by a female graduate of the Naval Academy. Also discusses training at the Air Force's Survival, Escape, Resistance, Evasion (SERE) School and service in the Philippines flying single-seat A-4Es. Article is abridged from an oral history interview with the author held in the U.S. Naval Institute Oral History Institute, Annapolis, Maryland.

340 *McKenzie, Colleen J.* **Attitudes of Male Unrestricted Line (URL) Officers towards Integration of Women into Their Designators and towards Women in Combat.** Monterey, CA: Naval Postgraduate School, 1983. 84p. OCLC 22606931.
The results of the 1978 Department of Defense Survey of officers and enlisted personnel were examined to survey attitudes of male Navy officers towards women serving as unrestricted line officers and in combat. It was shown that senior officers were less willing to accept women officers in their designators than were junior officers.

341 *Mumford, Sandra Jean.* **Similarities and Differences in the Organizational Perceptions of Female and Male Naval Officers.** Thesis (M.S.)--San Diego State University, 1977. 104p. OCLC 12433152.
Examines male and female managers in the Navy to determine what similarities and differences there are in attitudes towards and perceptions of the organization between gender groups. It was found that women felt less positive about the support provided to them by their supervisors and often felt left out of the decision making process.

342   *Regis, Elizabeth Ann.* **How Female Officers' Performance in Non-Traditional U.S. Navy Shipboard Jobs Compares to Male Officers' Performance.** Monterey, CA: Naval Postgraduate School, 1988. 39p. OCLC 22136289.
A research proposal, suggesting a way in which to analyze the performance of female officers in non-traditional shipboard jobs and compare that performance to male officers.

343   *Russell, Sandy.* **"High Flying Ladies."** *Naval Aviation News* 6-15, February 1981.
Provides a history of women in Naval aviation, from 1973, when women entered the Navy's flight program. Many excerpts from interviews with women Naval aviators. Photographs.

344   *Thomas, Patricia J.* **The Female Naval Officer: What Is Her Role?**
Paper presented at the Annual Convention of the American Psychological Association (Toronto, Canada), August 1978. 23p. ED 173723.
Discusses a 1972 survey of female and male Naval officers which found that most men doubted women should serve on active duty or as line or commanding officers. Women felt their status was one of inferiority. By 1977, women saw equal opportunity as essential. Recommends that junior female officers be encouraged to take on responsibilities previously undertaken only by male or senior female officers.

345   *Thomas, Patricia J.* **Women Officers' Performance Evaluations: Faint Praise May Affect Promotions.** Paper presented at the Annual Convention of the American Psychological Association (92nd, Toronto, Canada), August 24-28, 1984. 6p. ED 251745.
To determine whether gender influences Naval officers' evaluations, narrative information was extracted from the performance evaluations of 239 line officers (120 women, 189 men). There was a significant difference by gender in the words used to describe behavior.

346   *Turner, Robbie G.* **Minority Women Officers in the Navy: Past, Present, and Future Prospects.** Thesis (M.S.)--Naval Postgraduate School, 1991. 79p. OCLC 25291264.
An exploratory study, giving many statistics regarding female Naval officers, with an emphasis on black women. Concludes that the reduction in the size of the officer corps will result in the increased probability of the continued underrepresentation of minority women.

347   *Xenakis, Christopher I.* **"Lucy and Linus in the Wardroom."** *Proceedings: U.S. Naval Institute* 110(12): 90-92, December 1984.
Highlights problems faced by women officers, such as not seriously planning their careers, overspecializing, leadership styles, etc. Suggests women should take a more active role in managing their careers and develop a coherent career strategy.

WOMEN AT SEA

348 *Bertram, Jack Randolph.* **An Analysis of Attitudes toward the Integration of Women into U.S. Navy Shipboard Units.** Thesis (M.A.)-- United States International University, 1973. 74p. OCLC 2587867.
A study conducted to identify attitudes among male and female officers and enlisted personnel regarding the integration of women as crew members on board surface-type Navy ships. There was a significant difference found between male and female attitudes.

349 *Buchta, Katherine S.* **"Women at Sea: A Female Physician's Viewpoint."** *U.S. Navy Medicine* 72(9): 8-12, September 1981.
Describes how the medical needs of women sailors were met as part of the Women at Sea Program.

350 *Crooks, Robert A.* **Women-at-Sea from a Manager's Perspective.** Newport, RI: Naval War College, 1984. 31p.
Discusses problems caused by women on ships and some solutions. Based on the author's experience serving as commander of the USS *Norton Sound*, one of the first Navy ships to be assigned women. Concludes the problems with women on ships are the same of any minority, and women perform as well as men with comparable training.

351 *Dembert, Mark L.* **"Nobody Asked Me, but...Women Shouldn't Serve on Submarines."** *Proceedings: U.S. Naval Institute* 121(8): 72, August 1995.
Argues that women should not serve on submarines, although not due to the reason stated by the Navy, which is the expense of reconfiguring subs to accommodate women. Rather the author, a Navy psychiatrist, believes that an isolated submarine environment with a crew of men and women, would present too much of a psychologically complex environment for a submarine officer's training and role as a commanding officer to manage.

352 *Durning, Kathleen P.* **Women on Ships: Attitudes and Issues.** Paper presented at the Annual Convention of the American Psychological Association (Ontario, Canada), August 1978. 17p. ED 172091.
Results of a survey of 480 Navy women regarding women on Navy ships. Nearly ninety percent believed that women should be allowed to serve in ships exactly as men do, and over half declared themselves ready to go to sea. Found that there is sizeable resistance on the part of male officers to having women serve on ships.

353 *Edney, Leon A.* **"Interview: Leon A. Edney, Vice Admiral, U.S. Navy."** *Proceedings: U.S. Naval Institute* 114(5): 143-145, May 1988.
Interview with Vice Admiral Leon A. Edney, Chief of Naval Personnel and Assistant Chief of Naval Operations for Manpower, Personnel and Training. Outlines the Navy's policy on sending women to sea.

354 Greebler, Carol S., Patricia J. Thomas, and Judy D. Kuczynski. **Men and Women in Ships: Preconceptions of the Crews.** San Diego, CA: Navy Personnel Research and Development Center, 1982. 63p. ED 220665. Preintegration attitudes and expectations of 1,936 men and 346 women assigned to six Navy ships were measured before the women reported aboard. Results showed that the majority of men believed that integration would improve crew morale, but would have a negative impact on discipline. The women were most concerned with profanity, success in their job, and resentment from men.

355 Nice, Stephen D. and Susan Hilton. **"Sex Differences and Occupational Influences on Health Care Utilization Aboard U.S. Navy Ships."** Military Psychology 6(2): 109-123, 1994.
Assessed health care requirements of men and women aboard Navy ships. Collected data from twenty Navy ships over one year. Results indicated that the pattern of sex differences in health care use aboard ships was similar to that of the nation as a whole. Also showed that women in nontraditional occupations visited sick call at a significantly higher rate than women working in traditional occupations.

356 Regis, Elizabeth Ann. **How Female Officers' Performance in Non-Traditional U.S. Navy Shipboard Jobs Compares to Male Officers' Performance.** Monterey, CA: Naval Postgraduate School, 1988. 39p. See **342.**

357 Reichert, Paulette. **Women at Sea: A Sinking Ship?** Thesis (M.A.)-- Naval Postgraduate School, 1976. 95p. OCLC 3464842.
Examines different ways of utilizing women in the Navy and concludes that women are underutilized. Recommends women's roles be expanded to include sea and combat duty. Dated.

358 Sherrod, Joyce A. **Women at Sea: Welcome Aboard?** Thesis (M.S.)-- Naval Postgraduate School, 1983. 140p. OCLC 18327778.
Studies what actions Navy commands took in fiscal year 1978 to enhance the integration of the first shipboard women officers and what the women did or experienced that facilitated their integration. Also addresses what behaviors were considered acceptable for women officers and to what extent these behaviors could be considered typically masculine, feminine or androgynous.

359 Spillane, Roberta. **"Women in Ships: Can We Survive?"** Proceedings: U.S. Naval Institute 113(7): 43-46, July 1987.
Examines the issues surrounding the assignment of women to Navy ships, such as pregnancy, fraternization, and physical strength limitations, and proposes solutions. Brief, but good discussion. Concludes that the Women in Ships Program is needed to solve manpower shortages and further sexual equality within the Navy.

360 Thomas, Patricia J. **Men and Women in Ships: Attitudes of Crews After One to Two Years of Integration.** San Diego, CA: Navy Personnel

Research and Development Center, 1983. 67p.
Administered pre- and post-integration surveys to the first ten Navy ships to receive women. Found chief petty officers had a positive opinion of the impact of women on the ship and crew, nonrated men were enthusiastic about mixed-gender crewing, and petty officers felt women led to a decline in discipline and leadership and preferred all male crews.

361 *Thomas, Patricia J.* **Women in the Military: Gender Integration at Sea.**
San Diego, CA: Navy Personnel Research and Development Center, 1981. 27p.
Surveyed members of four Navy ships before integration, then resurveyed one ship nine months after integration. Found nonrated men had the most traditional beliefs about women's roles in the workplace, although they liked working with women more than any other group. Petty officers were the least positive about the success of integration. Women felt more performance pressure than men and experienced more problems aboard ship.

COAST GUARD

ARCHIVES AND MANUSCRIPTS

362 **Office of the Coast Guard Historian.** Washington, DC.
Contains nine boxes of materials on World War II SPARs, including reports, rosters of members, photographs and negatives, correspondence, manuals, newspaper articles, etc. Also holds video interviews with retired Coast Guard officers, including Dorothy Stratton, former director of SPARs in World War II.

363 **Records of the Bureau of Naval Personnel.** Record Group 24, National Archives.
Contains personnel policy and actions for the SPARs.

364 **Stratton, Captain Dorothy, USCGR**. Oral history Interview. United States Naval Institute Oral History Collection.
Captain Stratton was the Director of the SPAR during World War II. Her oral history interview and transcript are available at the Naval Institute. The transcript is also available at the Nimitz Library, United States Naval Academy and the Naval Historical Center in Washington, DC.

GENERAL WORKS

365 *Gooch, Robert H.* **"Coast Guard Example of Sending Women to Sea."**
Proceedings: U.S. Naval Institute 114(5): 124-133, May 1988.
Suggests the Navy study how the Coast Guard has sexually integrated its ships as the Navy prepares to do the same. Interviewed Coast Guard personnel on how integration was accomplished.

366 *Nelson, Cynthia Ann. "Dilemma: Coast Guard Women and Combat."*
Proceedings: U.S. Naval Institute 115(9): 78-82, September 1989.
Discusses the problems that would arise in wartime when the Coast
Guard comes under the direction of the Navy (written before women
were assigned to combatant ships). Analyzes whether or not Coast
Guard women would also be prohibited from serving on combatant ships.

367 *SPARS: The U.S. Coast Guard Women's Reserve.* Washington, DC:
U.S. Coast Guard, Office of Public Affairs, 1977. 114p. SuDocs
N24.39:22A; OCLC 14472797.
A collection of reprints about SPARs from the U.S. Coast Guard
Magazine (1944-1946, 1950, 1956) and press releases (1976-1977)
concerning women on active service in the Coast Guard.

368 *United States Coast Guard. Women in the Coast Guard Study.*
Washington, DC: U.S. Coast Guard, 1990. Not paged. SuDocs
TD5.2:W84; OCLC 22329155.
Results of a study chartered by the Commandant of the Coast Guard in
August 1989 to examine the utilization of women. Four major areas
were studied, force composition, recruitment and retention, nontraditional roles, and policy. Surveys and personal interviews were
conducted with men and women. Includes many useful statistics and
discussions on the attitudes towards women in combat, sexual
harassment, and pregnancy.

WORLD WAR II

369 *Harris, Mary Virginia. Guide Right: A Handbook of Etiquette and
Customs for Members of the Women's Reserve of the United States
Naval Reserve and the United States Coast Guard Reserve.* New York:
MacMillan Company, 1944. 105p.
See **295**.

370 *Lyne, Mary C. and Kay Arthur. Three Years behind the Mast: The
Story of the United States Coast Guard SPARS.* Washington, DC: n.p.,
1946. 126p. OCLC 3637904.
Includes personal anecdotes about SPAR training and job assignments.
One of the few books written at the time to mention any hostile reaction
by men towards women in service. Discusses experiences of SPARs
stationed in Alaska and Hawaii. Includes many photographs, lists SPAR
ratings, important dates in SPAR history, etc. Authors were lieutenants
in the SPAR.

371 *Schon, Marion B. "One Woman in Uniform: A Tale of Personal
Growth."* Minerva 5(2): 97-106, Summer 1987.
The author joined the Coast Guard in February 1943. She trained at the
Navy's boot camp, Hunter College in the Bronx. After serving in
Washington, DC, she was selected to attend Officer Training School and
was commissioned as an ensign.

372   *United States Coast Guard.* **The Coast Guard at War, Volume XX, Women's Reserve.**   Washington, DC: U.S. Coast Guard, Public Information Division, 1946. 259p.

A detailed official history of the Coast Guard Women's Reserve during World War II, covering organization, training, recruitment, job assignments, etc. Also covers housing, uniforms, personnel policies, and promotion policies.

5

MARINE CORPS

According to Marine Corps legend, Lucy Brewer was the first "girl marine." Disguised as George Baker, she is said to have served for three years on the USS *Constitution* during the War of 1812. The first woman to officially serve as a Marine was Opha Johnson, who enlisted on 13 August 1918. The Marine Corps enrolled 305 women, called Marine Reservists (F), in the last months of World War I. These women enlisted to assume clerical duties so that fighting men could be sent overseas. The Corps had no time for training, so only the most qualified women were selected. The majority of the women were assigned to Washington, DC, but a small number served in recruiting offices in several large cities. The women Marines received the same pay as enlisted men of equal rank, and at the end of the war, received full veterans benefits.

Women would not serve again as Marines until early in 1943, with the establishment of the Marine Corps Women's Reserve (MCWR). A small corps of officers, headed by the new Director of the Women Reserves, Major Ruth Cheney Streeter, was formed from a group of Navy WAVES.

By the end of the war, there were nearly 17,640 enlisted women and 820 officers. Restricted by law from serving overseas, at least until the last few months of the war, women Marines made up eighty-five percent of enlisted personnel at Marine Corps Headquarters and from one-half to two-thirds of personnel at large Marine Corps installations. They were working in 225 specialties in sixteen out of twenty-one functional fields.

The passage of the Women's Armed Services Integration Act of 1948 gave women Marines a permanent place in the Corps. The Corps, however, was home to a very small number of women. In June 1948, there were only eight officers and 159 enlisted women, for a total of 167 women Marines. Nearly all worked in administration and supply. At the end of the Korean War, numbers had grown to over 2,500, but women were still concentrated in only six or seven specialties and received very little job training.

Opportunities for women Marines were expanded during the 1960s and 1970s, with changes in training, assignments, and utilization. The Office of Director of Marines was abolished in 1977, signaling the Corps willingness to integrate women more fully.

While more jobs have opened for Marine women during the 1980s and 1990s, it is still the most restrictive of the services with the smallest number of women serving. Only thirty-four percent of available Marine Corps jobs are open to women, versus 99.7 percent in the Air Force. This is due partly to the fact that many jobs in the Corps are combat positions and are therefore closed to women.   It seems likely that even with some combat jobs now open to women, such as combat pilot, the numbers of Marine Corps women will remain small.

ARCHIVES AND MANUSCRIPTS

373   *Records of the United States Marine Corps.* Record Group 127, National Archives.
Contains general correspondence regarding Marine Reservists (F) from World War I, including uniforms, enrollment, pay and allowances, statistics, and photographs. Records for the World War II Marine Corps Women's Reserve (MCWR) include personnel records, correspondence of the Director, MCWR, and motion pictures.

374   *Streeter, Colonel Ruth Cheney, USMCWR (Retired).* Oral History Interview.   United States Naval Institute Oral History Collection, Annapolis, MD. 366p.
Transcript of four interviews conducted from April through July 1979. Streeter was the first Director of the MCWR. Discusses her younger years, World War I, and her work with the MCWR during World War II. Also held at the Schlesinger Library, Radcliffe College, Cambridge, MA.

375   *Towle, Colonel Katherine Amelia, Administration and Leadership.* Oral History Interview. Schlesinger Library, Radcliffe College, Cambridge, MA. Interview conducted in 1967 with Colonel Towle, the Director of Women Marines from 1948 to 1953.

376   *Women Marines in WW I Collection.* United States Marine Corps, History and Museums Division, Washington, DC.
Correspondence, a history, articles, photos, clippings and other memorabilia relating to the women of the Marine Corps Reserve in World War I. Also includes interviews with thirty-two veterans about their war experiences.

377   *Women Marines in WW II Collection.* United States Marine Corps, History and Museums Division, Washington, DC.
Histories, articles, pamphlets, clippings and other materials relating to the women Marines of World War II.

GENERAL WORKS

378   *Solis, Shirley A. Psychosocial Stress in Male and Female Marine Corps Officers.* Thesis (Ph.D.)--United States International University, 1988. 76p. OCLC 19074542.
The author wanted to see if female Marine Corps officers experience

significantly different levels of stress as compared to their male counterparts, and how each gender perceives their own level of stress. Surveyed 900 Marine officers (thirty-five women and 865 men) and found that majors and lieutenant colonels reported significantly greater total stress than did colonels. Female majors inaccurately perceived their stress to be greater than males.

379   *Williams, Christine L.* **Women Marines and Male Nurses: The Social Construction and Maintenance of Gender.** Thesis (Ph.D.)--University of California, Berkeley, 1986. 260p. OCLC 19736281.
Later revised for a book (see **697**), this dissertation contains an interesting discussion of femininity in the Marine Corps. Includes an analysis of the combat exclusion policies of all the services as well as the training given to women Marines. Also includes many quotations from men and women servicemembers on their views towards women in the service and in combat roles.

WORLD WAR I

380   *Hewitt, Linda L*. **Women Marines in World War I.** Washington, DC: History and Museums Division, Headquarters, United States Marine Corps, 1974. 80p. SuDocs D214.13:W84; OCLC 1448227.
Official history of Women Marines in World War I. Covers selection, training, housing, uniforms, duty assignments, etc. Includes photographs and a partial roster of women who served as Marines during the war.

WORLD WAR II

381   *Cone, Schuyler Eaton.* **Investigation of Fashion Characteristics 1937-1943 Incorporated in a Specific Type of Female Marine Corps Uniform, 1943.** Thesis (Ph.D.)--Ohio State University, 1994. 317p.
Research to determine if fashionable attributes of civilian apparel from 1937-1943 were present in the forest green winter uniform of the Marine Corps Women's Reserve. Found fashionable female civilian dress included a jacket with square shoulder and fitted waist and an A-line skirt; the marine uniform featured the same. Suggests a female uniform incorporating civilian fashion attributes provided social implications about the women who wore the uniform.

382   *Hahn, Milton E. and Cornelia T. Williams.* **"The Measured Interests of Marine Corps Women Reservists."** *Journal of Applied Psychology* 29(3): 198-211, June 1945.
Studied 667 enlisted Marine Corps women to determine the job satisfaction of women in military occupations, the measured interest in military occupations, and a comparison of claimed and measured interests of women performing military duties in the Marine Corps. Purpose was to help assign women to the type of military duty where they could most efficiently serve the Corps.

383 *Meid, Pat.* **Marine Corps Women's Reserve in World War II.**
Washington, DC: Historical Branch, G-3 Division, United States Marine
Corps, 1968. 98p. SuDocs D214.14/2:W84; OCLC 453689; ISBN
10802206.
Official history of women Marines during World War II. Discusses the
selection process, uniforms, assignment policies, promotions, relations
with the other services and demobilization. Has several appendices,
including biographies of the wartime directors of women Marines, the
jobs in which women served, etc.

384 *Nau, Erika S.* **"The Spirit of Molly Marine."** *Minerva* 8(4): 23-29,
Winter 1990.
Summary of the formation of, and the role played by, women Marines
during World War II. Brief description of boot training and job
assignments.

385 *Soderbergh, Peter A.* **Women Marines: The World War II Era.**
Westport, CT: Praeger, 1992. 189p. OCLC 25130970; ISBN
0275941310.
Outgrowth of a biography written by the author on a woman Marine who
was killed in a fire during World War II (see **387**). He sent a
questionnaire to 146 women who served as Marines in World War II.
This is a collection of their remembrances, not a history of women
Marines in World War II.

World War II - Personal Narratives

386 *Alsmeyer, Marie Bennett.* **Those Unseen Unheard Arkansas Women:
WAC, WAVES, Women Marines of World War II.** Conway, AR: Marie
Alsmeyer, 1988. 31p.
See **058**.

387 *Soderbergh, Peter A.* **Years of Grace, Days of Glory: The Legacy of
Germaine Laville.** Baton Rouge, LA: Boyd-Ewing Post 58, The
American Legion, Department of Louisiana, 1988. 184p. OCLC
20794652; ISBN 0962055700.
Germaine Laville was one of two women Marines killed in a fire at Cherry
Point, North Carolina on 3 June 1944, while at work. The book contains
many imagined details and conversations. Of interest only for the
description of the actual fire.

388 *Tonelli, Jerre C.* **Leathernecks in Pink Skivvies.** San Francisco, CA:
Pisani Press, 1968. 114p. OCLC 13233823.
The author enlisted in the Marines in February 1943. The book is an
account of her training at Camp LeJeune, North Carolina and ends with
her first assignment.

389 *Yianilos, Theresa Karas.* **Woman Marine: A Memoir of a Woman Who
Joined the U.S. Marine Corps in World War II "To Free a Man to Fight."**

La Jolla, CA: La Jolla Book Publishing Company, 1994. 459p. OCLC 30744726; ISBN 0962114243.
Author served from 1943-1945. Discusses her jobs, training, and life as a woman Marine. Worked as a post courier and in the post motor pool. Interesting and well written with good descriptions of sexual harassment.

POST WORLD WAR II

390 *Moore, Margaret L.* **"Memories of a Woman Marine 1950-1957: An Oral History."** *Minerva* 3(2): 128-137, Summer 1985.
Transcript of an oral history interview with Moore, who served as a sergeant in the Marine Corps. Discusses boot camp and administrative school.

391 *Soderbergh, Peter A.* **Women Marines in the Korean War Era.** Westport, CT: Praeger Publishers, 1994. 167p. OCLC 29952456; ISBN 0275948277.
More about the Korean War era than women Marines. Covers the signing of the Women's Armed Services Integration Act in 1948 to the withdrawal of the First Marine Division from Korea in the spring of 1955. Provides comments from questionnaires the author sent to women Marine veterans about their jobs and life as Marines.

392 *Stremlow, Mary V.* **A History of the Women Marines, 1946-1977.** Washington, DC: History and Museums Division, Headquarters, United States Marine Corps, 1986. 250p. SuDocs D214.13:W84/2; OCLC 14158802; ED 280948.
An official history of the Women Marines from the end of World War II to 1977. The author, a retired Marine colonel, discusses the Korean War years, women Marine's service in Vietnam, training, job assignments, uniforms, promotions, etc. Includes many photographs.

PERSIAN GULF WAR

393 *Rathmell, Anne E. and Kim T. Adamson.* **Women Marines: Their Perceptions from Southwest Asia.** Quantico, VA: Marine Corps Research Center, 1991. 25p.
The results of a survey done with 239 women Marines who served in Desert Shield/Desert Storm, to find out their perceptions of life in the desert and in combat, and how they were utilized. The women were generally satisfied with billeting and the availability of personal support items. They felt they had been treated equally by male Marines and had been given the opportunity to do their jobs. The majority believed women should be allowed to serve in the combat arms.

RECRUITMENT, TRAINING, AND ATTRITION

394   *Dunbar, Stephen B. and Melvin R. Novick.* **On Predicting Success in Training for Males and Females: Marine Corps Clerical Specialties and ASVAB Forms 6 and 7.** Arlington, VA: Office of Naval Research, Personnel and Training Research Program Office, 1985.   52p.   ED 255567.
Differences in prediction systems for male and female Marine performance were investigated in a study of clerical specialties in the Corps.

395   *Quester, Aline O. and Greg W. Steadman.* **Enlisted Women in the Marine Corps: First-Term Attrition and Long-Term Retention.** Alexandria, VA: Center for Naval Analysis, 1990.   Not paged.   OCLC 25814537.
Author found that during the first term of service, female attrition rates were about 1.5 times higher than male attrition rates. However, over the long term, women Marines have higher retention rates than males. One third of first term attrition for females was due to pregnancy or parenthood.

396   *Royle, Marjorie H.* **First-Term Attrition among Marine Corps Women: Some Associated Factors.** San Diego, CA: Navy Personnel Research and Development Center, 1983. 50p. OCLC 12176092; ED 231966.
Identifies factors which might be related to the high attrition of enlisted Marine Corps women, which was nearly fifty percent. The results of the study indicated that the difference in post-recruit training attrition between men and women was due to pregnancy (however women did not become pregnant to be discharged). Makes recommendations for changes in women's training and unit assignment.

6

ARMY 1942–1945

During World War I, women worked for, but did not serve in, the Army. First employed as telephone operators in France as civilian contract employees, they did not have military status. It was recognized by several Army agencies, including the Quartermaster General and the Chief of Ordnance, that a corps of women under military control would solve many manpower problems. Women were already serving with full military benefits in the Navy and later in the Marine Corps. The plan was considered unfavorably by the War Department. However, the end of the war did not bring an end to the planning for the utilization of women by the Army in a future war.

The position of Director of Women's Relations, United States Army, was established in 1920 to maintain a liaison between the War Department and the women of the United States. One of the first directors was Miss Anita Phipps, who spent ten years trying to expand her position into planner for a women's army corps and first director. Miss Phipps proposed that a women's corps should be established in the Army and not as an auxiliary. Questionnaires she sent to corps, chiefs of branches and similar services revealed that about 170,000 women would be needed in wartime. The Phipps plan was never enacted and was shelved after her resignation.

In 1928, Major Everett S. Hughes was appointed as the chief Army planner for a women's corps. Major Hughes recognized that women would be essential in the next war, and formulated a new plan to utilize women. The Hughes plan was based on the assumption that only women serving overseas or in danger zones would be militarized. He concluded that it was uneconomical and confusing to maintain separate organizations for men and women and that qualified women should be integrated into the men's army, with the same privileges and a similar uniform. Unfortunately, Major Hughes's plan ended up in a file and was not rediscovered until six months after the formation of the WAAC, and as Mattie Treadwell wrote, "War Department Planners had already made most of the mistakes he predicted" (see **408**).

It was not until 1939 that planning for a women's corps was resumed under Chief of Staff George C. Marshall. The earlier Phipps and Hughes plans had been forgotten. The new plan emphasized that women were not to receive full military status, and possible jobs would include hostesses, cooks and waitresses, chauffeurs and strolling minstrels. Nothing in the plan was implemented and by 1941, pressure began to build from women's groups for women's participation in the country's defense.

In May 1941, Congresswoman Edith Nourse Rogers introduced a bill to establish a Women's Army Auxiliary Corps (WAAC) for service with the Army. She wanted women to serve in, rather than with, the Army, but the resistance of the War Department and Congress to granting full military status to women would have ensured the bill's failure if this provision had been included. On 15 May 1942, Public Law 554, An Act to Establish a Women's Army Auxiliary Corps for Service with the Army of the United States, was signed by President Roosevelt and on 16 May, Oveta Culp Hobby was sworn in as the first Director of the WAAC.

The WAACs status as an auxiliary caused problems from the start. Women were not entitled to the same pay, benefits, or even the same ranks as men. The formation of the other women's corps, such as women Marines and Navy WAVES, where women were integrated with men from the start, made service in the WAAC less desirable, and the numbers of new recruits dropped. On 1 July 1943, a bill was signed establishing a Women's Army Corp (WAC) where women were given full military status. Members of the WAAC were given ninety days to join the WAC or leave the service.

WACs worked in many different types of jobs during the war, including as drivers, parachute riggers, mechanics, photographers, radio operators, aviation specialists, in intelligence, and weather forecasters. They served throughout the continental United States, as well as overseas, with over 17,000 WACs serving in all overseas theaters in July 1945. The numbers of WACs on active duty reached a high of nearly 100,000 in April 1945. The total number of women who served in the WAAC/WAC during World War II was over 150,000.

This chapter includes materials on Army women from the formation of the WAAC in 1942 to the end of World War II in 1945. Items on Army women from 1946 to present are in **Chapter 7**.

ARCHIVES AND MANUSCRIPTS

397   ***Hobby, Oveta Culp.   Papers, 1941-1952.***   Library of Congress, Manuscript Division. Washington, DC.
Hobby was the Director of the WAC from 1943 to 1945. Includes correspondence, engagement calendars, invitations, transcript of an interview, photos, clippings and printed matter such as yearbooks and army publications.

398   ***Long, Westray Battle Boyce.   Papers, 1945-1962.***   Harry S. Truman Library, Independence, MO.
Joined the WAAC in 1942 and was the Director of WACs from 1945-1947. Includes correspondence, memoranda, reports, publications, and clippings.

399   ***Records of the Adjutant General's Office, 1917-.***   Record Group 407, National Archives.
Includes records related to recruiting, training, uniforms, minorities,

medical examinations, orders, regulations, strengths, etc, of the WAC in World War II. Also contains records of general correspondence (formerly classified), statistics relating to WAC casualties, and lists of WAC officers.

400 ***Records of the War Department General and Special Staffs.*** Record Group 165, National Archives.
Contains a wealth of materials on the WAC, including recommendations for medals, overseas conditions, minorities, pregnancy, historical materials on the formation of the WAAC and WAC, and correspondence of the WAC Directors (formerly classified).

GENERAL WORKS

401 *Allen, Ann.* ***"The News Media and the Women's Army Auxiliary Corps: Protagonists for a Cause."*** *Military Affairs* 50(2): 77-83, April 1986.
Interesting account of how the WAAC used media coverage to build a positive public image. Analyzed newspaper and magazine articles to see how the WAAC were portrayed to the American public.

402 *Bellafaire, Judith A.* ***The Women's Army Corps: A Commemoration of World War II Service.*** Washington, DC: U.S. Army Center of Military History, 1993(?). 28p. SuDocs D114.2:W84.
Brochure summarizing the role of the WAAC/WAC during World War II. Covers the formation of the WAAC, recruitment and training, assignments, and overseas service. Good summary of WAC service.

403 ***"Benefits to Women's Army Auxiliary Corps."*** *Annals of the American Academy of Political and Social Science* 227: 156-157, May 1943.
Discusses the benefits available to members of the WAAC. As WAACs were not in, but served with the Army, they were not entitled to many benefits, such as free postage, dependent pay and uniform allowances.

404 *Hobby, O.C.* ***"Training of Women for New Tasks."*** *Proceedings of the Academy of Political Science* 20(3): 231-237, May 1943.
Writes that the WAAC have dispelled the notion that women cannot adjust themselves to discipline and communal living. Discusses the WAAC physical standards and classification tests. Good description of training.

405 *Hock, Cecilia.* ***"Creation of the WAC Image and Perception of Army Women."*** *Minerva* 13(1): 40-62, Spring 1995.
Describes how the first WAAC Director, Colonel Hobby, recognized the importance of portraying a positive image of the WAAC/WAC to the media and how this was accomplished. Emphasizing the femininity of the WAAC was done in many ways, including designing a uniform of a skirt and not pants. Discusses the slander campaign against the WAAC.

406   *Meyer, Leisa Diane.* **Creating G.I. Jane: The Women's Army Corps during World War II.** Thesis (Ph.D.)--University of Wisconsin, Madison, 1993. 619p.
An analysis of the creation and history of the Women's Army Corps. Emphasis on the process of how women were accepted into the Army, a masculine organization, and how this process can help to evaluate the discourse concerning gender and sexuality in modern American culture.

407   **Study of the Women's Army Corps in the European Theater of Operations.** Bad Nauheim, Germany: The General Board, U.S.F.E.T., 1945-1946. 3 volumes. OCLC 18486263.
Study to provide a factual and annotated report of the WAC in the European Theater and provide recommendations. An exhaustive analysis covering all aspects of women's service; assignments, uniforms and equipment, medical problems, housing, even the numbers of sheets and pillowcases needed for women's barracks. Includes many statistics and copies of correspondence. Originally a classified document (declassified in 1988).

408   *Treadwell, Mattie E.* **U.S. Army in World War II: Special Studies. The Women's Army Corps.** Washington, DC: Office of the Chief of Military History, Department of the Army, 1954. 841p. SuDocs D114.7:W84; OCLC 1028881.
Required reading for any researcher of the Women's Army Corps. A comprehensive, detailed official history of the Women's Army Corps in World War II, written by a former WAC lieutenant colonel. Covers all aspects of the WAC, from the establishment of the WAAC, regulations, uniforms, proposals to draft women, medical standards, the slander campaign, overseas service, etc. Indexed, with many photographs and appendices. Continued by *The Women's Army Corps, 1945-1978* (see **469**).

409   *United States. Army. Women's Army Auxiliary Corps.* **Women's Army Corps Regulations (Tentative).** Washington, DC: GPO, 1942. 21p. OCLC 17996500.
Regulations establishing the WAAC. Includes regulations regarding appointment and enrollment, promotion, discharge, discipline, training, uniforms, and pay and allowances.

410   *United States. War Department.* **WAC Life.** Washington, DC: War Department, 1945. 191p. OCLC 22287020.
A manual for women joining the WAC. Provides basic facts about the Army and Army Life and explains basic regulations.

AFRICAN-AMERICAN WACS

411   *Earley, Charity Adams.* **One Woman's Army: A Black Officer Remembers the WAC.** College Station, TX: Texas A & M University Press, 1989. 218p. OCLC 18321957; ISBN 0890963754.

Earley was a teacher who became the first black woman to receive a commission as an officer in the WAAC. Later became the commander of the 6888th Central Postal Directory, the only black WAC unit sent overseas. The unit, first stationed in England and later on the continent, consisted of thirty-one officers and 500 enlisted women, whose job was to redirect mail. Frankly discusses problems faced by black WACs, including segregation in training and units and the prejudices against them. One of the outstanding memoirs by military women.

412   *Newman, Debra L.* **"The Propaganda and the Truth: Black Women and World War II."** *Minerva* 4(4): 72-92, Winter 1986.
Describes the problems faced by black women in the WAC during World War II. The War Department tried to give the impression that it was doing everything possible to ensure the fair treatment of black WACs. However they remained segregated except in work areas.

413   *Pitts, Lucia M.* **One Negro WAC's Story.** Los Angeles, CA: Privately Published, 1968. 22p. OCLC 21697967.
Author enlisted in December 1943 and went to basic training at Ft. Des Moines, IA. First assignment was working for the Provost Marshall at Ft. Huachuca, AZ. Volunteered for overseas duty, was assigned to England, and later worked in the 6888th Central Postal Directory (see **411**).

414   *Putney, Martha S.* **When the Nation Was in Need: Blacks in the Women's Army Corps during World War II.** Metuchen, NJ: Scarecrow Press, 1992. 231p. OCLC 26217253; ISBN 0810825317.
History of black women who served as WACs in World War II. Discusses recruitment, problems caused by segregation, black units, assignments, and general problems faced by black WACs. Includes a discussion of the work of the 6888th Central Postal Battalion, the only black women's unit to serve overseas (see **411**). Appendices include statistical information. Author is a retired history professor who served as a WAC.

415   *Stoddard, Eleanor.* **"The Education of Margaret Jackson: Member of the Women's Army Corps: September 1943-March 1946."** *Minerva* 9(4): 56-77, Winter 1991.
Transcript of an oral history interview with Jackson. She completed basic at Ft. Des Moines, then attended Army Administration School before assignment to Ft. Benning, GA. Later was sent overseas as part of the 6888th Central Postal Battalion, the only black women's unit sent overseas (see **411**). Discusses segregation in the WAC.

HEALTH

416   *Glass, Albert J. and Robert J. Bernucci, editors.* **Neuropsychiatry in World War II. Volume 1: Zone of Interior.** Washington, DC: Office of the Surgeon General, Department of the Army, 1966. 898p. OCLC 3993673.

Chapter XV, "The Women's Army Corps", is a historical survey of psychiatric problems of WACs. Includes many statistics, including number of WACs discharged and reasons, rejection of enlistees, hospitalization rates, etc. Provides information on overseas assignments and effects on health and morale. Includes some data for Army nurses.

417   *Preston, Albert, Jr.* **"The Mental-Hygiene Unit in a W.A.C. Training Center."** *Mental Hygiene* 30: 368-380, July 1946.
The author headed an outpatient treatment center for problems of adjustment at Ft. Des Moines, IA. Describes how WACs were referred to the clinic, studied, and treated. Includes a detailed description of the typically maladjusted WAC.

418   *Wiltse, Charles M., editor.* **Physical Standards in World War II.** Washington, DC: Office of the Surgeon General, Department of the Army, 1967. 356p. OCLC 573215.
Contains information on physical standards for women in the Army in World War II, including members of the Army Nurse Corps. Includes policies for pregnancy and maternity care, as well as for psychiatric discharge, which was the reason for the largest number of discharges for the WAC until August 1943. Also contains a height and weight chart for WACs.

HUMOR, PLAYS, POETRY, AND SONGS

419   *Barsis, Max.* **They're All Yours, Uncle Sam!** New York: Stephen Daye, 1943. 103p.
See **292**.

420   *Douglass, CPT Ruby Jane, PVT Frank Loesser, PVT Hy Zaret and Arthur Altman.* **P.F.C. Mary Brown, A WAC Musical Review.** Washington, DC: Headquarters, Army Service Forces, Special Services Division, ASF, 1944. Not paged. OCLC 930937.
A musical distributed by the Army Service Forces for WACs to perform. Story is about Pallas Athene, who gets tired of Jupiter fooling around with other goddesses, comes down to earth and enlists in the WAC as PFC Mary Brown. Includes music and instructions for staging, costumes and scenery.

421   *Herman, Victor J.* **Winnie the Wac.** Philadelphia: David McKay Company, 1945. 119p. OCLC 1536363.
A collection of cartoons drawn for the camp newspaper at Aberdeen Proving Ground, MD, starring "Winnie the Wac," a fictional character who was portrayed as stupid and frivolous. Not very funny.

422   **Sound Off: A Collection of Verse Written by the WACS of the Mediterranean Theater of Operations.** WAC Public Relations Office, MTOUSA, 1943 (?). 84p. OCLC 8414638.
Collection of short poems written by WACs assigned to the

Mediterranean Theater of Operations during World War II. None are dated, but most are signed. Subjects range from army food, to holidays, jobs, and going home.

423   *Taggs, Margaret Jane.* **We Solemnly Swore.** Philadelphia: Dorrance & Company, 1946. 90p. OCLC 18491388.
Poems written by a WAC sergeant. Topics cover various areas of army life--physical training, inspections, charge-of-quarters, furlough, etc.

424   **Women's Army Corps Song Book.** Washington, DC: GPO, 1944. 41p. OCLC 20211765.
Published by the War Department, this booklet contains the words to patriotic songs, popular favorites, WAC songs, etc. Was distributed to members of the WAC.

PERSONAL NARRATIVES

General Works

425   *Allen, Sara Ann, editor.* **Daughters of Pallas Athene: Cameo Recollections of Women's Army Corps Veterans (WAC Vets).** n.p.: Women's Army Corps Veterans Association, 1983. 288p. OCLC 9701933.
Very short (one to three pages) recollections of women who served in the WAC during World War II. No explanation of where or how the material was compiled and provides little biographical information about contributors.

426   *Boles, Antonette.* **Women in Khaki.** New York: Vantage Press Inc., 1953. 240p. OCLC 7156662.
Author left her civilian teaching job in July 1943 to answer the WAAC's request for recruits with training in a foreign language. In sharp contrast to other memoirs, Boles is highly critical of the WAAC and WAC. Assigned to Ft. Rucker, AL, she was trained as an administrative and technical clerk, but ended up in a hospital ward doing manual labor. Descriptions of problems caused by low quality recruits.

427   *Chrisman, Catherine Bell.* **My War: W.W. II As Experienced by One Woman Soldier.** Denver, CO: Maverick Publishers, 1989. 196p. OCLC 20481969.
Author enlisted in the WAAC in November 1942. Served as a radio mechanic at Victorville Army Depot in California. There was not enough work, so she was reclassified as a clerk typist. Some photographs.

428   *Dahlgren, "Cyclone" Forbes.* **We Were First: Eglin Field WW II WACS: We Heard the Guns at Wewak.** Brownsville, TX: Springman-King Company, 1977. 150p. OCLC 10350238.
Forbes served as a WAC assigned to Eglin Field, Florida, where she worked in a weather station. Very disorganized. Provides some

information about the different types of jobs WACs held at Eglin and includes stories from WACs sent overseas. Many photographs.

429   *Flint, Margaret, editor.* **Dress Right, Dress: The Autobiography of a WAC.** New York: Dodd, Mead & Company, Inc., 1943. 174p. OCLC 362108.
The editor has taken letters from two women in the WAAC and edited them for publication, trying to give "an inside view." Majority of the letters were written by a woman Army photographer who later received a commission. Some incidents have been partially fictionalized.

430   *Grahn, Elna Hilliard.* **In the Company of WACs.** Manhattan, KS: Sunflower University Press, 1993. 195p. OCLC 30706530; ISBN 0897451597.
Grahn served from 1942-1946 as a major in the WAAC/WAC. She headed the WAAC in a top secret experiment in Washington, DC, using WAACs to see if a composite antiaircraft unit (using men and women) would be feasible; the goal was to determine if a sufficient number of women could be found to fill this type of position. She later attended the Command and General Staff College and commanded a WAC detachment. Indexed, photographs (see **454, 740**).

431   *Green, Anne Bosanko.* **One Woman's War: Letters Home from the Women's Army Corps, 1944-1946.** St. Paul, MN: Minnesota Historical Society Press, 1989. 308p. OCLC 20219263; ISBN 0873512464.
Collection of letters written by the author to her family during her service as a WAC. Worked in various hospitals in the U.S. as a surgical technician and later in occupational therapy. Includes some excerpts of letters from her family as well as background for some of the letters. Upbeat, written by someone who tried to get the best out of her service. Photographs.

432   *Harten, Lucille.* **"Life As a WAC: The Story of Louise Parkin."** *Rendezvous: Idaho State University Journal of Arts and Letters* 22(2): 87-89, 1987.
Short story of Parkin, who joined the WAC in 1944. After basic training, she was sent to Camp Stoneman, near Oakland, CA, where she worked as a service station attendant gassing officer's cars and later as a payroll clerk.

433   *Kelly, Emma Chenault. Alice E. Tolle, editor.* **Emmaline Goes to War.** Charleston, IL: BLT & J Publishing Company, 1992. 163p. OCLC 30129543.
Collection of letters sent from Kelly to her family during World War II. Joined the WAC in 1944 and worked in a public relations office of a camp newspaper in Florida. No explanatory materials (such as to whom the letters are written). Includes copies of articles she wrote for the base newspaper.

434   *Kochendoerfer, Violet A.* **One Woman's World War II.** Lexington, KY: University Press of Kentucky, 1994.   211p.   OCLC 3860160; ISBN 0813118662.
The first three chapters are about the author's eight months of service in the WAAC.   When the WAC was formed, she left the service as she felt the army was not utilizing her talents.   She spent the rest of the war in the Red Cross.   Consists of edited letters written to her family and friends.

435   *Perdue, Bernice.* **WAC Confidential.** New York: Exposition Press, 1963. 58p. OCLC 19817803.
Perdue enlisted in October 1944 and was sent to Ft. Oglethorpe, Georgia for basic training.   Short story of her basic training and later hospital work.

436   *Pollard, Clarice F.* **Laugh, Cry, and Remember: The Journal of a G.I. Lady.** Phoenix, AZ: Journeys Press, 1991. 218p. OCLC 25336282; ISBN 0962933406.
Enlisted in the WAAC in February 1943 and took basic training at Ft. Oglethorpe, GA. Later sent to Administrative School at Nacogdoches, TX. Stationed at Ft. Lawton, near Seattle, WA, where she worked as a draftsman, publications writer, entertainment specialist and a recruiter.

437   *Pollard, Clarice F.* **"WAACs in Texas during the Second World War."** *Southwestern Historical Quarterly* 93(1): 61-74, 1989.
Story of the author's training in the WAAC at Administrative School at the Stephen F. Austin State Teachers College in Nacogdoches, TX (see **436**).

438   *Pollock, Elizabeth R.* **Yes, Ma'am! The Personal Papers of a WAAC Private.** New York: J.B. Lippincott Company, 1953.   172p.   OCLC 1171377.
Collection of letters written during a three month period while Pollock was in WAAC training.   Was a member of one of the first classes of WAACs trained at Ft. Des Moines, IA.   Discusses her training, barracks life, uniforms, and adjustment to the army.   Later worked in an antiaircraft warning unit in Pennsylvania.

439   *Redmann, Betty Beyers.* **How Memories Are Made: The Journal of an Air WAC.** Hicksville, NY: Exposition Press, 1975.   181p.   OCLC 2187361.
After enlisting in the WAAC, author became a recruiter in Los Angeles, where she worked in the window of Bullocks Department Store and later at the corner of Hollywood and Vine.   She met many celebrities during her tour as a recruiter.   Poorly edited, but interesting due to her unusual job.

440   *Rosenthal, Rose.* **Not All Soldiers Wore Pants: A Witty World War II WAC Tells All.** Rochell Park, NJ: Ryzell Books, 1993.   239p.   OCLC 29780544; ISBN 0963693107.

Joined the WAAC in 1942 and trained at Ft. Des Moines, IA. An amusing account of her basic training, attendance at Administration School and Officer Candidate School. Later served as an officer at Ft. Devens, MA.

441 *Smith, Kathleen E.R.* **Lieutenant Colonel Emily U. Miller: A Biography.** Natchitoches, LA: Northwestern State University Press, 1984. 174p. OCLC 11572366; ISBN 0917898117.
Based on the author's master's thesis, Lieutenant Colonel Miller was a member of the second WAAC officer class. She later worked in recruiting until the end of World War II, when she left the service. In 1949, she rejoined the WAC and worked in logistics until her retirement in 1965. Briefly chronicles her World War II service, then reprints a collection of Smith's Christmas letters.

442 *Stoddard, Eleanor.* **"How it All Came Out: The Story of Florence Steinberg."** *Minerva* 8(3): 54-72, Fall 1990.
Transcript of an oral history interview with Steinberg, who was a WAC during World War II. After her husband was drafted, she joined the WAAC and was sent to basic at Daytona Beach, FL. Served with the Army Air Forces near Spokane, WA, working in photography. Later transferred to the Pentagon and served in Army intelligence.

Personal Narratives - Overseas Theaters

443 *Dammann, Nancy.* **A WAC's Story: From Brisbane to Manila.** Sun City, AZ: Social Change Press, 1992. 168p. OCLC 16335337; ISBN 0960937617.
After joining the WAAC in December 1942, the author worked as a classification specialist at Ft. Ogelthorpe, Georgia. Was sent to the Southwest Pacific Theater in June 1944, and later served in Australia, Hollandia, New Guinea, Leyte, and Manila. Illustrates the hardships suffered by WACs in the Pacific theater, including poor food, uniform shortages, inadequate housing, and long working hours with no leaves or passes allowed.

444 *Edgar, Louise E.* **Out of Bounds.** Philadelphia: Dorrance, 1950. 227p. OCLC 13677138.
Describes the author's service as a WAC in the Southwest Pacific, Dutch East Indies, Philippines and China.

445 *Green, Blanche.* **Growing Up in the WAC: Letters to My Sister, 1944-46.** New York: Vantage Press, 1987. 73p. OCLC 19570517; ISBN 0533071739.
Slim volume of short excerpts from the letters written by the author to her sister Bernice during World War II. Part of her tour was spent in Europe. Letters could have been written by anyone; the author seems more interested in her social life than in the war and its aftermath.

446   *Lutz, Alma, editor.* **With Love, Jane: Letters from American Women on the War Fronts.** New York: John Day Company, 1945. 199p. See **186**.

447   *Prior, Billy.* **Flight to Glory.** Belmont, CA: Ponce Press, 1985. 241p. OCLC 12550564; ISBN 0933829027.
Prior joined the WAAC in 1942, resigning her commission after attending Officer Candidate school to become an Air WAC. Was one of the ten WAC first sergeants stationed in Europe, and later founded Pallas Athene, a WAC veterans organization. Unique in that this was written by a noncommissioned officer and gives details about life in the corps.

448   *Samford, Doris E.* **Ruffles and Drums.** Boulder, CO: Pruett Press, 1966. 165p. OCLC 2120815.
Enlisted in December 1943 and went to basic training at Ft. Des Moines, IA, then worked in the Classified Message Center at the Pentagon. Later served overseas for one year in the Southwest Pacific Theater, stationed in Brisbane, Australia and Manila. There she worked in a classified intelligence unit processing enemy documents. Excellent descriptions of WAC life in the south Pacific.

449   *Siciliano, Peg Poeschl.* **The 6669th Women's Army Corps Headquarters Platoon: Path Breakers in the Modern Army.** Thesis (M.A.)--College of William and Mary, 1988. 176p. OCLC 19781560.
Story of the 6669th Women's Army Corps Headquarters Platoon, known as the Fifth Army WACs. These WACs served in North Africa and Italy, working closer to combat areas than any other World War II women's unit (excluding nurses). Interesting history based on questionnaires received by twenty-six former unit members, as well as diaries, letters and private manuscripts.

450   *Spratley, Delores R.* **Women Go to War: Answering the First Call in World War II.** Columbus, OH: Hazelnut Publishing Company, 1992. 140p. OCLC 26538522; ISBN 096328472X.
Author joined the WAAC in November 1942 and in 1943, was assigned to the 161st WAC Headquarters Company in Oran, North Africa. She worked in personnel and also did clerical work, eventually serving throughout Europe. She later became a warrant officer, then a commissioned officer, retiring from the service in 1962. Includes a good discussion of the living conditions of WACs in Europe, but little information about her service after World War II. Photographs.

451   *Stoddard, Eleanor.* **"One Woman's War: The Story of Joan Campbell, One Member of the Women's Army Corps World War II. April 1943-September 1945. Part 1."** *Minerva* 4(1): 122-166, Spring 1986.
Transcript of a two part oral history interview with Joan Campbell. Campbell joined the WAAC in April 1943. She served at Ft. Slocum, NY in a pharmacy and later served overseas in the Southwest Pacific Theater in cryptoanalysis (see **452**).

452   *Stoddard, Eleanor.* **"One Woman's War: The Story of Joan Campbell, One Member of the Women's Army Corps World War II. April 1943-September 1945. Part 2."** *Minerva* 4(2): 133-175, Summer 1986.
Part two of an oral history interview (see **451**).

453   *Summersby, Kathleen McCarthy-Morrogh.* **Eisenhower Was My Boss.**
New York: Prentice-Hall, Inc., 1948. 302p. OCLC 18388563.
Author was a British driver for General Eisenhower during World War II. She later was commissioned an officer in the WAC (through a loophole in the WAC legislation; her appointment was protested by WAC Director Colonel Hobby), became Eisenhower's secretary and probably his mistress. An adoring account of her time spent working for Eisenhower.

454   *Watson, Georgia B.* **World War II in a Khaki Skirt.** Moore Haven, FL: Rainbow Books, 1985. 155p. OCLC 13013104; ISBN 0935834508.
Watson was a member of one of the first officer candidate classes held at Ft. Des Moines, IA, for WAACs. Interesting for her description of her secret assignment to "Battery X" where women were placed in a 90 mm gun battery, the first composite tactical gun battery to defend Washington, DC (see **430, 740**). Later served in England, where she escorted Queen Elizabeth on a tour of the WAC detachment in London.

455   *Weirick, Dorothy Millard.* **WAC Days of WWII: A Personal History.**
Laguna Nigel, CA: Royal Literary Publications, 1992. 87p. OCLC 31191994; ISBN 0918329264.
Enlisted in September 1942, primarily to escape an unhappy marriage. Was assigned to the aircraft warning service in Boston, then sent to Camp Polk, LA for more training and was selected for overseas duty. Worked as a telephone operator in Algiers, and later in Italy. Excellent descriptions of her work and living conditions for WACs in Europe.

UNIFORMS

456   *Barnes, Elinor S.* **A Wardrobe for the WAAC: A Study of the Problems Encountered by the Quartermaster Corps, Particularly the Philadelphia Depot, in Clothing the Personnel of the Women's Army Auxiliary Corps, February 4, 1942-February 4, 1943.** Philadelphia, PA: Philadelphia Clothing Depot, 1943. 235p. OCLC 9834013.
A very detailed account of the design, procurement, and distribution of clothing for the WAAC. Discusses the problems of designing completely new uniforms and deciding which uniform items would be authorized. Includes many photographs which are difficult to see.

457   *Burns, Robert W.* **History and Development of the Field Jacket Wool OD; and, Nurses and Wac Uniforms in the European Theater.** Maryland (?): n.p., 1945. 32p.
See **215**.

458 *Peterson, George.* **American Women at War in World War II. Vol I: Clothing, Insignia, and Equipment of Army WACs and Nurses, American Red Cross, USO, AWVS, Civil Defense and Related Wartime Womens Organizations.** Springfield, VA: George A. Peterson, 1985. 29p.
See **217**.

459 *Risch, Edna.* **A Wardrobe for Women of the Army.** Washington, DC: Historical Section, General Administrative Services Division, Office of the Quartermaster General, 1945. 156p.
See **218**.

460 *Ross, Mary Steele.* **American Women in Uniform.** Garden City, NY: Garden City Publishing Company, 1943. 72p.
See **064**.

461 *United States.   Army Service Forces.   Quartermaster Corps.* **Quartermaster Supply Catalog. WACS' and Nurses Clothing and Equipment.** Washington, DC: Headquarters, Army Service Forces, 1943. 25p.
See **220**.

7

ARMY 1946–PRESENT

The passage of the Women's Armed Services Integration Act in 1948 ensured women a permanent place in the Army. The Integration Act placed restrictions on assignments for Air Force and Navy women, prohibiting their service on aircraft engaged in combat missions, and in the case of the Navy, to vessels except for transports and hospital ships. No such prohibition was set for Army women against serving in combat, however, the Army adopted its own policy of exclusion. Another unique aspect of the act, as applied to Army women, was that it gave permanent status to the Women's Army Corps (WAC) as a separate organization within the Army, requiring all women who were not members of the Nurse Corps or Women's Medical Specialist Corps, to be members of the WAC. The WAC would be responsible for women's Army careers, including training, promotions, and billeting. None of the other services maintained women in a separate organization.

The first enlisted women in the WAC Regular Army were sworn in on 8 July 1948, followed by women officers in December. Women were trained at the WAC Training Center, Camp Lee, Virginia, which was staffed entirely by WACs (In June 1954, the WAC Center and WAC school moved to Fort McClellan, AL). By June 1950, the WAC was permanently integrated into the Regular Army and Reserve and segregation of black and white women ended. Numbers of women in the WAC had dropped dramatically from a high of almost 96,000 in June 1945 to 7,259 by June 1950.

With the start of the Korean War, new strength goals of 1,000 officers and 12,000 enlisted women were set for the WAC by 30 June 1951 and 1,900 officers and 30,000 enlisted women by June 1952. Like all the women's services at this time, actual enlistments fell far short of the goals (with a high of only 11,456 WACs on active duty in June 1952), and the WAC was forced to recall reservists involuntarily to active duty, first enlisted women and later officers. A few individual WACs did serve in Korea on special assignments (such as stenographers and interpreters), however no WAC units were assigned to serve in country.

Army women once again served in a war zone during the Vietnam War. In January 1965, a WAC major and sergeant first class were sent to Saigon to serve as advisors to the Republic of Vietnam's Women's Armed Forces Corps (WAFC). Also in 1965, WAC stenographers arrived in Saigon to work in the

Military Assistance Command, Vietnam (MACV). WAC officers were assigned to administrative positions at MACV headquarters, in the support commands, and the headquarters of a new command, U.S. Army, Vietnam (USARV). A WAC detachment was later assigned to USARV headquarters. A total of about 700 WACs served in Vietnam between 1966 and 1972. None were killed, reported missing, or taken as prisoner of war.

In the 1970s, the end of the Vietnam War and the draft, and the expected passage of the Equal Rights Amendment, would have a great effect on the WAC. An expansion in WAC strength was implemented, as well as an increase in the number of military occupational specialties (MOS) available to women, and a change in regulations allowed women to command men except in combat units. The expansion also moved women into more nontraditional MOSs, causing training in defensive tactics and weapons to be made mandatory in WAC basic training. By December 1976, a WAC had to qualify on the M16 rifle before graduating from basic training. The WAC Center and School at Fort McClellan closed on 31 December 1976, as Army women were integrated with men in both basic and officer training.

A number of research studies were conducted during the WAC expansion to examine the effects a higher percentage of women would have on the effectiveness of the Army. One of the first of these was the Women Content in Units Force Development Test, known as MAX WAC (see **503**), which examined the effects of varying the percentage of women on a unit's ability to perform its mission under field conditions. MAX WAC showed that a content of up to thirty-five percent women had no adverse effect on a unit's ability to perform its mission. MAX WAC was followed by another test conducted during a major field exercise in Germany, the Women Content in the Army - REFORGER 77 (known as REF WAC 77, see **498**). REF WAC 77 found that a unit composed of up to ten percent women again had no adverse effect on unit performance. Another study, known as the Women in the Army (WITA) Study (see **494**) examined the WAC expansion, women's policies and procedures, and research on women. The WITA study group recommended the policies on pregnancy and single parents needed further study before any changes could be made. It also recommended closing six MOSs currently open to women and temporarily closing thirteen others. The Army conducted further research to determine how many women by MOS (or officer specialty) and grade could be assigned to a unit without reducing the unit's effectiveness or the Army's ability to accomplish its ground combat mission. This new study, called Evaluation of Women in the Army (EWITA) Study, showed the Army could achieve a strength of 75,000 enlisted women by fiscal year 1983 without lowering standards (see **500**). It further recommended that gender free strength requirements be established for each MOS and that the definition for combat exclusion should be prohibiting women from positions whose primary function was the crewing or operation of direct and indirect fire weapons.

The 1970s also saw the full integration of women with men in the Army. The Office of the Director, WAC, was abolished on 20 April 1978, followed on 20 October 1978, by the signing of Public Law 95-584, disestablishing the Women's Army Corps as a separate corps, the separate WAC promotion list, officer assignments only in the WAC branch, and other policies and procedures based on a separate women's corps.

In 1981, the Army initiated a new study on Army women, focusing on the combat exclusion. While the study was conducted, a ceiling of 65,000 female enlisted strength was imposed, keeping qualified women from enlisting. Before the study was completed in September 1982, twenty-three MOSs were closed to women, which brought the number of closed MOSs to fifty-two percent of all Army jobs. The reason for closure was these jobs would expose women to direct combat, but its effect was to further lower women's morale and force them out of jobs. When new report, titled Women in the Army Policy Review (see **504**), was released in November 1982, it was criticized by DACOWITS and later thirteen of the twenty-three MOSs which had been closed were reopened to women.

In 1983, the Army developed a new assignment system called Direct Combat Probability Coding (DCPC) which profiled the battlefield into areas ranging from high probability of enemy contact to low probability. All positions and units were coded according to the probability that they would be involved in direct combat. Women would not be assigned to positions determined to have a high probability of enemy contact. This policy caused problems both in the invasion of Grenada in 1983 and Panama in 1989, when the confusion over DCPC caused some women to be pulled from their units during deployment.

The failure of DCPC was evident during Desert Shield/Desert Storm, with the deaths of eleven Army women and the capture of two as prisoners-of-war. Clearly DCPC had not protected them from danger. Renewed debate on the issue caused a number of changes, the most significant of which was then Secretary of Defense Les Aspin's new combat ground assignment rule in 1994. This rule stated women were eligible to be assigned to all positions for which they were qualified, except those in units below brigade level with a primary mission to engage in direct combat on the ground. The effect of this new assignment rule was to open all Army units and positions except direct ground combat battalions and units which physically collocate with them, such as combat engineer companies, and air defense artillery batteries. Armor, infantry, special forces, cannon field artillery, combat engineer and forward area air defense artillery career fields remain closed. Over 32,000 new positions opened to women, and over ninety percent of the career fields and sixty-seven percent of the total positions in the Army are now open to women.

ARCHIVES AND MANUSCRIPTS

462 *Army War College Oral History Interviews.* **1974-1978.** Army War College, Carlisle Barracks, PA.
Holds transcripts of oral interviews of prominent women in the WAC, including Major General Mary E. Clarke, Brigadier General Mildred I.C. Bailey, and Colonel Mary Hallaren (all former WAC Directors).

463 *Records of the Army Staff.* Record Group 319, National Archives.
Includes many records on WACs after World War II, including assignments in Europe, uniform modifications, statistics, records relating to legislation, utilization of women, homosexuality, and physical training.

464   *WAC Historical Research Collection.* **1948-1976.** Women's Army Corps
Museum, Fort McClellan, AL.
Contains files of information concerning new or revised policies affecting
women requested by the Director of the WAC. Subjects range from
weapons training to assignments. Also includes reference files from the
WAC Center Commander's office and the Assistant Commandant of the
WAC School.

BIBLIOGRAPHIES

465   *Wood, Robert.* **Women in the Army: A Selected Bibliography.** Carlisle
Barracks, PA: United States Army War College Library, 1982. 21p.
OCLC 9846421.
A list of books, documents, and periodical articles regarding women in
the Army. Arranged by type, then alphabetically by author. Most entries
have very brief annotations.

GENERAL WORKS

466   *Davis, Richard D.* **Developing a Holistic Methodology for Counseling
Women in the Army.** Thesis (Th.M.)--Duke University, 1991. 68p.
OCLC 25360240.
The absence of a large number of women chaplains means male
chaplains must learn to effectively counsel women. Author defines three
problem areas for Army women, pregnancy, child care, and family
separation. Two groups of women have the most problems managing
their Army careers and families, single parents and women who are part
of a dual military couple. Proposes a holistic approach to counseling
these women.

467   *Harris, Beverly C., Alma G. Steinberg, and Jacquelyn Scarville.* **"Why
Promotable Female Officers Leave the Army."** *Minerva* 12(3): 1-23,
Fall 1994.
Study of why female Army officers selected for promotion would leave
the service and what issues were involved in their decision. Interviewed
by telephone thirty out of forty women officers selected for promotion
to major who chose to leave the Army with a monetary incentive. The
women gave multiple reasons for leaving, such as reduced opportunities
with downsizing of the military, issues of sex discrimination and sexual
harassment, and problems in obtaining joint domicile with their husbands.

468   *McKnight, James G.* **"Women in the Army: Experiences of a Battalion
Commander."** *Parameters, Journal of the US Army War College* 9(2):
20-26, June 1979.
Observations of the author while serving twenty-two months as a
battalion commander of a unit with eighty-five to 100 female members
(out of a total of 507). Discusses working with female soldiers in the
field, issues of pregnancy, women in combat, duty performance,

reactions of wives, male/female relationships, equipment, physical strength, and sole parents.

469 *Morden, Bettie J.* **The Women's Army Corps, 1945-1978.** Washington, DC: Center of Military History, U.S. Army, 1990. 543p. SuDocs D114.19:W84; OCLC 20055841.
The official Army history of the Women's Army Corps from 1945 to its disestablishment in 1978. Continues Treadwell's history (see **408**), includes discussions of WAC organization and training, the Korean and Vietnam Wars, the WAC Center and WAC School, etc. Appendices included of WAC strengths from 1942-1978 and women in the Army from 1979-1984, WAC uniforms from 1942-1978 with many color photographs, MOSs and Training, and a list of key WAC personnel. Indexed.

470 *Nabors, Robert L.* **"Women in the Army: Do They Measure Up?"** *Military Review* 62(10): 51-61, October 1982.
Examines concerns that women represent a liability to the Army's fighting capability. Focuses on physical strength, pregnancy and lost time rates, sexual harassment, and single parenthood. Recommends that a physical performance criteria for each military occupational specialty be developed, pregnant soldiers be eliminated from active duty, and a policy be established requiring single parents to prove they are deployable.

471 *Norman, Linda L.* **The Army of the 1990's: Women's Leadership Role.** Carlisle Barracks, PA: U.S. Army War College, 1989. 58p. OCLC 19611409.
Argues that the shortage of male recruits will result in the military being forced to open combat roles for women. Includes statistics on female soldiers, such as officer strengths by job specialty.

472 *Riolo, Augustine G.* **Women in the Army.** Thesis (M.M.A.S.)--United States Army Command and General Staff College, 1980. 75p. OCLC 9470447.
A very brief summation of women's roles in the military, with a discussion of women in the Army. Author admits he has no "deep experience" in the area of managing women soldiers and it shows in the lack of insightful analysis of women. On the basis of one year of data on hospital admissions for men and women in the Army, he concludes one of the biggest problems with women soldiers may be their health.

473 *Roberts, Joel E.L.* **"Women in the Army: A Commander's Perspective."** *Military Review* 58(5): 69-76, May 1978.
Author commanded the 533d Supply and Service Battalion at Fort Hood, TX, which had an average strength of about twenty-five percent women. Describes the jobs of the enlisted women and the problems of having no experienced women officers or noncommissioned officers, as well as the problems from a large increase of women assigned to the unit. Written to provide advice to unit commanders on working with women soldiers.

474 *Rogan, Helen.* **Mixed Company: Women in the Modern Army.** New York: Putnam, 1981. 333p. OCLC 7573662; ISBN 0399126546.
A widely cited work. The author interviewed ex-WACs, Army nurses, officers, cadets, etc. and mixes excerpts from these with her observations while following a group of recruits during women's basic training at Ft. McClellan, AL, and women at West Point.

475 *Rustad, Michael.* **Women in Khaki: The American Enlisted Woman.** New York: Praeger, 1982. 285p. OCLC 8451270; ISBN 0275908925.
Study of the emerging role of enlisted women in the Army. The first part examines enlisted women from a social-historical perspective, the second half describes the daily life of female soldiers in Europe (Germany). Presents a good discussion of sexual harassment and the problems women face in "fitting in."

476 **Survey of the Women's Army Corps As of 30 November 1966.** Washington, DC: Women's Army Corps, 1966. 92p. OCLC 1314353.
Compilation of statistical data on women in the WAC as of November 1966. Little text, mainly charts and tables. Covers a wide range of statistical material, such as ages, physical status, education, marital status, dependent information, etc., for both officers and enlisted women.

477 *United States. Women's Army Corps School.* **Role of the WAC.** Ft. McClellan, AL: Women's Army Corps School, 1962. 89p. OCLC 14961817.
A text written for women attending the Women's Army Corps School, tracing the history, organization, and function of the Corps.

478 **Women in the Army: Reference Book.** Fort Leavenworth, KS: U.S. Army Command and General Staff College, 1977. 64p. OCLC 21236707.
A quick reference source of facts and regulations pertaining to women in the Army (as of 1977). Provides examples from Army regulations regarding uniforms, assignment policies, ROTC, housing, etc. Includes references and a short bibliography.

ATTITUDE STUDIES

479 *Bundy, Hazel Buttrick.* **Attitudes of Enlisted Members of the Women's Army Corps toward the Army and Their Work.** Thesis (M.A.)--Leland Stanford Junior University, 1948. 90p. OCLC 16935710.
Author administered a questionnaire to sixty-five of the enlisted women on active duty in the Army in 1948 to investigate their attitudes towards the Army and their work. Generally, the women had good attitudes toward Army pay, the WAC uniform, their officers, non-commissioned officers and their peers. They had unfavorable attitudes toward red tape, recruiters, rate of promotions, recreational opportunities and Army food.

480   *Goehring, Dwight J. and James A. Thomas.* **U.S. Army Female Soldiers'**
Career and Racial Attitudes and Perceptions. Arlington, VA: U.S.
Army Research Institute for the Behavioral and Social Studies, 1978.
68p. OCLC 8738200.
Racial perceptions and attitudes as well as career orientations of 158
black and 187 white females from twenty-seven U.S. Army installations
were measured by questionnaire. Reports specific areas of satisfaction
with military life and general career orientation.

481   *Hall, Janice Cara Ryan.* **Attitudes of Army Females towards a Magazine**
for Career Army Women.   Thesis (M.A.)--University of Missouri,
Columbus, 1980. 205p. OCLC 8078503.
Conducted a survey of thirty-four officers and enlisted Army women at
Ft. Leonard Wood, MO, to determine interest in a magazine for career
Army women. Includes a discussion of previous magazines published for
military women. Survey results indicate a need for such a magazine, and
provides suggestions for how such a publication should be run and what
it should include.

482   *Savell, Joel M., John C. Woelfel and Barry Collins.* **Attitudes**
Concerning Job Appropriateness for Women in the Army. Arlington,
VA: U.S. Army Research Institute for the Behavioral and Social
Sciences, 1975. 9p. OCLC 3010058.
Presents results of a survey conducted to determine how the increase in
numbers of women in the Army had affected personnel (as of 1975).
Includes tables of jobs soldiers were asked to rate as to their
"appropriateness" for women.   Of twenty-four jobs, only one, rifle-
carrying infantryman, was judged by the majority to be inappropriate.
More women than men felt women could handle nontraditional jobs.

483   *Savell, Joel M., John C. Woelfel, Barry E. Collins, and Peter M. Bentler.*
Male and Female Soldiers' Beliefs about the "Appropriateness" of
Various Jobs for Women in the Army. Alexandria, VA: U.S. Army
Research Institute for the Behavioral Sciences, 1979. 18p. SuDocs
D101.60:352; OCLC 5963420.
Documents the expanding role of women in the Army and measures the
extent to which soldiers believe certain jobs are "appropriate" to women.
The majority of male and female soldiers thought all jobs (out of twenty-
four tested) were appropriate for women, with the exception of infantry
foot soldier.

DEPLOYMENTS AND WAR SERVICE

484   *Allen, E. Ann.* **The WAC Mission: The Testing Time from Korea to**
Vietnam. Thesis (Ph.D.)--University of South Carolina, 1986. 360p.
OCLC 21243253.
The author, a former noncommissioned officer in the Army, writes
authoritatively about the Women's Army Corps.   Includes a long
discussion of the events surrounding the passage of the legislation

leading to the Women's Armed Services Integration Act in 1948. Especially valuable for the information on WACs stationed in Vietnam.

485 *Hines, Jeffery F.* *"A Comparison of Clinical Diagnosis among Male and Female Soldiers Deployed during the Persian Gulf War."* *Military Medicine* 158(2): 99-101, February 1993.
Compares medical disorders between male and female soldiers during Desert Shield/Desert Storm. Found men were more likely to be diagnosed with orthopedic and dermatologic disorders and women with psychiatric and optometric disorders.

486 *Moskos, Charles C.* *"Female GIs in the Field."* *Society* 22(6): 28-33, September/October 1985.
Author made on-site observations and conducted interviews with soldiers in U.S. Army units in Honduras who were taking part in a field exercise in 1984. Wanted to actually study women during a long deployment/field exercise. Describes women's daily routine, living conditions, jobs, etc. Very interesting.

487 *Wright, Ann.* *"The Roles of U.S. Army Women in Grenada."* *Minerva* 2(2): 103-113, Summer 1984.
170 Army women deployed to Grenada. Describes their assignments and the problems faced by the women in being utilized properly.

PERSONAL NARRATIVES

488 *Nicely, Marian.* **The Ladies First Army.** Ligonier, PA: Fairfield Street Press, 1989. 202p. OCLC 21414244; ISBN 0935648275.
A unique personal account of life as a WAC in the 1950s. Author joined the WAC in 1953, and served as a recruiter, recreation specialist, and in an entertainment office. Includes many details of military life, including living in the WAC Detachment in Munich, Germany. Unfortunately the last chapter is a protest against women in today's military, where the author states women with children should not serve as they will refuse to deploy and women should not have command of combat support and service units.

UTILIZATION AND PERFORMANCE

489 *Boening, Suzanne S.* **What Are Little Girls Made Of? Individual Essay.** Carlisle Barracks, PA: U.S. Army War College, 1983. 16p. OCLC 13401270.
The author writes that since the demise of the Women's Army Corps, the U.S. Army has not had a basic philosophy on the proper utilization of women. Examines four ways of looking at women in society and the army, and suggests the Army needs to select one of these as a base for a consistent policy.

490 *Bolin, Stanley F., John S. Cowings, and Lois A. Johns.* **Women Soldiers in Korea: Command Concerns about Pregnancy, Facilities, and Other Issues.** Alexandria, VA: U.S. Army Research Institute for Behavioral and Social Sciences, 1977. 27p. OCLC 17458424.
One of two reports issued from questionnaires conducted in the summer and fall of 1976 (see **491**). Found that commanders were satisfied with women, but those assigned large numbers of women were concerned about pregnancy more than other problems. Commanders with lesser numbers of women assigned were more concerned about providing facilities for women. Pregnancy was perceived as lowering morale. Authors suggest the Army reexamine the policy of allowing pregnant soldiers to remain on active duty.

491 *Bolin, Stanley F., Lois A. Johns, and John S. Cowings.* **Women Soldiers in Korea: Troop Viewpoints.** Alexandria, VA: U.S. Army Research Institute for the Behavioral and Social Sciences, 1977. 146p. OCLC 22186530.
Second half of a two part study (see **490**) to identify problem areas associated with assigning women in larger numbers to the 8th U.S. Army in Korea. Questionnaires were sent to enlisted men and women. Both men and women were found to be against an expanded role for women in combat. Women were less satisfied with PX services. Primarily a collection of statistics and tables, little discussion.

492 *Boyd, H. Alton.* **Performance of First-Tour WAC Enlisted Women: Data Base for the Performance Orientation of Women's Basic Training. Final Report.** Arlington, VA: U.S. Army Research Institute for the Behavioral and Social Sciences, 1975. 150p. ED114612.
Presents results of a worldwide survey of 1,573 first-tour enlisted women and a representative sample of 156 of their supervisors. Found that the majority of basic training graduates have a high educational level, find basic and subsequent duty assignments different from what they expected, and reported a lack of correlation between what they learned at basic and what they needed to know at their jobs.

493 *Firestone, Juanita M.* **"Sexist Ideology and the Evaluation Criteria Used to Assess Women's Integration into the Army."** *Population Research and Policy Review* 3(1): 77-95, 1984.
A response to the 1978 Evaluation of Women in the Army (EWITA) (see **500**). Discusses in detail the criteria and findings of the women's evaluation in terms of the sexist ideology prevalent in the military system. Good evaluation of findings.

494 *Fox, Eugene A., Franklin D. Alexander, Jacquelin J. Kelly, George R. Kleb, Reinhard M. Lotz.* **Final Report of the Women in the Army Study Group.** Washington, DC: U.S. Department of the Army, Office of the Deputy Chief of Staff for Personnel, 1976. 322p. OCLC 2822299.
The Women in the Army Study Group was established as an ad hoc group to revalidate the Army's program for women. This report reviews current and planned policy on the utilization of women in the Army.

Commanders surveyed indicated pregnancy and single parent policies caused no problems and some believed women could serve in some specialties in combat units who did not enter the battle zone. They also agreed men accepted women in leadership roles.

495   *Greene, Byron D., III and Kenneth L. Wilson.* **"Women Warriors: Exploring the New Integration of Women into the Military."** *Journal of Political and Military Sociology* 9(2): 221-254, Fall 1981.
Gathered data from training records and questionnaires on 800 men and women in basic Army training in 1979 to determine whether or not different sex integration alternatives exerted any kind of effects on the attitudes and performance of soldiers.

496   *Herbert, Melissa S.* **"From Crinoline to Camouflage: Initial Entry Training and the Marginalization of Women in the Military."** *Minerva* 11(1):41-57, Spring 1993.
Examines the initial entry, or basic, training in the military as a resocialization process and its potential impact on women soldiers. Author believes military training depends on the development of combat skills and the denigration of women to reinforce masculinity. This emphasis causes women to be marginalized within the military. Concludes that only by opening combat positions to women can women be fully integrated into the military.

497   *Hicks, Jack M.* **"Women in the U.S. Army."** *Armed Forces and Society* 4(4): 647-657, August 1978.
Discusses results of a questionnaire given to enlisted men and women about their Army background, attitudes towards the Army, stereotypical concepts of the military, attitudes towards women in the Army, and demographic information. Found that women worked less time than men did in their primary specialty, that men and women agreed that combat and heavy equipment jobs should be held by men, that women were slightly more satisfied than men with the Army and more men than women felt the sexes should be treated equally in the Army.

498   *Johnson, Cecil D., Bertha H. Cory, Roberta W. Day, and Laurel W. Oliver.* **Women Content in the Army - REFORGER 77 (REF WAC 77).** Alexandria VA: U.S. Army Research Institute for the Behavioral and Social Sciences, 1978. 353p. OCLC 21235775.
The Army followed the performance of female soldiers and male counterparts during the annual REFORGER (Return of Forces to Germany) exercises, which involved one and a half weeks of realistic war games. Results supported the conclusion that a unit composition of ten percent women had negligible effect on unit performance. Also observed a number of leadership and management problems involving women.

499   *Racelis, Pedro E., III.* **Use of Demographic and Biographical Data to Investigate Occupational Success for Enlisted Women Soldiers in the United States Army.** Thesis (M.A.)--Middle Tennessee State University, 1981. 38p. OCLC 11631702.

441 enlisted female soldiers were surveyed in Spring 1981. Found that an enlisted woman was more likely to pursue a traditional job if she had a low skill qualification test score, had spent less time in the service, had high motor maintenance and clerical scores and attended more military schools. Enlisted women who had a higher educational level, higher general technical scores and more time spent overseas were more likely to hold nontraditional jobs.

500   *Roberts, Grace L., Charles Baker, Doris L. Caldwell, Sonya R. Laubscher, and James Sampson.* **Evaluation of Women in the Army: Final Report (EWITA).** Washington, DC: Department of the Army, 1978. One volume. OCLC 4146034.
The final report of the Women in the Army Study Group. Analyzed all military occupational specialties (MOS) excluding infantry and armor, currently closed to women to determine if they should be opened. Also calculated the maximum female content of each MOS, identified which units should open to women, and analyzed other factors that impact on Army women.

501   *Schreiber, E.M. and John C. Woelfel.* **"Effects of Women on Group Performance in a Traditionally Male Occupation: The Case of the U.S. Army."** *Journal of Political and Military Sociology* 7:121-134, Spring 1979.
Effects of up to twenty-five percent women on company performance during three-day field exercises were investigated in twenty-nine combat support and combat-service support companies in the Army during 1976-1977. Found companies with higher proportions of women did not perform less well than those with less or no women.

502   *Sweeney, R.W., Jr., A. DiValentin III, and Earl L. Halbrook.* **Women in the Army: The Right Numbers, the Wrong Skills.** Carlisle Barracks, PA: United States Army War College, 1987. 42p. OCLC 20966452.
Presents the results of a group study project at the Army War College. Found the most growth of women in the Army occurred almost entirely in traditional fields, such as administration and medicine. Concluded women must be trained in more nontraditional areas.

503   *United States. Army Research Institute for the Behavioral and Social Sciences.* **Women Content in Units Force Development Test (MAX WAC).** Arlington, VA: The Institute, 1977. 142p. OCLC 3741148; ED 152826.
Results of a study to determine the effects of varying the percentages of female soldiers assigned to non-combat Army units on the unit's ability to perform its mission under field conditions. A comparison of companies that went from zero percent to fifteen percent enlisted women and those that went from fifteen percent to thirty-five percent enlisted women showed that while the former showed a slight decrease in performance scores, the latter showed a slight increase. Neither score was statistically significant. A widely cited report.

504   ***Women in the Army Policy Review.*** Washington, DC: Office of the
Deputy Chief of Staff for Personnel, Department of the Army, 1982.
255p. SuDocs D101.2:W84/5; OCLC 9001835.
Report presenting the results of the Women in the Army Policy Review
Group's analysis of Army personnel policies as they relate to mission,
combat readiness, quality of life aspects, and the utilization of female
enlisted soldiers in the Army. Also introduces the Military Entrance
Physical Strength Capacity Test, which rates military occupational
specialties according to the number of pounds a soldier will be required
to lift.

8

WOMEN AIRFORCE SERVICE PILOTS (WASP)

In 1940, Jacqueline Cochran, an accomplished woman pilot, proposed the formation of a women's flying unit as part of the Army Air Corps, later renamed the Army Air Forces (AAF). Her plan was for these women to fly noncombat missions, releasing male pilots for combat flights. The commander of the Corps, General Henry H. "Hap" Arnold, felt that women pilots were not needed when there were male pilots available. However, he did send Jackie Cochran to England to study how women were being used as pilots in the Air Transport Auxiliary (ATA). In March 1942, Jackie left for England, taking along twenty-five American women pilots to join the ATA.

While Jackie studied the ATA in England, another woman pilot, Nancy Love, had her own plan for a women's flying corps. Nancy was working for the Ferrying Division of the Air Transport Command, under the direction of General Harold George. She suggested that experienced women pilots be used to help ferry planes from factories and depots to Army Air Force bases. Nancy would lead an elite corps of experienced women pilots who would fly as civilians for the Ferrying Command. Nancy's plan was approved by her boss, Colonel William Turner, and in September 1942 General George announced the formation of the Women's Auxiliary Ferrying Squadron (WAFS). Nancy Love would serve as the director.

Jackie was furious when she heard about the WAFS, returned from England, and confronted General Arnold. General George decided that while Nancy Love would remain as head of the WAF, Jackie would be in charge of the Women's Flying Training Detachment (WFTD). The WFTD, based in Texas, would train pilots not as experienced as the original WAFS, and prepare them eventually to enter the WAFS. After the first classes graduated from the WFTD, the women began assuming duties other than ferrying. In August 1943, a new name, Women's Airforce Service Pilots (WASP) was selected for the WAFS and the WFTD. Jackie gained overall control of the WASP, but the ferrying division remained under Nancy Love.

According to Jackie Cochran's *Final Report on Women Pilot Program* (see **512**), 1,074 women graduated from the WASP training program, flying more than sixty million miles, with thirty-eight fatalities. The women did ferrying, target towing, tracking and searchlight missions, simulated strafing, smoke laying, engineering test flying, and instruction. They flew nearly every type of aircraft in the AAF. The women pilots had as much endurance and flew as regularly and as long as the male pilots. However, in the second half of 1944, the war was winding down. The pilot shortage was not as acute. The WASP were seen as a threat to male pilots, and Jackie's push to militarize the WASP, with her at the head, alienated many (see **522**). General Arnold decided to deactivate the WASP on 20 December 1944. Women would not fly again as military pilots for over thirty years.

After the war, the former WASP did not push again for militarization until 1976, after the Air Force selected ten women to train as the "first women to fly for the military." The WASP, feeling their service had been forgotten, began a campaign to gain veteran's status. With the help of Colonel Bruce Arnold (son of "Hap" Arnold), the WASP finally received military recognition in 1977.

This chapter contains entries for general histories of the WASP as well as biographies of individual members and some of the larger archival collections. Modern day Air Force pilots are covered separately in **Chapter 9, Air Force**.

ARCHIVES AND MANUSCRIPTS

505 *Cochran, Jacqueline. Papers, 1932-1975.* Dwight D. Eisenhower Library, Abilene, Kansas.
Most of the collection is arranged by subject. Includes files on work as director of the WASP, 1942-1945, and service as a reserve officer in the Air Force, as well as photographs, tape recordings, and other memorabilia.

506 *Records of the Army Air Forces.* Record Group 18, National Archives. Contains many records for the WASP, including correspondence documenting the origin of the WASP, sketches of uniforms, Cochran's *Final Report on Women Pilot Program* (see **512**), and press releases.

507 *Women Air Force Service Pilots Records 1942-1945.* Albert F. Simpson Historical Research Center, Maxwell Air Force Base, Alabama.
Contains miscellaneous records of the WASP, including reports, data on WASP uniforms and insignia, and correspondence. *USAF History of Women in the Armed Forces: A Selected Bibliography* by Eleanor E. Peets (see **027**), indexes some of these records.

508 *Women Air Force Service Pilots (WASPs) Records, 1942-1945.* Air Force Museum, Wright-Patterson Air Force Base, Ohio.
Correspondence, rosters, slides, photographs, medical reports and histories of commands where the WASP trained and served, are included. Some personal papers.

509 *Women's Air Force Service Pilots Records, 1943-1975.* Southwest Collection, Texas Tech University, Lubbock, Texas.
Contains correspondence, photographs, scrapbooks and other materials on the WASP.

510 *Women's Airforce Service Pilots.* Texas Woman's University, Blagg-Huey Library, Denton, Texas.

Extensive collection of personal papers of individual WASPS, transcripts and tapes of oral history interviews, photographs, uniforms and equipment, and official records.

GENERAL WORKS

511   Chun, Victor K. **"The Origin of the WASP."** *American Aviation Historical Society Journal* 14:259-262, Winter 1969.
A history of the WASP, primarily taken from *Women Pilots with the AAF: 1941-1944* (see **513**).   Good brief summary of the formation of the WASP, their training, and push for militarization during World War II. Some photographs.

512   Cochran, Jacqueline.   **Final Report on Women Pilot Program.** Washington, DC: n.p., 1945. 53p. OCLC 18875019.
An after-action report written by the Director of the WASP to summarize the accomplishments of the WASP and their training. Gives details about recruiting, the objectives of the training program, requirements for applicants, curriculum, pay and living costs, etc. Recommends a future pilot training program should be militarized. This report is reprinted in Keil's book (see **516**).

513   England, J. Merton, Martha E. Layman, Chase C. Mooney and Joseph Reither. **Women Pilots with the AAF: 1941-1944.** Manhattan, KS: MA/AH Publications, 1987. 122p. OCLC 19022135; ISBN 0891261389. Reprint of the official Army Air Force history of the WASP. A clear, balanced account of the women pilots who flew for the AAF. Frankly discusses problems and issues. Originally a restricted document.

514   Granger, Byrd Howell. **On Final Approach: The Women Airforce Service Pilots of W.W. II.**   Scottsdale, AZ: Falconer Publishing Company, 1991. 661p. OCLC 249050; ISBN 0962626708.
An exhaustive history of the WASP, written by a former member from research conducted to help the WASP be recognized as military veterans. It has an unusual chronological journal arrangement (September 28, 1938 to March 30, 1945) and is written in the present tense. Very heavily footnoted with many primary source documents cited.   Detailed appendices of WAF and WASP class lists, bases where WASP served, WASP fatalities, pursuit pilots, uniforms, etc. Many photographs. Good for anyone who has read basic WASP histories and is interested in a more detailed work. Photographs.

515   Johnson, Ann R. **"The WASP of World War II."** *Aerospace Historian* 17(2-3): 76-82, Summer-Fall 1970.
The author, an Air Force Lieutenant Colonel, prepared this article for the Air Force Historical Foundation. Includes an introduction by Jacqueline Cochran.   A brief, but accurate summary of the WASP program. Includes information about pay, uniforms, physical requirements, and lists of women killed during different phases of the program. Photos.

516 *Keil, Sally Van Wagenen.* **Those Wonderful Women in Their Flying Machines: The Unknown Heroines of World War II.** Revised and expanded edition. New York: Four Directions Press, 1990. 418p. OCLC 23177610; ISBN 0962765902.
An often recommended general history of the WASP. Includes many stories of individual members from the founding to the deactivation of the WASP. Covers training, types of missions, problems, accidents, etc. Some photographs. The *Final Report on Women Pilot Program*, written by Jacqueline Cochran (see **512**) is included as an appendix. A good book to start research on the WASP.

517 *Noggle, Anne.* **For God, Country, and the Thrill of it: Women Airforce Service Pilots in World War II.** College Station, TX: Texas A&M University Press, 1990. 160p. OCLC 20417857; ISBN 0890964017.
General history of the WASP written by a member of the WASP class 44-1. Includes many photographs accompanied by personal accounts of individual WASP members.

518 *Schamel, Wynell B. and Richard A. Blondo.* **"Correspondence Concerning Women and the Army Air Forces in World War II. Teaching with Documents."** *Social Education* 58(2): 104-107, February 1994.
Presents a brief article about the WASP, then gives a lesson plan for teaching about the WASP. Includes questions for discussion, research activities and suggested readings.

519 *Stewart-Smith, Natalie Jeanne.* **The Women Airforce Service Pilots (WASP) of World War II: Perspectives on the Work of America's First Military Women Aviators.** Thesis (M.A.)--Washington State University, 1981. 81p. OCLC 7611278.
Brief history of the WASP written as a Master's thesis. Mainly of interest for the epilogue, which details the fight of WASP members to gain recognition as military veterans.

520 *Tanner, Doris Brinker.* **"We Also Served."** *American History Illustrated* 20(7):12-21,47-49, 1985.
Very good summary of the WASP program, from its inception to the recognition of the WASP as military veterans. Written by a former WASP, emphasizes the training program, describing each phase. Photos.

521 *Tanner, Doris Brinker.* **Who Were the WASP?: A World War II Record.** Sweetwater, TX: Sweetwater Reporter, 1989. Not paged, 1 volume. OCLC 22275993.
Reprinted collection of articles originally published in the *Fifinella Gazette* at Houston and the *Avenger* at Sweetwater, Texas (both base papers printed for the WASP trainees), from 1942 to 1944. Not a history, but gives an interesting glimpse of WASP life.

522 *United States. Congress. House. Committee on Military Affairs.* ***Providing for the Appointment of Female Pilots and Aviation Cadets of the Army Air Forces.*** Washington, DC: GPO, March 22, 1944. 10p. SuDocs Y4.M59/1P:64.
Testimony on H.R. 4219, known as the "WASP Bill", which was introduced to make the WASP officers in the Army Air Forces. Includes testimony by General Henry H. Arnold, Commanding General of the Army Air Forces, commenting on why the WASP could not be officers in the Women's Army Corps, and that as long as they were not part of the Army, did not receive normal benefits, such as insurance and medical treatment.

523 *United States. Congress. House. Committee on Veterans' Affairs. Select Subcommittee to Review WASP Bills.* ***To Provide Recognition to the Women's Air Force Service Pilots for Their Service during World War II by Deeming Such Service to Have Been Active Duty in the Armed Forces of the United States...*** Washington, DC: GPO, September 20, 1977. 461p. SuDocs Y4.V64/3:W84.
Hearings held to determine whether or not to give veterans status to the WASP. Includes a legislative history compiled by the Congressional Research Service, testimony highlighting the military nature of WASP duties.

524 *Verges, Marianne.* ***On Silver Wings: The Women Airforce Service Pilots of World War II, 1942-1944.*** New York: Ballantine Books, 1991. 255p. OCLC 23767444; ISBN 0345365348.
A brief, one volume history of the WASP. Good general summary, not particularly detailed. Basic book for introducing the WASP.

525 *Williams, Vera S.* ***WASPs: Women Airforce Service Pilots of World War II.*** Osceloa, WI: Motorbooks International Publishers & Wholesalers, 1994. 156p. OCLC 29386555; ISBN 0879388560.
General history of the WASP, notable for its extensive use of photographs. Includes excerpts of author interviews with former WASPs. Worth viewing for the excellent photographs.

PERSONAL NARRATIVES

526 *Chaffey, Kay Gott.* ***WASP; Women Airforce Service Pilots, World War II: Class 43-W-2.*** 2nd edition. Eureka, CA: Broadway Printing, 1991. 154p. OCLC 25249433.
Collection of photographs and short (one to two page) biographies of women in the WASP training class 43-W-1. Includes a brief history of the class, of which the author was a member.

527 *Churchill, Jan.* ***On Wings to War: Teresa James, Aviator.*** Manhattan, KS: Sunflower University Press, 1992. 184p. OCLC 26835770; ISBN 0897451309.
A short biography of Teresa James, a member of the WAFS and later a

WASP. Good descriptions of WASP life. James later joined the Air Force Active Reserve and helped to fight for the recognition of WASP pilots as military veterans. Photographs, indexed.

528   *Cochran, Jacqueline and Maryann Bucknum Brinkley.* **Jackie Cochran: An Autobiography.** New York: Bantam Books, 1987. 358p. OCLC 15428885; ISBN 055305211X.
Written by Brinkley using the notes and papers of Jacqueline Cochran, the director of the WASP; calls this an "autobiographical biography." More detailed than *The Stars at Noon* (see **529**), but does not have much information about Jackie's involvement in the WASP program.

529   *Cochran, Jacqueline, with Floyd Odlum as Wingman.* **The Stars at Noon.** Boston· Little, Brown and Company, 1954. 274p. OCLC 669880.
Read to get a feel for Jacqueline Cochran's personality, not for information about the WASP or the author's other military activities. Recounts selection of the WASP uniform and discusses her role in the formation of the WASP, but provides no dates or other information. Not particularly revealing or candid.

530   *Cole, Jean Hascall.* **Women Pilots of World War II.** Salt Lake City: University of Utah Press, 1992. 165p. OCLC 24283724; ISBN 0874803748.
The author was a WASP in the tenth class to complete the pilot training program, Class 44-W-2. The story of thirty-five members of the author's training class, written from interviews. Discusses their training and what happened to them while serving in the WASP and in their later lives.

531   *Gott, Kay.* **Women in Pursuit: Flying Fighters for the Air Transport Command Ferrying Division during World War II: A Collection & Recollection.** McKinleyville, CA: K. Gott, 1993. 230p. OCLC 28056091; ISBN 0963307509.
Written by a former WASP, the story of the 184 WASP who flew pursuit aircraft (fighters) for the Air Transport Command. Discusses jobs, assignments, and training in chapters on each ferrying group. Many excerpts from WASP interviews. Photographs.

532   *Klick, John R.* **"WASP with a Fifinella Heart."** *Aerospace Historian* 29(1):31-33, March 1982.
Brief story of Leoti Deaton, who served as the staff executive for training the WASP. Was in charge of securing housing, dining, recreational and medical facilities for the WASP.

533   *Noggle, Anne.* **"Return of the WASPs: Women Airforce Service Pilots Seen through One Member's Eyes."** *Air & Space Smithsonian* 5(2):82-87, June/July 1990.
An excerpt from *For God, Country, and the Thrill of It* (see **517**), the author's story of her WASP class, 44-1, and her memories of her classmates and WASP training. Photographs.

534 *Scharr, Adela Riek.* **Sisters in the Sky. Volume 1-The WAFS.** Gerald, MO: The Patrice Press, 1986. 531p. OCLC 14377404; ISBN 093528446X.
First volume in the autobiography of Adela Scharr, an original member of the WAFS; insider story of the WAFS (see **535**).

535 *Scharr, Adela Riek.* **Sisters in the Sky. Volume 2-The WASP.** Gerald, MO: The Patrice Press, 1988. 758p. OCLC 19379440; ISBN 0935284559.
Primarily the autobiography of Adela Scharr, an original member of the WAFS and later the WASP, until the program was deactivated in 1944. A fascinating and candid behind-the-scenes look at everyday life in the WASP, discussing everything from the rivalry between Jackie Cochran and Nancy Love to flying assignments, to stories of other women pilots. Not a general WASP history; insider story of the WASP (see **534**).

536 *Stowell, Philip M.* **Duty with the Flying Fifinellas.** Maxwell Air Force Base: Air University, Air Command and Staff College, 1955. 15p.
A brief account of the author's tour of duty as a check pilot for WASP trainees.

537 *Tanner, Doris Brinker.* **"Cornelia Fort: A WASP in World War II, Part 1."** *Tennessee Historical Quarterly* 40(4):381-394, Winter 1981.
Part 1 of a two part article (see **538**) about Cornelia Fort, the first WASP to be killed during World War II. Covers her early life and flying experiences. Fort was invited by Nancy Love to join the WAFS in September 1942, and became one of the original members. Photographs.

538 *Tanner, Doris Brinker.* **"Cornelia Fort: Pioneer Woman Military Aviator, Part 2."** *Tennessee Historical Quarterly* 41(1):67-80, Spring 1982.
Part 2 (see **537**) of an article on one of the first WAFS. Details Fort's life as a member of the WAFS through excerpts from letters to her family. Covers the time from her initial acceptance into the WAFS until her death in a flying accident. Photographs.

539 *Wood, Winfred.* **We Were WASPS.** Coral Gables, FL: Glade House, 1945. 196p. OCLC 4128147.
A personal account by a woman who became a WASP in 1943, trained at Sweetwater, TX on various aircraft and was assigned to Biggs Field, El Paso, TX. She worked briefly towing targets until the WASP was disbanded. Ms. Wood is the aunt of Janet Reno, the Clinton administration U.S. Attorney General.

9

AIR FORCE

Women officially became part of the Air Force with the passage of the Women's Armed Services Integration Act of 1948. Women remaining on active duty after World War II, who had served as "Air WACs" with the Army Air Forces, had to choose between going into the Army, transferring to the newly formed Air Force, or becoming civilians. About 160 women officers and 1,400 enlisted women chose to transfer to the Air Force shortly after the Act was passed. Out of 349 Air Force enlisted specialties, 158 were closed to women in peacetime. Women were not eligible to become pilots, despite the success of the WASP during World War II.

Recruiting efforts were increased with the advent of the Korean War. However, the Air Force failed to meet its goal of 50,000 members, reaching a maximum strength of 13,000 members. By the late 1950s, enlisted Air Force women were reassigned from jobs where only a small number were assigned, and were no longer allowed to enter fields such as control tower operation, weather, intelligence, and flight attendance. This led to the highest rates of turnover in the history of the women's program.

The 1960s and 1970s saw a number of significant events for Air Force women. From 500-600 served in Southeast Asia, and in fact the proportion of women officers serving overseas was greater than that of male officers, twenty-eight percent versus twenty-six percent. In 1969, the Air Force was the first service to accept women into its Reserve Officer Training Corps (ROTC) programs. In 1971, the director of women, Colonel Jeanne Holm, became the Air Force's first woman brigadier general (see **543**). The position of Director of Women in the Air Force was abolished in 1976.

One of the most important changes for Air Force women was the opening of new job specialties. Pilot training was opened to women in 1976, when twenty female commissioned officers were sent to Williams Air Force Base in Arizona for a forty-nine week undergraduate pilot training program (see **555-559**). Missile maintenance and other support positions in Minuteman and Titan systems opened in the early 1970s, and by the late 1970s, women could serve as missile launch officers (see **560-563**).

The 1980s saw more changes for Air Force women. In 1983, women pilots flew troops and equipment to Grenada in support of Operation Urgent Fury. In 1989, Congress stopped the Air Force from setting minimum or maximum gender limits on first term enlistments of men and women, allowing them to compete equally for available slots. More than 2,700 new positions were opened to women under the DOD Risk Rule in 1988 on combat exclusion.

The Persian Gulf War renewed debate regarding assignments for women. During the war, Air Force women flew cargo planes as well as jet tankers which refueled fighters and bombers, serviced planes, and worked on AWACs aircraft, among other duties. In April 1993, the Secretary of Defense directed the services to permit women to serve in aircraft engaged in combat missions and in 1994, the Air Force assigned its first women combat pilot. By the mid-1990s, 99.7 percent of all Air Force jobs were open to women.

ARCHIVES AND MANUSCRIPTS

540 *Records of Headquarters, U.S. Air Force (Air Staff).* Record Group 341, National Archives.
Records from the Director of Women in the Air Force, including procurement, training, and housing, statistical summaries, and women's mobilization plans.

541 *Records of the Office of the Secretary of the Air Force.* Record Group 340, National Archives.
Contains many items on Air Force women, including administrative records for women, correspondence, studies on utilizing military women, records relating to motion pictures, and records from the office of the Director of women.

542 *United States Air Force Historical Research Agency*. Maxwell Air Force Base, AL.
Contains oral history interviews, as well as documents, including reports, histories from the Office of the Director, Women in the Air Force, scrapbooks, etc. Partially indexed by *USAF History of Women in the Air Force* (see **027**).

GENERAL WORKS

543 *Gauch, Tracey L.* **Air Force Leadership: Major General Jeanne M. Holm.** Maxwell Air Force Base, AL: Air University. Air Command and Staff College, 1985.
Analyzes the leadership strengths of General Holm during her tenure as Director, Women in the Air Force from 1965-1973. She was the first Air Force woman line officer to be promoted to brigadier general. Holm used her influence to enhance women's status in the military.

544 *Harris, John L.* **The Utilization of the WAC within the Regular Air Force.** Maxwell Air Force Base, AL: Air University, Air Command and Staff School, 1948. 27p.
A discussion of the way women should be integrated into the Air Force from the Army Air Forces after World War II.

545   *Kosier, Edwin J.* **"Women in the Air Force... Yesterday, Today and Tomorrow."** *Aerospace Historian* 15(2): 18-23, Summer 1968.
Short history of women in the Air Force, from those who served as Air WACs during World War II, to their integration into the Air Force. Discusses job assignments for Air Force women. Some photographs.

546   *Peets, Eleanor E.* **USAF History of Women in the Armed Forces: A Selected Bibliography.** Maxwell Air Force Base, AL: Historical Reference Branch, Albert F. Simpson Historical Research Center, 1976. 18p.
See **027**.

ENLISTED WOMEN

547   *Down, Marcia L.* **Job Strain and Job Satisfaction of Air Force Enlisted Women in Traditional and Nontraditional Career Fields.** Thesis (M.S.)--University of Wisconsin, Stout, 1981. 45p. OCLC 8145533.
Investigates the differences between enlisted Air Force women in traditional and nontraditional jobs by surveying enlisted women at Pope Air Force Base, North Carolina. Results indicated that women in nontraditional fields experienced significantly higher job stress than those in traditional fields. There was no difference in job satisfaction.

548   *United States. General Accounting Office.* **Losses of Air Force Women in Nontraditional Occupations.** GAO/FPCD-83-7. Washington, DC: GAO, 1982. 6p.
Before October 1982, the Air Force followed a policy of maintaining the same percentage of women in all noncombat operations. This caused many women to be placed in nontraditional occupations who would have preferred assignment to traditional occupations. Attrition rates in nontraditional occupations have been higher than in traditional occupations. Surveyed men and women in ten specialties, but found problems for women in nontraditional occupations were not the same in different specialties.

549   *Vitola, Bert M. and James H. Wilbourn.* **Comparative Performance of Male and Female Enlistees on Air Force Selection Measures.** Brooks Air Force Base, TX: Air Force Human Resources Lab, 1971. 22p. ED 056094.
Male and female enlistee samples were compared for total groups and by enlistment region in terms of their performance on the Airman Qualifying Exam and the Armed Services Vocational Aptitude Battery. A positive relationship was demonstrated between educational level and aptitude index.

OFFICERS

550   *Bartholomew, Charles W.* **Personal Value Systems and Career Objectives of Men Vis a Vis Women Air Force Officers.** Thesis (M.S.)-- Air Force Institute of Technology, 1973. 282p. OCLC 18755751; ED 090368.
Used a personal values questionnaire to compare the personal values and career objectives of Air Force women officers to Air Force men officers.

551   *Cashel, William Francis.* **The Perception of the USAF Company Grade Officer Role by Women Officer Trainees.** Thesis (Ph.D.)--Ohio State University, 1975. 93p. OCLC 2077805.
Studied thirty-five women officer trainees at the USAF Officer Training School to find out what role behaviors the women thought were important for women officers and how they rated their ability to perform these roles. Women had significant agreement on these roles and upon completing school, felt they would be able to fulfill them.

552   *Dunivin, Karen O'Donnell.* **Adapting to a Man's World: United States Air Force Female Officers.** Thesis (Ph.D.)--Northwestern University, 1988. 239p. OCLC 22970077.
Author interviewed thirty-five active duty female Air Force officers to study their marginal status in the military social world and how they adapt to a masculine world. Found that women officers formulate a role identity that is compatible with the male reference group and that they accentuated rewarded work and deemphasized devalued gender roles.

553   *Dunivin, Karen O.* **"Gender and Perceptions of the Job Environment in the U.S. Air Force."** *Armed Forces and Society* 15(1): 71-91, Fall 1988.
Using data from an Air Force survey, the author found that women felt they had less career opportunity and power than did men. However, while the organizational climate was less satisfactory to women, they liked the work they did.

554   *Neugebauer, Susan Hitchcock.* **A Comparative Study on the Promotion of Women Line Officers to Field Grade Ranks in the United States Air Force during Fiscal Years 1972 Through 1976.** Thesis (M.P.A.)-- Southwest Texas State University, 1976. 110p. OCLC 2757829.
Examines promotions of female officers compared to male officers in the Air Force from 1972 to 1976. Found the percentage of male and female officers receiving promotions were not equal, particularly in promotion to Major, and that non-rated officers status (those not having an aeronautical rating) decreased a woman officer's chances for promotion.

PILOTS

Items primarily about women pilots flying aircraft in combat are included in
Chapter 13, Women in Combat.

555 *Bateman, Sandra L.* **Female Air Force Pilots and Combat Aircraft: "The Right Stuff" Has No Gender.** Maxwell Air Force Base: United States Air University, Air Command and Staff College, 1987. 14p.
A short history of the role played by female pilots in the Air Force. Discusses the combat exclusion law and its consequences and examines the myths surrounding female pilots.

556 *Dunivin, Karen O.* **"Gender Identity among Air Force Female Aviators."** *Minerva* 9(1): 17-28, Spring 1991.
Examines gender identity in Air Force female aviators. Found that they displayed more masculine and androgynous identity than other military women and civilian women. Suggests female aviators adapt more masculine identities in order to succeed in the male dominated flying world.

557 *Kantor, Jeffrey E.* **Air Force Female Pilots Program: Initial Performance and Attitudes.** Brooks Air Force Base, TX: Air Force Human Resources Laboratory, 1978. 40p. SuDocs D301.45/27:78-67; OCLC 4602760.
Research conducted to establish a data base from female pilot selectees, composed of pre-training measures found to be predictive of training performance for men, to compare these data with that of male trainees, and to monitor flying performance of women. Few significant differences were found between women and men entering pilot training.

558 *Lyons, Terrence J.* **Women in the Military Cockpit.** Brooks Air Force Base, TX: Air Force Systems Command, 1991. 43p. OCLC 25533009.
Written by an Air Force physician, this report addresses the physical, psychological and medical differences between men and women. Contains an excellent summary comparing men and women in the areas of strength, hypoxia, aerobic fitness, etc. Concludes that pregnancy and the possibility of fetal damage in early pregnancy are women's greatest concerns in aviation.

559 *White, Anthony G.* **U.S. Servicewomen--Air Combat Debate: A Selected Sourcelist.** Monticello, IL: Vance Bibliographies, 1986. 6p. OCLC 17296164.
A very brief list of articles about women in military aviation, primarily from military periodicals. Arranged alphabetically by author. No annotations.

WOMEN ON MISSILE CREWS

560   *Donovan, John L. **The Integration of Women into Minuteman Missile Crews.*** Thesis (M.A.)--Central Missouri State University, 1991. 237p. OCLC 25504682.
Very detailed and interesting discussion and analysis of the factors detailing the Strategic Air Command's policy on the successful integration of women to Minuteman missile crews. The author, an Air Force officer, worked as a Missile Launch Officer, and provides unique insights into problems due to pregnancy, spouse reaction, and the option of officers to refuse duty with members of the opposite sex.

561   *Ideen, Dana R. and Jeffrey E. Kantor. **Introduction of Women into Titan II Missile Operations.*** Brooks Air Force Base, TX. Air Force Human Resources Lab, Air Force Systems Command, 1981. 50p. SuDocs D301.45/27:80-55; OCLC 7643688.
Evaluates the performance of women entering Titan II launch career fields to determine if women encounter any gender specific problems during Titan II operations. Women entering these fields and male peers were surveyed. Overall, few differences were found between men and women concerning their attitudes, perceptions and performance in Titan II training and operations.

562   *Vaughn, Arthur D. **Is it Feasible to Employ Women on Minuteman Missile Crews?*** Maxwell Air Force Base, AL: Air Command and Staff College, Air University, 1975. 37p. OCLC 21266634.
Presents an implementation program for women entering Minuteman missile crews. Author concludes that social attitudes assuming women could not handle the stress of missile crew duty were due to cultural conditioning and that women were as capable as men in working as missile launch operators.

563   *White, James R. **Women on Minuteman Missile Crews.*** Maxwell Air Force Base, AL: Air Command and Staff College, Air University, 1979. 65p. OCLC 5897824.
Author believes that by restricting women from working on Minuteman missile crews, the Air Force denies two-thirds of available crew opportunities to women. Proposes ways the Air Force could reduce opposition to mixed sex missile crews.

10

SERVICE ACADEMIES

The push to integrate the service academies began in 1972, when Senator Jacob Javits of New York nominated Barbara J. Brimmer to the United States Naval Academy. While her application was denied, the Senate passed a resolution that women should not be denied entrance to the service academies on the basis of sex. Lawsuits were filed by women desiring admission to the academies and by several members of Congress, who protested that they were being forced to discriminate against female applicants. The military services prepared for a fight.

In May 1974, the House Military Personnel Subcommittee began hearings on the admission of women to the service academies. The services argued that the academies existed to provide officers for combat roles in the Armed Forces. Training at the academies was so expensive that it should be reserved for those with potential for serving in combat. The services insisted that Congress needed to decide on the issue of women in combat before admitting women to the academies. Evidence was collected to oppose this view. A Government Accounting Office report, issued in April 1975, pointed out that of all service academy graduates then on active duty, 12.3 percent had never held a combat assignment. Proponents of integrating the academies argued that the academies did not exist solely to train officers for combat. Members of Congress were persuaded that it was time to integrate and voted 303 to ninety-six to approve an amendment to the Defense Authorization Bill of 1976 to admit women to the academies. It was approved by the Senate on 6 June. On 7 October 1975, President Gerald R. Ford signed Public Law 94-106, making women eligible for admission to the service academies. In June 1976, 119 women entered the United States. Military Academy at West Point, eighty-one entered the United States Naval Academy at Annapolis, and 157 entered the United States Air Force Academy at Colorado Springs.

The services prepared for the admission of women in different ways. The Army conducted an extensive research program, from 1975 to 1980, called "Project Athena" (see **598-604**), examining the effect of attending the Military Academy on female cadets, as well as the effect female cadets had on the Academy. The Air Force conducted studies examining the attitudes, beliefs, and interactions of male and female cadets at the Air Force Academy (see **575-576**). The Navy also examined the effects of integration (see **631-632, 639-640**).

The first women to attend the service academies graduated in 1980. Of the 357 women who entered, sixty-six percent graduated (for the men of the class of 1980, seventy percent graduated). It was found that twice as many men as women dropped out due to academic failure.

Despite the fact that women have attended the service academies for nearly twenty years, and have graduated at the top of their classes, been selected as Rhodes Scholars, and served as Brigade Commander and First Captain of the West Point Corps of Cadets, they have not been fully assimilated into the academies. A January 1994 Government Accounting Report on sexual harassment at the Air Force, Military, and Naval Academies concluded between half to three quarters of academy women experienced various forms of harassment at least twice a month in academic year 1991 (see **573**). It concluded the academies have not met DOD's policy of providing an environment free of sexual harassment. A March 1995 update (see **574**) confirmed earlier findings, while women at the Naval and Air Force Academies reported a statistically significant increase in levels of harassment from the 1990-91 levels.

The downsizing of the military has also raised questions of the cost effectiveness of the academies. The Government Accounting Office estimates the cost of providing an academy education at $250,000 per graduate, while ROTC costs about $60,000 per officer and Officer Candidate School (OCS), about $25,000 per officer. The GAO also found no proof that academy graduates make better officers than those commissioned through ROTC or OCS. While military tradition is strong, the costs of maintaining the academies in their present form is sure to lead to continued debate about their usefulness in providing officers for the military.

The entries in this chapter are primarily reports of research conducted to study the effects of integration at the service academies, including physical and academic differences between male and female cadets, attitudes held by cadets regarding integration, and the ways in which the academies adapted to women. It also includes two first hand accounts of life as a female cadet and Army officer written by women who graduated from the United States Military Academy (**596-597**).

BIBLIOGRAPHIES

564   *White, Anthony G. U.S. Servicewomen--Academy Cadets: A Selected Bibliography*. Monticello, IL: Vance Bibliographies, 1986. 5p. OCLC 22711065.
Very brief list of articles dealing with women at the service academies. Citations are primarily from military periodicals.

GENERAL WORKS

565   *Baldi, Karen A. "An Overview of Physical Fitness of Female Cadets at the Military Academy."* Military Medicine 156(10): 537-539, October 1991.
Examined the performance in physical fitness progress of female cadets

at the military academies from 1979 to 1989. Found that women were capable of much higher levels of physical performance than had previously been anticipated.

566   Clark, Albert P.   **"Women at the Service Academies and Combat Leadership."** Strategic Review 5(4): 64-73, Fall 1977.
Author was a former Superintendent of the United States Air Force Academy. Discusses legal developments and congressional action which opened the academies to women. Also comments on how women have fared at the academies physically. Includes information on what the prohibition against women in combat (at the time the article was written) will have on women academy graduates and their military careers.

567   Heinzman, Richard R.   **A Policy Analysis of the Admission of Women by the U.S. Military Academies.**   Maxwell Air Force Base, AL: Air War College,   Air University, 1986.   30p.   OCLC 26206489.
An analysis of the law, enacted in October 1975, directing the admission of women to the service academies. Includes a discussion of the law making process and briefly, how the Air Force Academy handled the admission of women. Emphasizes the admission of women was beneficial to the services.

568   Ponte, Lucille M.   **"Waldie Answered: Equal Protection and the Admissions of Women to Military Colleges and Academies."**   New England Law Review 25(4): 1137-1160, Summer 1991.
A lengthy and detailed article which discusses the issues that the Waldie case (which addressed the issue of female admissions into the military academies in light of equal protection concerns), and the Supreme Court have struggled with regarding gender-based distinctions in military settings. Concludes that based on case law development and statutory and regulatory changes, all military academies should be open to men and women and that allowing some military colleges to operate single-sex admissions violates equal protection guarantees, and statutory and regulatory requirements.

569   Schoonmaker, Linda Lee.   **The History and Development of the Programs of Physical Education, Intercollegiate Athletics, Intramurals, and Recreational Sports for Women at the United States Military Service Academies.**   Thesis (Ph.D.)--Ohio State University, 1983.   276p.   OCLC 10660572.
Examines the history of women in the U.S. military and describes events leading to the admission of women to the service academies. It primarily details the history of each service academy and its programs rather than critically analyzing them. Interviews were conducted with key personnel involved in the development of the women's sports programs.

570   United States Department of Defense.   Defense Equal Opportunity Management Institute. **The Service Academies As a Source of Minority and Female Officers.**   Washington, DC: The Institute, 1986.   35p.
Discusses the application process for all academies, including the Coast

Guard, giving statistics for women and minority cadets. Primarily a collection of statistics for women and minorities at service academies.

SEXUAL HARASSMENT

571 *United States. Congress. Senate. Committee on Armed Services.* **Honor Systems and Sexual Harassment at the Service Academies:** Hearing Before the Committee on Armed Services, United States Senate. Washington, DC: GPO, 1994. 256p. SuDocs Y4.AR5/3:S.HRG103-550; ISBN 0160443946.
Transcript of a hearing on the honor code and sexual harassment at the service academies. Reprints the GAO report *DOD Service Academies: More Action Needed to Eliminate Sexual Harassment* (see **573**).

572 *United States. General Accounting Office.* **DOD Service Academies: Further Efforts Needed to Eradicate Sexual Harassment.** Testimony Before the Subcommittee on Force Requirements and Personnel, Committee on Armed Services, U.S. Senate. GAO/T-NSIAD-94-11. Washington, DC: GAO, February 1994. 7p. SuDocs FA1.512:T-NSIAD-94-111.
Transcript of statements by Mark E. Gebicke, Director of Military Operations and Capabilities Issues, National Security and International Affairs Division. Discusses a review of sexual harassment at the service academies (see **571**) and defines sexual harassment. Found sexual harassment continues at the service academies, that between one-half and three-quarters of the women were harassed at least twice a month, usually verbally.

573 *United States. General Accounting Office.* **DOD Service Academies: More Actions Needed to Eliminate Sexual Harassment.** GAO/NSIAD-94-6. Washington, DC: GAO, January 1994. 64p. SuDocs GA1.13:NSIAD-94-6.
Reviews sexual harassment at the Military Academy, Air Force Academy, and Naval Academy. Addresses the extent to which sexual harassment occurred, forms it took, effects on those subjected to it, and evaluates the academies' efforts to eradicate it. Found ninety-three to ninety-seven percent of women reported experiencing sexual harassment. Presents many statistics and results of questionnaires. Recommends actions to improve climate for women.

574 *United States. General Accounting Office.* **DOD Service Academies: Update on Extent of Sexual Harassment.** GAO/NSIAD-95-58. Washington, DC: GAO, March 1995. 34p.
Presents results from a 1994 follow-up survey to earlier studies on sexual harassment at the service academies. Questionnaires were administered at the Naval Academy, the Military Academy and the Air Force Academy in May 1994. The majority of women reported experiencing at least one form of sexual harassment on a recurring basis in the academic year 1993-1994. The proportion of women at the Naval

and Air Force Academies who reported sexual harassment a couple of times a month or more increased significantly from 1990-1991. Many statistics on sexual harassment.

UNITED STATES AIR FORCE ACADEMY

Sex Integration

575 *DeFleur, Lois B. and David Gillman.* **Cadet Beliefs, Attitudes, and Interactions during the Early Phases of Sex-Integration**. Colorado Springs, CO: United States Air Force Academy, 1978. 26p. ED 188503.
Attitudes, beliefs and interactions of male and female cadets at the Air Force Academy during the first year of integration are discussed. A survey was conducted with men and women six months after entering the Academy. Results showed that women felt less accepted than men, and less understood. Men felt women did not receive a fair share of assignments and were very uncomfortable with female cadets.

576 *Defleur, Lois B. and Frank Wood.* **Four Years of Sex Integration at the United States Air Force Academy: Problems and Issues.** Colorado Springs, CO: United States Air Force Academy, 1985. 191p. OCLC 13180017.
Results of a study conducted over the first four years of sex integration at the Air Force Academy. Information was gathered using questionnaires distributed to the same sample of male and female cadets at least once a year during their attendance at the Academy. The main areas studied were the assessment of the sex-integration process, a monitoring of changes in cadet career and family plans and some comparisons of male and female cadets experiences. Good coverage of issues facing cadets and includes many tables and statistics.

577 *DeFleur, Lois B., David Gillman and William Marshak.* **"Sex Integration of the U.S. Air Force Academy: Changing Roles For Women."** *Armed Forces and Society* 4(4): 607-622, August 1978.
Focuses on the integration process at the USAF Academy by examining attitudes of upper-class cadets, as well as the characteristics of the first integrated class. Data was obtained through two questionnaires. Found men at the Academy tended to be traditional towards women's roles while women were significantly less traditional.

578 *Dinsmore, John C.* **Women As Cadets: An Analysis of the Issue**. Maxwell Air Force Base, AL: U.S. Air University, Air Command and Staff College, 1974. 80p. OCLC 1929012; ED 107194.
Traces the history of the women's movement and the specific ways by which the Air Force policy (in 1974) against admitting women to the Air Force Academy could be changed. Policy and planning for the admission of women is reviewed. Concludes that women will be admitted to the Academy and that Air Force planning for their admission is satisfactory.

579   *Fincher, Michele S.* **Gender-Role Orientation of Female Cadets at the United States Air Force Academy.** Thesis (M.S.)--Air Force Institute of Technology, Wright-Patterson Air Force Base, OH, 1993. 62p.
Effects of a masculine service academy environment on the gender-role development of female cadets was studied. Gave fifty-five female cadets the Bem Sex-Role Inventory to determine if orientation changed as the women spent more time in the masculine environment. Found that while the majority of women in general were not masculine in gender-role orientation, women at the Air Force Academy have become more so since they were last studied.

580   *Furdek, Dennis T.* **History of the Integration of Women at the Air Force Academy, 1972-1979.** Maxwell Air Force Base, AL: Air Command and Staff College, Air University, 1980. 31p. OCLC 18668093.
The author was assigned to the Academy from 1976-1979, when women were admitted for the first time. The purpose of the paper is to present a "detailed account" of the integration of women. An overly optimistic evaluation of the success of integration, mentioning none of the many problems women cadets were actually experiencing.

581   *Heinzman, Richard R.* **A Policy Analysis of the Admission of Women by the U.S. Military Academies.** Maxwell Air Force Base, AL: Air War College, Air University, 1986. 30p.
See **567.**

582   *Hughes, Richard L.* **Who Goes to a Service Academy?** Colorado Springs, CO: United States Air Force Academy, 1982. 9p. OCLC 22292243; ED 223164.
Personality characteristics of females admitted to the Air Force Academy were compared to those of male cadets and to females entering other colleges. All 217 female cadets and one-half of the male cadets entering the academy were surveyed. Found that female cadets were similar to men in personality, but were relatively non-traditional, while the male cadets were relatively traditional. Concludes that the Academy attracts achievers and relatively dominant or assertive individuals.

583   *Petosa, Scott.* **"Women in the Military Academies: U.S. Air Force Academy (Part 2 of 3)."** *Physician and Sports Medicine* 17(3): 133-136, 139-140, 142, March 1989.
Since women first entered the Air Force Academy, their fitness levels have improved and now male and female cadets take the same physical fitness test. Describes the evolution and structure of the fitness program for women from 1977-1987 and provides test statistics.

584   *Stiehm, Judith.* **Bring Me Men and Women: Mandated Change at the U.S. Air Force Academy.** Berkeley: University of California Press, 1981. 348p. OCLC 6532683; ISBN 0520040457.
For sixteen months, the author was allowed to interview persons involved with planning and implementing women's admission to the Air Force Academy. Provides a unique insiders' view to not only the changes

which took place at the Academy, but also problems caused by the admittance of women to the Military Academy and the Naval Academy. The best overall source for information on how the service academies handled women's admission. Extensive bibliography.

585 *Thomas, James Carl.* **Women's Integration Project: Project "Blue Eyes."** 3 volumes. Colorado Springs, CO; United States Air Force Academy, 1976. OCLC 6156435.
Research project implemented to smoothly and efficiently integrate the class of 1980 women cadets into the Air Force Academy physical education program. Three phases: 1. Preparation period to see how women could perform physically; 2. Women's integration to focus on female physiological response to cadet basic training; 3. Description of physical training program for women. Includes many statistics on women cadets.

586 *United States. General Accounting Office.* **Air Force Academy: Gender and Racial Disparities.** GAO/NSIAD-93-244. Washington, DC: GAO, 1993. 62p. SuDocs GA1.13:NSIAD/93-244.
Addresses differences in performance indicators between men and women and between whites and minorities, cadets' perceptions of the fairness of the treatment that female and minority cadets receive, and actions the Academy has taken to enhance the success of women and minorities. Many statistics.

587 *Wallisch, William Joseph, Jr.* **The Admission and Integration of Women into the United States Air Force Academy.** Thesis (Ed.D.)--University of Southern California, 1977. 227p. OCLC 3834555.
Written by an Air Force officer who was a member of the faculty at the Air Force Academy at the time of female integration, this is a record of the planning and the processes necessary for the admission of women. Good "insiders" view.

588 *Williams, John W., Jr.* **The Integration of Women into the Air Force Academy (An Update).** Paper presented at the Annual Meeting of the American Psychological Association (New York), September 1979. 12p. ED 188556.
Reviews changes at the Air Force Academy since women entered in 1976, focusing on male student attitudes and female performance. Women were doing well. Male cadets, were not convinced female cadets could succeed but were more accepting of women at the Academy.

United States Air Force Academy - Graduates

589 *DeFleur, Lois B. and Rebecca L. Warner.* **"Air Force Academy Graduates and Nongraduates: Attitudes and Self-Concepts."** *Armed Forces and Society* 13(4): 517-533, Summer 1987.
Considers whether or not the Air Force Academy provides a different socialization experience for men and women and compares Academy

dropouts with graduates to determine how men's and women's attitudes change after four years of military experience. Graduates were more likely to retain traditional family life-style expectations than dropouts.

590 *Roffery, Arthur E., Frank R. Wood, Bridgett R. Proce, and Melissa R. Kallett.* **"Work and Family Issues Affecting Early Career Decisions of the First Women Graduates of the Air Force Academy."** *Minerva* 7(3-4): 25-40, Fall/Winter 1989.
Authors conducted telephone interviews of forty-six of the ninety-seven women graduates of the Air Force Academy class of 1980. In 1986, they were voluntarily leaving the military at twice the rate of men. Major reasons given for leaving were problems of balancing family responsibilities and military duties.

UNITED STATES COAST GUARD ACADEMY

591 *Cheatham, Harold E.* **"Integration of Women into the U.S. Military."** *Sex Roles* 11(1/2): 141-153, July 1984.
Study to assess male attitudes towards women admitted to the Coast Guard Academy. Administered attitude surveys to male members of the classes of 1979-1983. Male attitudes toward women in the military worsened after women started at the Academy, but then improved.

592 *Rottman, Myrna.* **"Women Graduates of the U.S. Coast Guard Academy: Views from the Bridge."** *Armed Forces and Society* 11(2): 249-270, Winter 1985.
Discusses research conducted at all the different service academies regarding the integration of women. Studied the experiences of the first women to graduate from the Coast Guard Academy and how they affected the women's subsequent service as officers.

593 *Safilios-Rothschild, Constantina.* **"Young Women and Men Aboard the U.S. Coast Guard Barque "Eagle": An Observation and Interview Study."** *Youth & Society* 10(2): 191-204, December 1978.
The author observed 120 Coast Guard Academy cadets (ten were women), during a four day training cruise aboard the barque *Eagle* in August 1977. Data was collected through systematic observation and focused interviews. Found that when there was only one women cadet in a training group she tended to become marginal and had difficulty receiving adequate training. Good discussion of reactions of male cadets and officers to women at the Coast Guard Academy.

594 *Stevens, Gwendolyn and Sheldon Gardner.* **"But Can She Command A Ship? Acceptance of Women by Peers at the Coast Guard Academy."** *Sex Roles* 16(3/4): 181-188, February 1987.
Study replicating an earlier study (1977-1978) to assess whether or not male Coast Guard cadets' attitudes have changed. The earlier study reported male cadets were not favorable to women at the academy. This study showed a more positive attitude towards women cadets.

595 *Stevens, Gwendolyn, Alyce Hemstreet and Sheldon Gardner. **"Fit to Lead: Prediction of Success in a Military Academy Through Use of Personality Profile."*** *Psychological Reports* 64(1): 227-235, February 1989.
Studied personality traits of cadets from the Coast Guard Academy classes of 1984 and 1985, including 134 female cadets and 150 male cadets to try and predict attrition. Found that personality traits were not accurate predictors of attrition and that it was likely that the traits measured were not crucial in the decision to continue to completion at a military academy.

UNITED STATES MILITARY ACADEMY

Personal Narratives

596 *Barkalow, Carol with Andrea Raab. **In the Men's House: An Inside Account of Life in the Army by One of West Point's First Female Graduates.*** New York: Poseidon Press, 1990. 283p. OCLC 21524184; ISBN 0671673122.
The author was a member of the first class of women admitted to West Point. Written from diaries the author kept while she was at school. After graduation, she served in the Air Defense Artillery in Germany, then transferred to the Transportation Corps. Later served as a company commander. An excellent source of information on challenges faced by military women today as well as what it was like being in the first class of women at West Point.

597 *Peterson, Donna. **Dress Gray: A Woman at West Point.*** Austin, TX: Eakin Press, 1990. 254p. OCLC 2209674; ISBN 0890157820.
The author graduated from West Point in the class of 1982, the third class to admit women as cadets. Presents an interesting contrast with the experiences of Carol Barkalow from the first class of women (see **596**). Spends too much time detailing her romances with male cadets, trivializing her accomplishments. Worth reading, if only for the observations about the women who preceded the author at the Academy. After graduation, she became a helicopter pilot before resigning her commission.

"Project Athena"

598 *Adams, Jerome. **"Attitudinal Studies on the Integration of Women at West Point."*** *International Journal of Women's Studies* 5(1): 22-28 January/February 1982.
Reviews the attitudinal studies conducted at West Point in support of the longitudinal study of the integration of women (see **599-600, 603-604**). Good summary of previous research.

599 *Adams, Jerome*. **Report of the Admission of Women to the U.S. Military Academy: Project Athena III.** West Point, NY: Department of Behavioral Sciences and Leadership, United States Military Academy, 1979. 236p. OCLC 5637029.
Analyzes the third year of integration of women at West Point, from May 1978-May 1979. The major finding was that women who did not perform well physically received poorer leadership ratings by men than women who were physically fit. Includes many statistical tables, including applicant profiles, injury rates, leadership ratings and physical aptitudes. Part three of a four part study (see **600, 603-604**).

600 *Adams, Jerome*. **Report of the Admission of Women to the U.S. Military Academy: Project Athena IV.** West Point, NY: Department of Behavioral Sciences and Leadership, United States Military Academy, 1980. 146p. OCLC 7852517.
Covers June 1979-June 1980. Completes the first three phases of Project Athena, conducted as a long-term research program as women were integrated into the academy. Concludes that women's integration was successful, however, women as a group had not reached their potential and sexism still existed. Many statistical tables are included. Part four of a four part study (see **599, 603-604**).

601 *Adams, Jerome*. **"Women at West Point: A Three-Year Perspective."** *Sex Roles* 11(5/6): 525-541, September 1984.
A discussion of the longitudinal research conducted during Project Athena (see **599-600, 603-604**). Examines the personality characteristics of men and women to seek gender related differences, describes the leadership evaluation system to determine if leadership ratings are influenced by gender of the person being rated, and finally, discusses social aspects of the integration process after three years.

602 *Priest, Robert F., Howard T. Prince, and Alan G. Vitters*. **"The First Coed Class at West Point: Performance and Attitudes."** *Youth & Society* 10(2): 205-224, December 1978.
Summarizes some of the findings of Project Athena (see **599-600, 603-604**). Good discussion of batteries of tests and questionnaires given to the West Point class of 1980 and their results.

603 *Vitters, Alan G. and Nora Scott Kinzer*. **Report of the Admission of Women to the U.S. Military Academy: Project Athena**. West Point, NY: Department of Behavioral Sciences and Leadership, United States Military Academy, 1977. 208p. OCLC 3664981; ED163828.
Summarizes the actions taken from June 1975 to June 1977 to integrate women into the Academy. Found that more women than men resigned during the first summer and academic year. Women tended to be rated lower on leadership skills than men. Many statistics are included. Part one of a four part study (see **599-600, 604**).

604 *Vitters, Alan G*. **Report of the Admission of Women to the U.S. Military Academy: Project Athena II**. West Point, NY: Department of

Behavioral Sciences and Leadership, United States Military Academy, 1978. OCLC 4286067; ED 165516.

Part two of a four part project studying women's integration at West Point (see **599-600, 603**). Presents a great deal of data obtained through surveys, interviews, and observations of officers and cadets. Found men and women differed in physical aptitude, attitudes toward appropriate roles for women in society and in the Army, and in personal life-style preferences.

United States Military Academy - Sex Integration and Gender Issues

605 *Adams, Jerome, Robert W. Rice, Debra Instone and Jack M. Hicks.* ***Follower Attributional Biases and Assessments of Female and Male Leaders' Performance.*** Alexandria, VA: Army Research Institute for the Behavioral and Social Sciences, 1981. 20p. ED 209609.

Male and female cadets at the Military Academy completed questionnaires describing their unit leaders at two training activities. Results showed that egalitarian followers and traditional followers did not make different attributional or evaluative judgements regarding male and female leaders.

606 *Adams, Jerome, Robert W. Rice and Debra Instone.* **"Follower Attitudes toward Women and Judgements Concerning Performance by Female and Male Leaders."** *Academy of Management Journal* 27(3): 636-643, September 1984.

Studied cadets at the USMA during two six week summer courses, Cadet Basic Training and Cadet Field Training. Studied attitudes of male and female cadets toward male and female leaders. Found that female cadets had more egalitarian attitudes, while male followers of male leaders were more satisfied with their peers and summer assignments.

607 *Adams, Jerome, Howard T. Prince II, Jan D. Yoder and Robert W. Rice.* **"Group Performance at West Point: Relationships with Intelligence and Attitudes toward Sex Roles."** *Armed Forces and Society* 7(2): 246-255, Winter 1981.

Primary concern of this study was with the possible effects of the following variables on group performance: the leader's sex (male versus female), follower's sex role attitude (measured with the Attitude Toward Women Scale) and the SAT or ACT scores for both leaders and followers. Subjects studied were thirty-six men and thirty-six women freshmen cadets at the USMA. Each cadet led a three-man group which conducted two experimental tasks. Found that when a leader is male and intelligent, group performance on a structured task was maximized when the followers hold traditional attitudes towards women. More intelligent groups performed well on the structured task when the followers were supportive of an egalitarian role for women and the leader is a women.

608 *Adams, Jerome, Howard T. Prince II, Robert F. Priest and Robert W. Rice.* **"Personality Characteristics of Male and Female Leaders at the U.S. Military Academy."** *Journal of Political and Military Sociology* 8(1): 99-105, Spring 1980.
Reviews the evidence of personality characteristics of a leader that predict group performance using male and female cadets at West Point. The data suggests that in general, the higher the intelligence of the leader, the more productive was group performance on structured tasks and that male cadets resisted the leadership attempts of the appointed female leaders in their group.

609 *Campbell, D'Ann.* **"Servicewomen and the Academies: The Football Cordon and Pep Rally As a Case Study of the Status of Female Cadets at the United States Military Academy."** *Minerva* 13(1): 1-14, Spring 1995.
Reviews the actions taken by the Military Academy after a football spirit run in October 1994, when several female cadets reported being touched on the breast by football players. Author believes the emphasis at West Point (versus that at the Naval Academy) on zero tolerance for sexual harassment and discrimination was responsible for a swift and appropriate reaction and punishment of those responsible.

610 *McKeon, Jane Perkins.* **Predicting Attrition for Women at West Point: Is it a Function of Adopting the Male Dominant Culture?** Thesis (M.A.)--University of Richmond, 1990. 53p.
The author, a member of the first class of women to graduate from West Point, conducted a survey of 3,305 men and 314 women in the Academy classes of 1990 and 1992 to see if attrition of women could be predicted. Compared women's scores on the Student Information Form and found that attriters and non-attriters could be predicted with a seventy percent accuracy rate. Sloppily done (tables are in the wrong place) and filled with jargon.

611 *Priest, Robert F. and John W. Houston.* **Analysis of Spontaneous Cadet Comments on the Admission of Women**. West Point, NY: Office of the Director of Institutional Research, 1976. 14p. OCLC 13020243.
In March 1976, cadets in the classes of 1977, 1978, and 1979 at West Point were given a sixty-four item questionnaire concerning their attitudes towards women. The largest number of comments (forty-two percent) argued against the admission of women to West Point. Many of the cadet's comments are included (see **614**).

612 *Priest, Robert F.* **Cadet Attitudes toward Women**. West Point, NY: Office of the Director of Institutional Research, United States Military Academy, 1976. 40p. OCLC 8920600.
Results of a survey of all cadets done in August 1975, measuring their attitudes toward women in the army, society and women at West Point. Cadets were found to have a more conservative, traditional opinion about women than did college students in general. They were quite negative about women in the army.

613 *Priest, Robert F.* **Cadet Perceptions of Inequitable Treatment during Cadet Basic Training, 1976**. West Point, NY: Office of the Director of Institutional Research, United States Military Academy, 1977. 11p. OCLC 13035163.
After Cadet Basic Training, cadets in the class of 1980 (the first to admit women), were asked three questions about perceived discrimination due to race, ethnicity, or sex. Only a few cadets reported that they frequently or on other occasions had been treated more harshly due to their group membership.

614 *Priest, Robert F.* **Changes in Cadet Attitude toward the Admission of Women to West Point**. West Point, NY: Office of the Director of Institutional Research, United States Military Academy, 1976. 15p. OCLC 11723383.
A repeat of the survey conducted in 1975 (see **612**), this time taken in March 1976. Between the time of the two surveys, cadets were briefed by the Superintendent, heard several lectures on women in the military, participated in discussions about women, etc. It was found that on most items of the questionnaire, no significant change in attitude occurred (see **611**).

615 *Priest, Robert F., Alan G. Vitters and Howard T. Prince.* **"Coeducation at West Point."** *Armed Forces and Society* 4(4): 589-606, August 1978.
Details preparations made for the admittance of women to the Military Academy, entrance characteristics of women cadets, cadet basic training, and the academic year. Good summary of women's integration.

616 *Priest, Robert F.* **A Comparison of Faculty and Cadet Attitudes toward Women**. West Point, NY: Office of the Director of Institutional Research, United States Military Academy, 1976. 18p. OCLC 8920629.
Cadets and faculty at West Point were given a questionnaire in March 1976 regarding their attitudes towards women (see **611, 614**). The results showed that the faculty were less traditional in their attitudes toward the women than were the cadets. The reasons for these differences are discussed.

617 *Priest, Robert F.* **Content of Cadet Comments on the Integration of Women**. West Point, NY: Office of the Director of Institutional Research, United States Military Academy, 1977. 11p. OCLC 13020319.
In April 1977, cadets in the classes of 1978, 1979, and 1980 were surveyed regarding their attitudes toward the integration of women at West Point. Most cadets, male and female, felt that women had not been effectively integrated into the corps of cadets. Many cadet comments are included.

618 *Priest, Robert F. and Howard T. Prince.* **Women at West Point: Their Performance and Adjustment**. West Point, NY: Office of the Director of Institutional Research, United States Military Academy, 1979. 43p.

OCLC 8641838; ED 174887.
The performance correlates of perceptions of discriminatory treatment, satisfaction, and self-concept for male and female cadets in the classes of 1980 and 1981 at the Military Academy were investigated. Results indicated that women with the same performance and entrance motivation as men were given higher leadership ratings. Women also perceived greater discriminatory treatment than did men.

619 *Rice, Robert W., Debra Instone and Jerome Adams. **"Leader Sex, Leader Success, and Leadership Process: Two Field Studies."** Journal of Applied Psychology* 69(1): 12-31, February 1984.
Effects of leader sex were examined in two six week cadet training programs at West Point to determine, among other factors, if there are differences in the degree of leadership success achieved by male and female leaders. Freshmen and sophomore cadets were subordinates and more senior cadets were leaders. Found that leader sex effects were nonsignificant nearly ninety percent of the time.

620 *Rice, Robert W., Jan D. Yoder, Jerome Adams, Robert F. Priest and Howard T. Prince II. **"Leadership Ratings for Male and Female Military Cadets."** Sex Roles* 10(11/12): 885-901, June 1984.
Examined leadership ratings for 1,096 male and ninety-one female cadets at West Point for gender differences. Males were rated significantly higher than females for two of three ratings periods. Physical ability and performance were most highly correlated with leadership ratings during summer training, while academic ability and performance were most highly correlated with these ratings during the academic year.

621 *Stauffer, Robert W. **Comparison of United States Military Academy Men and Women on Selected Physical Performance Measures... "Project Summertime."*** West Point, NY: Office of Physical Education, United States Military Academy, 1976. 248p. OCLC 5166128.
Report on "Project Summertime", a response to Public Law 94-105 directing that women be admitted to the U.S. service academies. The study's purpose was to determine what adjustments in performance standards would be made to accommodate women. Tests on male and female cadets at the Academy in the summer of 1976 determined that adjustments should be made. It was also recommended that women increase their upper body and leg strength.

622 *United States. General Accounting Office. **Military Academy: Gender and Racial Disparities.*** GAO/NSIAD-94-95. Washington, DC: GAO, March 1994. 63p. SuDocs GA1.13:NSIAD-94-95.
Addresses differences in indicators of performance between men and women and whites and minorities, perceptions of fairness of treatment that women and minorities receive, and actions the Academy has taken to enhance the success of women and minorities. Found women's physical education grades were often higher than men's, but their military development grades were often lower. Includes many statistics and tables.

623   *Vitters, Alan G. and Nora Scott Kinzer.* **"Women at West Point: Change within Tradition."** *Military Review* 58(4): 20-28, April 1978.
Reviews some of the significant events of the first year of women at West Point. Presents data on characteristics of entering cadets, resignation rates, academic and physical performance, and attitudes and adjustment problems of men and women.

624   *Welch, Michael J.* **"Women in the Military Academies: U.S. Army (Part 3 of 3)."** *Physician and Sportsmedicine* 17(4): 89-92, 95-96, April 1989.
Describes the physical education program and fitness training at the Military Academy. Women's fitness has improved since they first entered the Academy, but fitness scores are difficult to compare because the Army physical fitness test has changed several times since 1976. However, women in the class of 1990 improved significantly over women in the class of 1980 on the Physical Aptitude Test, required only for first year cadets.

625   *Yoder, Janice D., Jerome Adams, Stephen Grove and Robert F. Priest.* **"To Teach Is to Learn: Overcoming Tokenism with Mentors."** *Psychology of Women Quarterly* 9(1): 119-131, March 1985.
Studied the failure of women in the first class to accept women at West Point to develop a sponsoring or mentoring relationship with women in the following class. Interviewed the sixty-two women in the class of 1980 just before graduation. Confirmed that women in the class of 1980 had failed to offer help to the women of the class of 1981. Reasons given were the first women were reluctant to damage their peer relationship with male members of their class, it would jeopardize the "specialness" they felt as the first women, and they had problems of their own. Authors suggest ways to foster mentoring.

United States Military Academy - Graduates

626   *Adams, Jerome.* **Early Career Preparation, Experiences, and Commitment of Female and Male West Point Graduates**. West Point, NY: United States Military Academy, 1983. Not paged. OCLC 11627652.
Contains a descriptive analysis of the Postgraduate Questionnaire of the West Point classes of 1980 and 1981. Mainly a collection of statistics used in Project Proteus (see **627**).

627   *Adams, Jerome.* **Project Proteus: Early Career Preparation, Experiences, and Commitment of Female and Male West Point Graduates**. West Point, NY: Science Research Lab, United States Military Academy, 1984-1985. 3 volumes. OCLC 17826760.
A three volume set that presents data and discussions from interviews with West Point graduates, as well as questionnaires and small group interviews (see **626**). Volume three contains very interesting excerpts from interviews conducted with the graduates one, two, and three years after entering active duty. Many graduates were beginning to experience

conflicts between career and family (including those who were part of a dual career couple), and between their expectations of military service and the reality of their jobs.

628   *Yoder, Janice D. and Jerome Adams.* **A Report on Women West Point Graduates Assuming Nontraditional Roles**. Paper presented at the Annual Meeting of the Midwestern Psychological Association (56th, Chicago), May 3-5, 1984. 15p. ED 247484.
Thirty-five female and 113 male graduates of West Point were surveyed regarding career assessment and planning, commitment and adjustment, and satisfaction. Forty percent of the women and nineteen percent of the men planned to leave the Army at the completion of their service obligation. Women were less satisfied than men with their adjustment, and were less satisfied with their overall job. The author suggests that gender differences arise when the role demands of the officer conflict with other roles, such as that of mother.

629   *Yoder, Janice D. and Jerome Adams.* **"Women Entering Nontraditional Roles: When Work Demands and Sex-Roles Conflict: The Case of West Point."** *International Journal of Women's Studies* 7(3): 260-272, May/June 1984.
Studies how women from the class of 1980 at the Military Academy were adjusting to active duty. Results of a questionnaire from thirty-five women and 113 men are presented. Found women had a role conflict with a leadership role, and women are not benefitted as much as men by relationships with superior officers. No difference was found between men and women in job satisfaction.

United States Military Academy - Miscellaneous

630   *Hancock, Cynthia Riffe.* **Women Officers at the United States Military Academy: A Study of Acceptance Patterns and Coping Mechanisms**. Thesis (Ph.D.)--University of North Carolina at Chapel Hill, 1991. 297p. OCLC 26296855.
Presents the results of interviews with fifty-one women officers assigned to West Point during 1989. While these women were not attending the Academy, they were serving as role models for female cadets. The author found that women working in the most and least traditional jobs in both the Army and at West Point felt less accepted than women in mid-range traditional jobs.

UNITED STATES NAVAL ACADEMY

Sex Integration

631   *Durning, Kathleen P.* **"Women at the Naval Academy: An Attitude Survey."** *Armed Forces and Society* 4(4): 569-588, August 1978.
Surveyed members of the Naval Academy class of 1980 twice, as well

as members of the classes of 1977, 1978, and 1979. Found that exposure to women as peers tended to break down stereotyping and traditionalism in the class of 1980 men during the first year of coeducation. Concludes that as more women attend the Academy, acceptance of women will increase.

632 *Durning, Kathleen P.* **Women at the Naval Academy: The First Year of Integration.** San Diego, CA: Navy Personnel Research and Development Center, 1978. 39p. OCLC 4269437; ED 152199.
Studied the first year of integration of women midshipmen at the Naval Academy and found that the majority of men perceived women as receiving favored treatment, while women felt resented and less accepted than their male peers. Plebe men were more favorable to integration than upperclassmen. The author concludes that more peer contact between men and women and greater numbers of women midshipmen will lead to greater acceptance.

633 *Good, Jane E. and Karl M. Klein.* **"Women in the Military Academies: U.S. Navy (Part 1 of 3)."** *Physician and Sports Medicine* 17(2): 99-102, 105-106, February 1989.
Describes the physical training program for men and women, including statistics for physical fitness tests. While modifications were made for women in physical fitness training when they first entered the Academy in 1976, they have been raised over the years. Notes that the attrition rate for women on varsity sports teams is lower than for non-athletic women.

634 *Harrison, Patrick R. and Beth Ledbetter.* **Comparison of Men and Women at the U.S. Naval Academy: Outcomes and Processes in Their Development.** Annapolis, MD: United States Naval Academy, 1980. 42p. ED 201222.
Analyzes the integration of women at the Naval Academy. Areas of concern before the arrival of women were fraternization, acceptance, physical conditioning, berthing, leading and counseling females, weight and diet concerns, etc. These issues are examined with reference to other issues such as admissions and military performance. Found that women have successfully adapted and have shown equivalent performance on a majority of outcome measures.

635 *Klein, Karl M. and Jane E. Good.* **"Women in the Brigade."** *Proceedings: U.S. Naval Institute* 114(4): 103-108, April 1988.
Discusses the results of the Women Midshipmen Study Group (1987, see **639**). Studied academic performance, leadership roles, physical performance, and brigade life of Academy women. Recommends corrective actions.

636 *Neuberger, Carmen Guevara.* **A Comparative Study of Environmental Expectations of Female Versus Male Midshipmen Entering the United States Naval Academy.** Thesis (Ph.D.)--American University, 1977. 148p. OCLC 4014010.

Compares and contrasts the pre-attendance expectations of the male and female members of the class of 1980 at the Naval Academy. Fifty entering male and fifty entering female plebes were given the College and University Environment Scales test during the first week of summer training in July 1976. Contrary to the author's hypothesis, the environmental expectations of the male and female plebes entering the Academy were essentially similar.

637   *Neumann, Idell and Norman M. Abrahams.* **Validation of Naval Academy Selection Procedures for Female Midshipmen.** San Diego, CA: Navy Personnel Research and Development Center, 1982. 17p. OCLC 10995127.
Assessment of the selection procedures for female midshipmen. Found the present method for predicting plebe-year academic performance, military performance, and choice of major was effective for female midshipmen. However, the method of predicting female disenrollment was not effective.

638   *United States. General Accounting Office.* **Naval Academy: Gender and Racial Disparities.** GAO/NSIAD-93-54. Washington, DC: GAO, April 1993. 68p. SuDocs GA1.13:NSIAD-93-54.
Addresses differences in performance indicators between men and women and whites and minorities, student perceptions of the fairness of treatment of women and minorities, and Academy actions to address disparities and improve assimilation of women and minorities.

639   *United States Naval Academy.* **Report to the Superintendent on the Assimilation of Women in the Brigade of Midshipmen.** Annapolis, MD: The Academy, 1990. 89p. OCLC 23466964.
Results of the Women Midshipmen Study Group, formed to review the status of the 1987 report (see **640**), to assess the current Brigade climate and to propose additional measures to achieve fair and equal treatment of female midshipmen. Among other findings, the report found women midshipmen were still not totally accepted. In fact, one-third of all male midshipmen believed women were not an integral part of the Academy. Contains many statistical tables, including attrition from 1980-1990 of all the service academies, number of women faculty, etc.

640   *United States Naval Academy.* **Report to the Superintendent on the Integration of Women in the Brigade of Midshipmen.** Annapolis, MD: United States Naval Academy, 1987. 109p. OCLC 18568061.
The Superintendent of the Academy convened the Women Midshipmen Study Group to review the progress toward integrating women into the Brigade of Midshipmen and to develop recommendations for improving their assimilation. Contains an excellent discussion of the problems faced by women midshipmen and possible solutions. One interesting finding was that the principal support system for women was their membership on varsity sports teams and that one out of two women not playing on a varsity team left the Academy before graduation.

11

FAMILY AND PREGNANCY ISSUES

When women first officially became part of the military, with the formation of the Army Nurse Corps in 1901, family issues were not a problem. Nurses were not allowed to marry or to be parents. In fact, prior to World War II, marriage of an Army nurse could lead to her dishonorable discharge.

Contrary to popular belief, women who served in the military during World War II could marry and marriage did not prevent a woman from enlisting. However, marriage between two servicemembers in the European Theater resulted in one spouse's transfer to prevent pregnancy. Women were barred from enlisting in the Army if they had children under fourteen or dependents between fourteen and eighteen and were discharged for medical reasons if they became pregnant.

After the war, these rules generally remained in effect. If a servicewoman married after she enlisted, she could then ask for a discharge based on this marriage. This policy was reexamined in 1964, when a Government Accounting Office Report found that over seventy percent of women enlistees left the service before the end of their first enlistment, primarily for unsuitability, pregnancy, and marriage. Policies were modified to require women to serve at least a year of their current enlistment before requesting discharge for marriage. By the late 1970s, optional discharge for marriage was no longer available.

Married servicewomen did not enjoy the same benefits as their male counterparts. A civilian husband did not receive dependency benefits or allowances unless his wife could prove that he was dependent on her for more than fifty percent of his support (men automatically received support for their wives without showing such proof). This policy would remain in effect until 1973, when as the result of a suit brought by Air Force Lieutenant Sharron Frontiero, the U.S. Supreme Court declared the policy unconstitutional unless it was also applied to spouses of male servicemembers.

Pregnancy and parenthood have been more difficult issues to resolve. Until the 1970s, a servicewoman who became pregnant or a parent of minor children was automatically discharged. A series of lawsuits filed in the 1970s caused the services to stop their policies of requiring these mandatory discharges for pregnancy or parenthood. However, discharge would remain an option if requested by an enlisted woman. Women who stayed on active duty after pregnancy remained available for worldwide deployment. The problems this would cause became clear during deployment for Operation Desert Storm/Desert Shield, when women soldiers, single parents (both male and female), and dual military couples had to leave their children behind. It also highlighted the increase in the number of dual military couples. Besides dealing with the dilemma of having both parents in a dual career couple deploy, there is the added difficulty of finding joint assignments where the careers of both will be enhanced.

DUAL CAREER COUPLES/MARRIAGE

641   *Adams, Kerry G.* **Dual Army Couples and Their Impact on Readiness.** Carlisle Barracks, PA: United States Army War College, 1990. 45p. OCLC 21889562.
The author believes dual career couples adversely affect readiness in two ways; they are not as likely to be available and responsive to national emergencies/war as their single or married to civilian counterparts, and the conflicting requirements for joint domicile versus career enhancing assignments mean one member of the couple will accept assignments which are not career enhancing in order to be assigned with a spouse.

642   *Edwards, Laura Nell.* **Effects of Marital/Dependency Status on Reenlistment Behavior of Second-Term Enlisted Females.** Thesis (M.S.)--Naval Postgraduate School, 1989. 76p. OCLC 25565622.
Author used the 1985 DOD Survey of Officer and Enlisted Personnel to examine reenlistment behavior of 8,916 male and female second-term enlisted personnel responding to the survey. Among women, those who were single or married with children reenlisted at higher rates than women with no children.

643   *Johnson, Vanessa Olivia.* **Stress and Overload on the Woman in the Dual Career Navy Family.** San Diego, CA: San Diego State University, 1987. 71p. OCLC 17925646.
Written as part of a master's degree project. The author, a Navy officer, analyzed the results of questionnaires given to thirty-eight active duty dual career women Naval officers in the San Diego area to determine the stress and overload on women in dual career Naval families. The top stressors were career planning, spending time with family, transfers, and separation from spouses.

644   *Leeds, Sara Ann.* **Dual Navy Couples: Their Assignment and Retention.** Monterey, CA: Naval Postgraduate School, 1988. 96p. OCLC 20083319.
Describes the issues surrounding dual career Navy couples. The author uses data from the 1985 DOD Survey of Officer and Enlisted Personnel. She found that enlisted Navy couples had less sea duty than non-dual couples and fewer permanent change of station moves. Found that dual-career couples were not utilized efficiently, with some couples taking co-location over career enhancing billets that would separate them.

645 *McGee, Peggy J.* **Civilian Spouses of Female Soldiers: A Forgotten Breed?** Carlisle Barracks, PA: United States Army War College, 1990. 127p. OCLC 22152463.
Gives background information on female soldier/civilian spouse couples. The author gathered her information from surveys sent to Army Community Service offices. She found that in 1988, fifty-six percent of all female enlisted soldiers were married to civilians. She suggests the military should focus more on the needs of these women and their spouses to enhance their retention in the military.

646 *Raiha, Nancy Kay.* **Dual-Career Couples in the U.S. Army: A Descriptive Study.** Thesis (Ph.D.)--University of Washington, 1986. 349p. OCLC 15340081.
The author, herself part of a dual-career couple in the military, discusses the results of an Army survey which included 1,350 dual career members. Provides a general review of the literature, with a focus on family separation, work schedules, pay and benefits, childcare, etc. Suggests some modifications for dual career couples be made.

647 *Schneider, Dorothy.* **"Soldier, Sailor, Airman, Marine --and Wife."** Minerva 4(3):101-115, Fall 1986.
Written from 300 interviews with women in all branches of the military to discuss the problems faced by married servicewomen.

648 *Stoddard, Ellwyn R.* **"Married Female Officers in a Combat Branch: Occupation, Family Stress and Future Career Choices."** Minerva 12(2) 1-14, Summer 1994.
Examines present and future career plans of sixteen married female officers in the Air Defense Artillery Command at Ft. Bliss, TX. Found the greatest predictor of intention to stay in the service was the officer's source of commission and perceived support of her husband. West Point officers were more committed than those commissioned through ROTC or Officer Candidate School.

649 *Teplitzky, Martha L.* **Dual Army Career Couples: Factors Related to the Career Intentions of Men and Women.** Alexandria, VA: U.S. Army Research Institute for the Behavioral and Social Sciences, 1988. 29p. OCLC 20511299.
In 1985, 149 officers and 405 enlisted personnel in dual career Army marriages were surveyed to determine relationships between career intentions and a number of work and family related factors. For both men and women, family concerns accounted for variance in career intentions more than work related variables.

650 *Teplitzky, Martha L., Shelley A. Thomas and Glenda Y. Nogami.* **Dual Army Career Officers: Job Attitudes and Career Intentions of Male and Female Officers.** Alexandria, VA: U.S. Army Research Institute for the Behavioral and Social Sciences, 1988. 90p. OCLC 20612925.
In 1985, 149 dual Army career officers were surveyed about their job attitudes and career intentions. Female officers in dual marriages were

much less likely than male officers to have plans to stay in the Army until retirement. Almost half of the women would leave the Army rather than face a lengthy separation from their husbands, and many felt that the demands of a dual Army career lifestyle are incompatible with family life.

PREGNANCY

651   *Caldenhead, Julia T.* **"Pregnancy on Active Duty: Making the Tough Decisions."** *Proceedings: U.S. Naval Institute* 121(4): 52-53, April 1995.
The author, a Navy Chaplain, discusses the difficulties faced by active duty women who become pregnant. Some interesting points made are women should plan pregnancies around operational commitments, i.e. don't become pregnant right before assuming a command, and that women should be prepared to deal with the stresses of being pregnant and working in an environment which will not always be supportive.

652   *Correnti, Elizabeth E. and Peter S. Jensen.* **"Support of the Pregnant Soldier in the Workplace: A Comparison of Her Assessment with that of Her Supervisor."** *Military Medicine* 115(11): 571-573, November 1989.
Compares pregnant soldiers' responses to statements concerning job performance, job satisfaction, and support in the workplace with those of their supervisors. Found that there was no real discrepancy between soldier and supervisor perception of support from coworkers and supervisors.

653   *Hoiberg, Anne.* **Motherhood in the Military: Conflicting Roles for Navy Women?** San Diego: Naval Research Center, 1979. 16p. OCLC 20546752.
Report of a study to determine the effects of pregnancy on the performance, retention, and hospitalization of Navy women who entered the service after 1972. It was found that parenthood separations accounted for 10.9 percent of discharges. It also determined that service in the Navy and motherhood were compatible.

654   *Hoiberg, Anne and John Ernst.* **"Motherhood in the Military: Conflicting Roles for Navy Women."** *International Journal of Sociology of the Family* 10(2): 265-280, July-December 1980.
Studied all Navy women who enlisted between 1973-1977 to determine the effects of pregnancy-related conditions upon subsequent performance, retention, and hospitalization. Found that more active duty than discharged mothers were married and that a higher percentage of non-white mothers stayed in the Navy. The roles of mother and sailor seemed to be compatible.

655   *Landrum, Cecile S.* **"The Changing Military Family: Impacts on Readiness."** *Parameters, Journal of the US Army War College* 10(3): 78-85, September 1980.

Suggests the military's demand that the mission come before the family is not accepted by some of today's military families. Discusses some of the issues faced by military families, such as dual service couples, pregnancy and nontraditional jobs, and conflicts between family and mission. Concludes that the military must set practical policy guidelines that resolve the conflicts between mission and family responsibilities.

656 *McClintock, Virginia Marie.* ***Effects of Pregnancy in Active Duty Enlisted Navy Women on Workplace Morale and Navy Readiness.*** Thesis (M.S.)--San Diego State University, 1990.   107p.   OCLC 22738878.
Examines the perceived effects of pregnancy on a Navy woman's workplace, by comparing the viewpoint of the woman with that of her supervisor.   426 active duty pregnant enlisted Navy women and their supervisors were interviewed.   Pregnant women were often seen as "slackers" and received negative comments from their supervisors. The women tended to underestimate the effects of their pregnancy on their co-worker's workload and morale.

657 *Maxson, Thomas J.* ***Effects of Pregnancies in Maintenance-Related AFSCs.*** Maxwell Air Force Base, AL: Air Command and Staff College, 1986. 37p.
Determined the impact of pregnant airmen serving in maintenance related jobs. Pregnant airman may be required to be temporarily reassigned to reduce their exposure to hazards.   Reviews medical considerations, assignment and utilization policy, and addresses the impact of pregnant airmen on training, unit readiness, and day-to-day operations.

658 *Meg, G. and Royle, M.H.* ***Predicting Pregnancy and Pregnancy Attrition.*** San Diego, CA: Navy Personnel Research and Development Center, 1985. 27p.
Investigates the effects of traditional family/career orientation, feelings of isolation, and feelings of dissatisfaction with the Marine Corps on incidence of pregnancy and pregnancy attrition among enlisted Marine Corps women. Pregnant women who attrited were less committed to a Marine Corps career than those who became pregnant and remained in the Marines.   Neither feelings of isolation or dissatisfaction with the Corps were predictors of pregnancy or pregnancy attrition.

659 *Munley, Judyann L.* ***The Perception of Pregnancy Among Enlisted Work Group Members.*** Thesis (M.A.)--Air Force Institute of Technology, Wright-Patterson Air Force Base, OH, 1986. 115p.
Examines how over 11,000 Air Force enlisted work group members stationed at thirty bases throughout the world perceived pregnant co-workers. Data suggested only fifteen and one-half percent perceived pregnancy as a problem and less than ten percent indicated pregnant women don't carry their own weight on the job.   There was no difference between how male and female members perceived pregnant co-workers.

660   *Sadler, Georgia C. and Patricia J. Thomas.* **"Rock the Cradle, Rock the Boat?"** *Proceedings: U.S. Naval Institute* 12(4): 51-56, April 1995.
Discusses the work of the Navy Personnel Research and Development Center's research on pregnancy in the Navy. Found that pregnancy rates for enlisted Navy women ranges from 8.4 percent to 8.9 percent at any point in time and that this pregnancy rate is comparable for the civilian birth rate for women ages twenty to twenty-nine. Provides information on early separations, predeployment pregnancies, workplace absences, and performance. Concludes the overall impact of pregnancy on the Navy is manageable. Includes information on the Department of the Navy's new Pregnancy Policy (February 1995).

661   *Thomas, Marie D., Patricia J. Thomas, and Virginia McClintock.* **"Pregnant Enlisted Women in Navy Work Centers."** *Minerva* 9(3): 1-32, Fall 1991.
Reports the second phase of a three year project to investigate the impact of pregnancy and single parents on mission accomplishment in the Navy (see **663-664**). Determined the total amount of time lost due to pregnancy was one day for most of the pregnant women in the study.

662   *Thomas, Patricia J. and Marie D. Thomas.* **"Effects of Sex, Marital Status, and Parental Status on Absenteeism among Navy Enlisted Personnel."** *Military Psychology* 6(2): 95-108, 1994.
Compared the lost time of Navy enlisted women and men, with particular emphasis on the contribution of pregnancy to women's absences. Results showed that sex had no significant effect on absenteeism except where pregnant women from ships were temporarily reassigned. Marital status and parental status seldom reduced time available for work.

663   *Thomas, Patricia J. and Marie D. Thomas.* **Impact of Pregnant Women and Single Parents upon Navy Personnel Systems.** San Diego, CA: Navy Personnel Research and Development Center, 1992. 29p. OCLC 26873746.
A review of policies created to manage pregnant women and single parents and to evaluate the impact of these two groups on recruitment, assignment, and separations (see **661, 664**). In addition, the policies at housing offices, child development centers and family service centers regarding pregnant women and single parents were investigated. Found that dual career couples were more time consuming to assign than single parents, that single parents are more likely to receive a hardship discharge and that less than twenty percent of single parents have a Dependent Care Certificate.

664   *Thomas, Patricia J. and Jack E. Edwards.* **Incidence of Pregnancy and Single Parenthood among Enlisted in the Navy.** San Diego, CA: Navy Personnel Research and Development Center, 1989. 36p. OCLC 22536544.
This survey is the first phase of a planned three year project investigating the impact of pregnancy and single parents on mission accomplishment in the Navy (see **661, 663**). Some significant findings were five times as

many women as men were found to be single parents, women on ships had a lower pregnancy rate than those on shore, and Navy policies regarding pregnant women and single parents were not well known among Navy personnel. Includes many statistical tables.

PARENTHOOD

665 *Bowen, Gary L. **"Single Mothers for the Defense."** Conciliation Courts Review* 25(1): 13-18, June 1987.
Presents data from a survey of sixty-nine single mothers in the Air Force, which examined the work, personal and family demands and adjustments made by Air Force mothers. Found most single mothers are coping well with the demands of military and family life.

666 *Edwards, Laura Nell.* **Effects of Marital/Dependency Status on Reenlistment Behavior of Second-Term Enlisted Females.** Thesis (M.S.)--Naval Postgraduate School, 1989. 76p.
See **642**.

667 *Kelley, Michelle L., Peggy A. Herzog-Simmer and Marci A. Harris.* **"Effects of Military-Induced Separation on the Parenting Stress and Family Functioning of Deploying Mothers."** *Military Psychology* 6(2): 125-138, 1994.
Examined the responses of 118 Navy deploying mothers on the Parenting Stress Index, the Maternal Separation Anxiety Scale, the Parenting Dimension Inventory and two subscales of the Family Environment Scale. Found women anticipating deployment reported significantly higher levels of parenting stress and more sensitivity to children. Single mothers reported more separation anxiety, less family cohesiveness, and less family organization than did married mothers.

668 *Marino, Charley, Jr.* **Sole-Parents and Their Impact on Readiness.** Carlisle Barracks, PA: United States Army War College, 1990. 101p. OCLC 21588615.
Studies the impact that sole parents and dual career parents have on military readiness. Provides a summary of the sole-parent issue in the Army, as well as a review of the literature. Concludes that the military does not yet meet the needs of sole and dual career military parents.

669 *Morrison, Peter A., George Vernez, David W. Grissmer, and Kevin F. McCarthy.* **Families in the Army: Looking Ahead.** Santa Monica, CA: Rand, 1989. 68p. OCLC 19268817.
An examination of Army families. Discusses dual career Army families and single parent families, providing many statistics.

670 *Rider, Maradee W.* **Single Parents in the Military.** Thesis (M.S.)--Naval Postgraduate School, 1980. 105p. OCLC 8038359.
A study of how single parent families affect mission accomplishment of the Navy. Sole parents end up having to choose between their job and

their family.   The author recommends the Navy try to accommodate single parents by providing twenty-four hour child care facilities and through a child care referral service.

671   *Rupkalvis, Carol Anne Cude.* **The Relationship of Health with Role Attitudes, Role Strain, and Social Support in Enlisted Military Mothers.** Thesis (M.S.)--University of Arizona, 1987. 116p. OCLC 16393966.
Forty enlisted mothers were surveyed to examine the relationship of health with social support.   Mothers with partners showed significant correlation between role attitude, role strain, social support and stress.

672   *Teplitsky, Martha L., Mark Hedlund and Glenda Nogami.* **Case Studies of Officer and Enlisted Single Parents in the Army: Performance, Retention, and Quality of Life.** Alexandria, VA: U.S. Army Research Institute for the Behavioral and Social Sciences, 1987. 90p. OCLC 19905031.
Based on in-depth interviews with twenty-seven single parents and their immediate supervisors.   Found that supervisors did not attribute performance problems or strengths with single parent status.   Major problems faced by single parents included child care problems and difficulties caused by frequent relocations.

673   *United States.   Congress.   House.   Committee on Armed Services. Military Personnel and Compensation Subcommittee.* **Parenting Issues of Operation Desert Storm.** Washington, DC: GPO, 1991. SuDocs Y4.Ar5/2a:991-92/5; OCLC 26481091; ISBN 0160356350.
Hearing discussing the impact of Desert Storm deployment on military families, especially single parent and dual service families.   Good discussion of issues of sole parents, two deploying parents, etc. Describes each service's policies regarding deploying parents.

674   *United States.   General Accounting Office.* **Army Needs Better Data to Develop Policies for Sole and Interservice Parents.** GAO/FPCD-82-50. Washington, DC: GAO, 1982. 37p. SuDocs GA1.13:FPCD-82-50.
Discusses the actual and expected availability and performance of sole parents and interservice parents (servicemembers married to other servicemembers).   Also identifies ways the Army can improve its management of these individuals. Concludes the Army cannot restrict service of these individuals because the Army lacks reliable data on which to base restrictions. Includes many statistics.

12

SEX ISSUES

Among the top issues related to women's service in the military are homosexuality, sexual harassment and discrimination, and sex integration. These issues, along with women's combat roles (discussed in Chapter 13), make press headlines and serve as political hot buttons.

Women serving on active duty have often been labeled as lesbians, which can be seen as an attempt to both discredit their participation and as an excuse to discharge women. In a June 1992 Government Accounting Office report (see **687**), an examination of homosexual discharges from the years 1980-1990, showed that in each military service, women were discharged for homosexuality at a rate consistently higher than their rate of representation. They constituted ten percent of all personnel serving, but twenty-three percent of homosexual discharges. This discrepancy was most noticeable in Marine Corps women, who represented just five percent of the personnel serving, but twenty-eight percent of the homosexual discharges. There is a widely held view that military service attracts lesbians and results in an above-average representation in the service as compared to the U.S. population; however, no reliable research exists to prove or disprove this speculation. As stated in the GAO report (see **687**), scientific and medical studies disagree with the military's policy holding that homosexuality is incompatible with military service.

Sexual harassment of military women and discrimination against them are issues which are being reexamined, especially in light of the wide publicity received by the events of the 1991 Tailhook Convention and subsequent investigations. Women have faced gender discrimination from sex-based physical standards and other institutional inequities promulgated through official policies that have prohibited their equal military participation with men. Sexual harassment has been a special problem at the service academies, as discussed in Chapter 10; perhaps due to the combination of the persistence of sexist traditions and immaturity of younger men and women. Some believe sexual harassment is more prevalent in the military than civilian life because of the traditionally male environment and small numbers of women. Each service has developed comprehensive policies to handle harassment complaints and instituted educational programs to help prevent harassment from occurring. However, with the recent opening of many of the formerly all male military jobs, especially combat jobs, it is likely sexual harassment will continue to be a problem for each branch of the services.

   This chapter includes materials on homosexuality, sexual harassment and discrimination, and sex integration and sex role orientation. Materials on these issues at the service academies are covered in **Chapter 10, Service Academies**.

HOMOSEXUALITY

675   Benecke, Michelle M. and Kirstin S. Dodge. **"Military Women in Nontraditional Job Fields: Casualties of the Armed Forces' War on Homosexuals."** Harvard Women's Law Journal 13: 215-250, Spring 1990.
   In a detailed article, the authors assert that military men don't want women around and are getting rid of them by labeling them lesbians. Divided into five sections: a history of the use of homosexual discharges against women, the types of investigations against women alleged to be lesbians, the personal stories of two of these women, a description of a sociological study on gender identity formation, and the consequences of lesbian baiting on servicewomen. Concludes with recommendations for change, such as abolishing the DOD's homosexuality policy.

676   Bérubé, Allan and John D'Emilio. **"The Military and Lesbians during the McCarthy Years."** Signs: Journal of Women in Culture and Society 9(4): 759-775, Summer 1984.
   Reproduces indoctrination lectures on homosexuality designed for WAVE recruits in 1952. Also includes correspondence from 1951 between the American Civil Liberties Union and lesbians being purged from the Air Force as evidence of the "homosexual scare" of the 1950s. Notes that women were particularly vulnerable to anti-homosexual policies, and discusses how these policies affected servicewomen in the 1950s.

677   Harry, Joseph. **"Homosexual Men and Women Who Served Their Country."** Journal of Homosexuality 10 (1/2): 117-125, Fall 1984.
   Examines the effectiveness of U.S. military policies in excluding homosexual men and women from the armed forces by comparing the percentages of homosexuals who have served with matched samples of heterosexuals. Used interview data from 1,456 respondents from 1969-1970. Found that homosexual and heterosexual men were equally likely to have served, while lesbians were more likely than heterosexual women to have served. Indicates the policies excluding homosexuals from the service are ineffective.

678   ***Homosexuality and the Military: A Sourcebook of Official, Uncensored U.S. Government Documents.*** n.p.: Diane Publishers, 1991-1993. Not paged.
   Reproduces four government documents on homosexuality in the services, including *DOD's Policy on Homosexuals* (see **687**), the *Crittenden Report* (Navy), the *Pen and Schoen Poll* and the *Homosexuality and Personnel Security Report*.

679 *Katzenstein, Mary Fainsod.* **"The Spectacle As Political Resistance: Feminist and Gay/Lesbian Politics in the Military."** *Minerva* 11(1): 1-16, Spring 1993.
Addresses the question of why President Clinton campaigned on the military and homosexuality issue and if the opening of combat aircraft assignments to women is linked to the probable end of the homosexual ban in the military.

680 *Kohn, Richard H.* **"Women in Combat, Homosexuals in Uniform: The Challenge of Military Leadership."** *Parameters, Journal of the US Army War College* 23(1): 2-4, Spring 1993.
A brief argument for military leaders who oppose the end of the ban on homosexuals in the military and women in combat. Believes that in the long run, the services will find their effectiveness will be enhanced by women in combat and allowing homosexuals to serve, as the armed forces are stronger when they reflect the values and ideals of the society they serve.

681 *Meyer, Leisa D.* **"Creating G.I. Jane: The Regulation of Sexuality and Sexual Behavior in the Women's Army Corps during World War II."** *Feminist Studies* 18(3): 581-601, Fall 1992.
Interesting discussion of the sexual stereotyping of WACs as camp followers, prostitutes and lesbians. When fraternization issues arose between male officers and WAC enlisted, usually the WAC was the only one punished. WAC Director Hobby felt that homosexual discharges would result in too much public scrutiny and disapproval of WACs, so she attempted to portray WACs as sexless.

682 *Rand Corporation.* **Sexual Orientation and the U.S. Military Personnel Policy: Options and Assessment.** Santa Monica, CA: Rand Corporation, 1993. 518p.
Results of a study undertaken by the Rand Corporation at the request of then Secretary of Defense Les Aspin to help formulate an Executive Order ending discrimination on the basis of sexual orientation in the armed forces. Covers a wide range of subjects, such as history of the services' treatment of homosexuals, sexual behavior, attitudes towards homosexuals in the military, etc. Also examines how foreign services deal with homosexuality. Recommends a policy that focuses on conduct rather than sexual orientation and provides recommendations for implementation.

683 *Ray, Ronald D.* **Gays: In or Out? The U.S. Military & Homosexuals - A Sourcebook/DOD's Policy on Homosexuality.** New York: Brassey's, 1993. 205p. OCLC 27726187; ISBN 0028810805.
A combination of two works, a Government Accounting Office report titled *DOD's Policy on Homosexuality* (see **687**) and *Military Necessity and Homosexuality.* Colonel Ray presents his arguments as to why homosexuals should not be allowed to serve while the GAO report analyzes the military's policies regarding homosexuals.

684   *Scott, Wilbur J. and Sandra Carson Stanley, editors.* **Gays and Lesbians in the Military: Issues, Concerns, and Contrasts.** New York: Aldine De Gruyter, 1994. 278p. ISBN 0202305406.
A collection of chapters on the issues surrounding homosexuals in the military. Includes an overview of the gay and lesbian literature, comparison of gays and women in the U.S. armed forces, and integration of homosexuals into the service.

685   *Shilts, Randy.* **Conduct Unbecoming: Gays and Lesbians in the U.S. Military.** New York: St. Martin's Press, 1993. 784p. OCLC 27681806; ISBN 031209261X.
A massive work investigating the situation of gays and lesbians in the military. The author interviewed over 1,000 gay service members and tells many of their stories. The emphasis is on gay men, but does include information on gay women. Many details of life as a homosexual in the military and a discussion of the various gay purges.

686   *United States. Congress. House. Committee on Armed Services.* **Policy Implications of Lifting the Ban on Homosexuals in the Military.** Washington, DC: GPO, 1993. 364p. SuDocs Y4.Ar512A:993-94/18; ISBN 0160417783.
Presents various views expressed during hearings on lifting the ban on homosexuals in the military. Very detailed information and good discussion of the implications of lifting the ban.

687   *United States. General Accounting Office.* **DOD's Policy on Homosexuality.** GAO/NSIAD-92-98. Washington, DC: GAO, 1992. 63p. SuDocs GA1.13:NSIAD-92-98.
Covers fiscal years 1980-1990. A collection of charts and tables, statistics on active duty gender and race by service, discharges by race, gender and rank, discharges for homosexuality, etc. Information was taken from the DOD's Defense Manpower Data Center.

688   *United States. General Accounting Office.* **Statistics Related to DOD's Policy on Homosexuality.** GAO/NSIAD-92-98S. Washington, DC: GAO, 1992. 63p. SuDocs GA1.13:NSIAD-92-985.
Supplements *DOD's Policy on Homosexuality* (see **687**), by providing statistics from 1980 to 1990 on personnel discharged for homosexuality, data on cases involving homosexuality investigated by the service's criminal investigative agencies, etc.

Homosexuality - Bibliographies

689   *Wilson, Donna L.* **"Women and Homophobia in the Armed Services: An Annotated Bibliography. Part 1."** *Minerva* 7(1): 63-80, Spring 1989.
Part one of a selective annotated bibliography of books and journal articles on homosexuality and women in the armed forces. Covers sources prior to 1987 (see **690**).

690   *Wilson, Donna L.* ***"Women and Homophobia in the Armed Services: An Annotated Bibliography. Part 2."*** *Minerva* 7(2): 60-68, Summer 1989.
Part two of a selective annotated bibliography of books and journal articles on homosexuality and women in the armed forces (see **689**). Covers the period after 1987 and includes a resource list of organizations for further information.

Homosexuality - Personal Narratives

691   *Bérubé, Allan.* ***Coming Out under Fire: The History of Gay Men and Women in World War Two.*** New York: Free Press, 1990. 377p. OCLC 20671784; ISBN 0029031001.
An excellent history of gay and lesbian participation in the service during World War II. Author interviewed seventy-one men and women, some of whom were discharged for homosexuality, others who stayed in the military.   Includes chapters on the military's policy towards gay enlistment, gay rights, problems with fitting in, and what happened to veterans who received a "blue" or undesirable discharge because of homosexuality. Includes photographs and is indexed.

692   *Cammermeyer, Margarethe with Chris Fisher.* ***Serving in Silence: The Story of Margarethe Cammermeyer.*** New York: Viking, 1994. 308p. OCLC 30671428; ISBN 0670851671.
The author, an Army nurse who won the Bronze Star for her service in Vietnam, admitted that she was a lesbian during an interview for a top secret clearance she needed to attend classes at the Army War College. The book details her military career and life and the subsequent investigation of her homosexuality and ultimate discharge from the service (she was reinstated in the Army reserves in June 1994). Well done. Includes photographs.

693   *Humphrey, Mary Ann.* ***My Country, My Right to Serve: Experiences of Gay Men and Women in the Military, World War II to the Present.*** New York: HarperCollins Publishers, 1990. 286p. OCLC 21196731; ISBN 0060164468.
Contains the stories of gay and lesbian servicemembers who served or are currently serving in the military. Divided in chapters by era, World War II and Korea, Vietnam, post-Vietnam years and the present. Most of the interviews include brief biographical information and photographs, although a few are anonymous. Includes appendices and references.

694   *Webber, Winni S.* ***Lesbians in the Military Speak Out.*** Northboro, MA: Madwoman Press, 1993. 136p. OCLC 27683002; ISBN 096308223X.
The author, writing under a pseudonym, is an active duty Army physician.   A collection of stories, each two to four pages, told by officers and enlisted women of the Army, Navy, Coast Guard, Marine Corps and Air Force about their experiences as lesbians in the service.

Includes a list of resource organizations and publications of interest to lesbians in the military.

SEXUAL DIFFERENCES

695   *Dowdell, Faye E. **Gender Differences in Orientations toward Military Service.***   Alexandria, VA: U.S. Army Research Institute for the Behavioral and Social Sciences, 1979. 37p. OCLC 17962530.
The purpose of this study was to integrate existing data on the attitudes of women towards the military with theories of the changing nature of military service.   Concludes that males are more positively oriented towards military service than are females.

696   *Valentine, Mary-Blair Truesdell. **An Investigation of Gender-Based Leadership Styles of Male and Female Officers in the United States Army.*** Thesis (DPA)--George Mason University, 1993. 225p.
Focuses on the leadership and gender role styles of Army officers by rank and gender. Administered surveys to 660 Army officers (330 male and 330 female) in Combat Support and Service Support branches. Found the females were primarily androgynous and masculine in gender role styles at all ranks. Male and female officers used the same leadership styles.

697   *Williams, Christine L. **Gender Differences at Work: Women and Men in Nontraditional Occupations.*** Berkeley, CA: University of California Press, 1989. 191p. OCLC 17806943; ISBN 0520063732.
Expansion of the author's dissertation (see **379**). She chose women Marines and male nurses because they represent less than five percent of the work force in their occupation and she was interested to discover how they maintain their gender identity. Includes a good discussion of women's roles in the armed forces, as well as a summation of the various studies conducted to examine the effects of differing levels of males and females in the military.

698   *Yarbrough, Jean. **"The Feminist Mistake: Sexual Equality and the Decline of the American Military."*** *Policy Review* #33: 48-52, Summer 1985.
Argues that the military is not a civic instrument or a social welfare agency and cannot function as a democratic society.   Provides arguments for the case that women cannot function equally with men and concludes the prejudice against military women is based on the natural differences between men and women, is valid, and should influence policy.

SEX DISCRIMINATION

699   *Beans, Harry C. **"Sex Discrimination in the Military."*** *Military Law Review* 67: 19-83, Winter 1975.

Addresses the state of the law (as of 1975) with respect to the utilization of sex as a basis for discrimination. Reviews military statutes and regulations that provide special treatment for either sex. Suggests ways to achieve compliance with statutory and constitutional requirements barring discrimination.

700 *Ernst, Robert W. and Robert J. Gildeau.* **Gender Bias in the Navy.** Monterey, CA: Naval Postgraduate School, 1993. 129p.
Investigates issues of sexual harassment, gender bias, and women in combat via personal interviews with male Navy and Marine Corps officers. Addresses the issues from a male point of view. Concludes women should be fully integrated into all military fields, there should be one standard for each job, and more training should be provided on working with members of the opposite sex.

701 *Goodman, Jill Laurie.* **"Women, War, and Equality: An Examination of Sex Discrimination in the Military."** *Women's Rights Law Reporter* 5(4): 243-269, Summer 1979.
Argues that sex discrimination in the military should end. Discusses the role of women in the military and their status, as well as combat restrictions and legal challenges to policies.

702 *Kenyon, Cynthia A.* **Relationship of Gender to Promotion and Retention Rates in the United States Air Force.** Thesis (M.S.)--University of Florida, 1989. 112p. OCLC 22783552.
Studied all Air Force Nurse Corps (female-dominated), Biomedical Science Corps (male-dominated), and Medical Service Corps (male-dominated) officers eligible for promotion between 1977 and 1987. Found consistently lower promotion rates experienced by Nurse Corps members than male-dominated corps. Also found a strong positive relationship between promotion and retention rates.

703 *McKenny, Betsy B.* **"Frontiero v. Richardson: Characterizations of Sex Based Classifications."** *Columbia Human Rights Law Review* 6(1): 239-247, Spring 1974.
Studies the case of *Frontiero v. Richardson*, where a female Air Force officer and her dependent husband attacked the statutes requiring female servicemembers to prove their husbands were actually dependent on them for support before they were paid benefits while male members were not required to do the same for their wives. Concludes the immediate effect of the case was to strike down statutory provisions which discriminated against women in the military.

704 *Rogers, Robin.* **"A Proposal for Combatting Sexual Discrimination in the Military: Amendment of Title VII."** *California Law Review* 78(1): 165-195, January 1990.
Promotes the idea that the combat exclusion laws encourage sex-based discrimination in the military and should be reformed or eliminated. Analyzes the combat exclusion, how it harms women and how the military uses the exclusion to rationalize other discriminatory practices.

Proposes Congress amend Title VII of the Civil Rights Act of 1964, which is the primary federal law used to combat employment discrimination based on race, sex, religion, or national origin.

705 *Schenkenberger, Henry C.* **Petticoats and Prejudice: Sexual Discrimination in the Air Force.** Maxwell Air Force Base, AL: Air Command and Staff College, Air University, 1974. 74p. OCLC 21271307.
Discusses some of the common arguments and cultural values that lead to discrimination against women. Also examines the nature and extent of sexual discrimination in the Air Force. Concludes sexual discrimination does exist in the Air Force and presents recommendations for correcting the problem. Dated.

706 *Stremlow, Mary V.* **Coping with Sexism in the Military.** New York: Rosen Publishing Group, 1990. 171p. OCLC 21904709; ISBN 0823910253.
Written by a retired Marine Corps Colonel (see **392**), provides a brief history of the women's services and discusses issues of women in combat, sexual harassment, marriage, etc. While the title implies this is about sexism in the military, it is really an advice book for high school women considering entering the military. Gives entrance requirements for the service academies as well as enlistment requirements and officer procurement programs.

707 *United States. Congress. House. Committee on Armed Services.* **Gender Discrimination in the Military.** Washington, DC: GPO, 1992. 128p. SuDocs Y4.Ar5/2A:991-92/60; ISBN 0160396379.
Hearings held to examine gender discrimination in the military and sexual harassment. Testimony by Major General (Ret.) Jeanne Holm, Admiral Frank Kelso, Admiral Elmo Zumwalt and others. Covers several issues, including homosexuality and weight control, and provides statistics on discharge rates, Tailhook, women in combat, and sexual harassment complaints. Good discussion of the issues.

SEXUAL HARASSMENT

708 *Beck, Lois M.* **"Sexual Harassment in the Army: Roots Examined."** *Minerva* 9(1): 29-40, Spring 1991.
The author, an Army major, believes that sexual harassment is caused by cultural sexism. She defines sexual harassment, problems it causes in the Army, and ways commanders can reduce it.

709 *Dean, Donna M.* **Warriors without Weapons: The Victimization of Military Women.** Thesis (Ph.D.)--The Union Institute, Cincinnati, OH, 1994. 255p.
Discusses how women are victimized in the military, by being sexually harassed and assaulted, facing hostility from men, being investigated for homosexuality, etc. The author served for eighteen years in the Navy

and describes her experiences with sexual harassment, assault and post-traumatic stress disorder.

710   *Firestone, Juanita M. and Richard J. Harris.* **"Sexual Harassment in the U.S. Military: Individualized and Environmental Contexts."** *Armed Forces and Society* 21(1): 25-43, Fall 1994.
Focuses on individual experiences and understanding of sexual harassment in the military workplace. Studied results of the DOD Survey of Sex Roles in the Active Duty Military. Over fifty-four percent of respondents know of individuals who had been sexually harassed on duty. The Air Force had the lowest level of harassment. Concludes that sexual harassment should be controlled to produce a positive work situation.

711   *Krohne, Kathleen Anne.* **The Effect of Sexual Harassment on Female Naval Officers: A Phenomenological Study.** Thesis (Ed.D.)--University of San Diego, 1991. 255p. OCLC 26627267.
A timely discussion of sexual harassment in the Navy, providing an in-depth examination of eight female Naval officers who were sexually harassed between 1985-1990. Results indicate that there are significant long term consequences of sexual harassment, including an increased desire for privacy, reluctance to socialize with co-workers and a reduced ability to trust others.

712   *McMillian, Willie.* **Women in the Military: Sexual Harassment.** Carlisle Barracks, PA: United States Army War College, 1993. 42p.
Discusses sexual harassment, examines reasons for its persistence and identifies ways to prevent and eliminate this behavior. Concludes sexual harassment continues to be a serious problem in all of the services.

713   *Mangione-Lambie, Mary Giselle.* **Sexual Harassment: The Effects of Perceiver Gender, Race and Rank on Attitudes and Actions.** Thesis (Ph.D.)--California School of Professional Psychology, San Diego, 1994. 180p.
Purpose of this study was to identify perceiver characteristics that may influence how sexual harassment is viewed and dealt with in the workplace. Studied 410 active duty Army personnel. Found the most junior ranking personnel had the most tolerant attitudes towards sexual harassment, viewed it as less serious and recommended less severe actions than any other rank group. White women viewed incidents as more serious than non-white women and both white and non-white men.

714   *Martindale, Melanie.* **Sexual Harassment in the Military: 1988.** Arlington, VA: Defense Manpower Data Center, 1990. 80p. OCLC 22590054.
Interprets results of the 1988 DOD Survey of Sex Roles in the Active Duty Military, which surveyed over 20,000 active duty military. Focuses on the frequency of sexual harassment among active duty servicemembers, how harassment occurred, and effectiveness of programs to eliminate sexual harassment. Found women were four times

more likely to be harassed than men and women harassed tended to be enlisted personnel and to have fewer years of active service. Includes many statistics.

715 *Miller, Laura L.* ***"Creating Gender Detente in the Military."*** *Minerva* 13(1): 15-18, Spring 1995.
Author believes military women who successfully manage gender issues such as sexual harassment, can offer insight as to how to prevent such harassment from occurring. Suggests women should employ specific strategies to create gender detente, specifically, desexualize the workplace, focus on job performance, and confront harassment directly.

716 *Stewart, Shelley Ann.* ***A Causal Model of Behavior Applied to Sexual Harassment and Reenlistment Behavior of Enlisted Navy Women.*** Thesis (M.S.)--San Diego State University, 1983. 107p. OCLC 9958737.
Studied the relationship between sexual harassment and reenlistment behavior in a cohort of 114 enlisted Navy women. Found women who worked in jobs previously open only to men perceived more sexual harassment by the end of their first enlistment and women reporting sexual harassment were less satisfied with the Navy and less likely to reenlist.

717 *United States. Congress. House. Committee on Armed Services.* ***Sexual Harassment of Military Women and Improving the Military Complaint System.*** Washington, DC: GPO, 1994. 276p. SuDocs Y4.Ar 5/2A:993-94/44; ISBN 0160462207.
Presents very interesting testimony from military women on their experiences with sexual harassment. Also reproduces each services' policy on dealing with sexual harassment.

718 *Wilds, Nancy G.* ***"Sexual Harassment in the Military."*** *Minerva* 8(4): 1-16, Winter 1990.
Sexual harassment continues to be a problem in the military, lowering unit cohesion, morale and productivity and increasing attrition rates, lost time, and human misery. A detailed account of surveys taken to measure harassment, suggests what women who are harassed should do, and discusses the question of whether or not men are sexually harassed.

Sexual Harassment - Tailhook

719 ***The Tailhook Report: The Official Inquiry into the Events of Tailhook '91.*** New York: St. Martin's Press, 1993. 250p. OCLC 28533303; ISBN 031203928.
Reprints Part 2 of the official inquiry into the events of Tailhook '91, but excludes the photographs (see **722**).

720 *United States. House. Committee on Armed Services.* **Women in the Military: The Tailhook Affair and the Problem of Sexual Harassment.** Washington, DC: GPO, 1992. 121p. SuDocs Y4.Ar5/2:W84; OCLC 27178113; ISBN 0160392624.
A report examining how to deal with sexual harassment and how to achieve cultural change in the military. Discusses the findings of the Tailhook report and reprints the various services' sexual harassment policies.

721 *United States. Department of Defense. Office of the Inspector General.* **Tailhook '91. Part 1: Review of Navy Investigations.** Arlington, VA: Department of Defense, Office of the Inspector General, September 1992. Not paged. SuDocs D1.2:T13/Pt 1.
Details a review of the investigations of Tailhook '91 made by the Navy's Office of the Inspector General and related matters. Concludes that the scope of the Navy's earlier investigations should have been expanded beyond the indecent assaults to encompass other violations of laws and regulations as they became apparent and should have addressed individual accountability for the leadership failure that allowed such events to occur. See **722**.

722 *United States. Department of Defense. Office of the Inspector General.* **Tailhook '91. Part 2: Events at the 35th Annual Tailhook Symposium.** Arlington, VA: Department of Defense, Office of the Inspector General, February 1993. Not paged. SuDocs D1.2:T13/Pt 2; ISBN 0160416639.
Describes what transpired at the Las Vegas Hilton between 8-12 September 1991 at the annual Tailhook convention. Very detailed accounts of activities and statements by victims. Includes photographs and diagrams. See **719, 721**.

723 *Zimmerman, Jean.* **Tailspin: Women at War in the Wake of Tailhook.** New York: Doubleday, 1995. 336p. ISBN 0385477899.
Discusses how the Tailhook scandal resulted from the combat exclusion laws and helped lead to their repeal. Detailed information about Tailhook, its effects on the lives of female Naval aviators, as well as excerpts from interviews conducted with Navy officers. An excellent and current discussion of women's roles in the Navy and how the lifting of combat exclusion laws will affect them. Includes photographs and a list of selected sources. Indexed.

SEX INTEGRATION AND SEX ROLE ORIENTATION

724 *DeFleur, Lois B.* **"Organizational and Ideological Barriers to Sex Integration in Military Groups."** *Work and Occupations* 12(2): 206-228, May 1985.
Summarizes factors affecting sex integration in traditionally all male fields that have emerged from previous studies. The operation of these variables in military groups is illustrated through the use of existing

literature and data from a four year study at the Air Force Academy. Concludes that women in the military have been accommodated, but not assimilated.

725   Devilbiss, M.C. *"Gender Integration and Unit Deployment: A Study of GI Jo."* Armed Forces and Society 11(4): 523-552, Summer 1985.
The author studied her own mixed sex unit (a radar squadron of the Air National Guard), during a Joint Chiefs of Staff exercise of the rapid deployment force. A very detailed, interesting account of what it is like for women in the field.

726   Dunivin, Karen O. *"There's Men, There's Women, and There's Me: The Role and Status of Military Women."* Minerva 6(2): 43-68, Summer 1988.
Examines how military women define their roles and status as a minority group in a male military. Found that women didn't identify with the feminist movement, women's issues and didn't network with other military women; they instead adapted to the male standards.

727   Elster, Richard S., editor. **Gender Integration in the Military: Presentations Given at the Naval Postgraduate School.** Monterey, CA: Naval Postgraduate School, 1982. 151p. OCLC 8891895.
To identify manpower, personnel and training policy issues and research and development requirements associated with changes in the numbers and roles of women in the Army, experts in various disciplines address the pertinent issues involved. A transcript of these sessions.

728   Franke, Suzanne. **Sex Role Orientation and Career Decisions of Women in the Army.** Thesis (Ed.D.)--University of Louisville, 1984. 97p. OCLC 26642354.
Used a questionnaire to determine if sex role orientation would be a significant predictor of certain career decisions for women in the Army. Found sex role orientation was a poor predictor of both career decisions of military women and their degree of commitment to a military career.

729   Greene, Byron D. **The Effects of Sex Integration on the Attitudes and Behavior of Military Personnel.** Thesis (M.A.)--University of South Carolina, 1980. 64p. OCLC 7216173.
Gave a questionnaire to 813 recruits in Army basic training to see what attitudes were held toward women in the Army as well as job satisfaction. Found women performed the best in the most integrated setting while men performed best in the least integrated setting.

730   Herbert, Melissa Sheridan. **Feminism, Militarism, and Women in the Military.** Thesis (M.A.)--University of Massachusetts at Amherst, 1990. 46p. OCLC 23090409.
Examined the relationship between feminism, militarism, and gender integration in the military to assesssee to what extent the ideologies of feminism and militarism are in opposition. Found those with a feminist ideology were likely to support the rights of women to equal participation

in the military, while those with a militaristic ideology were less like to support women's equal participation.

731 *Mitchell, Brian.* **Weak Link: The Feminization of the American Military.** Washington, DC: Regnery Gateway, 1989. 232p. OCLC 18959615; ISBN 0895265559.
Presents the author's beliefs that women have no place in the military. States "the presence of women inhibits male bonding, corrupts allegiance to the hierarchy, and diminishes the desire of men to compete for anything but the attentions of women." Includes many "facts" but no sources. Totally ridiculous, but worth reading as an illustration of the kinds of attitudes towards women that persist today.

732 *Stoddard, Ellwyn R.* **"Female Participation in the U.S. Military: Gender Trends By Branch, Rank, and Racial Categories."** *Minerva* 11(1): 23-40, Spring 1993.
Speculative analysis of increases in female sex ratios in different services and service jobs over time. Concludes that the Air Force has not done as much as the other services to attract servicewomen, relative to organizational constraints such as the number of non-combat positions.

733 *Wilcox, Clyde.* **"Race, Gender, and Support For Women in the Military."** *Social Science Quarterly* 73(2): 310-323, June 1992.
Takes data from the 1982 General Social Survey conducted by the National Opinion Research Center, which included a series of questions about women in the military. Found most Americans favored allowing women in non-traditional roles, even those involving combat, although only a minority favored women in ground combat.

13

WOMEN IN COMBAT

There are few issues surrounding the role of women in the military as controversial as that of women in combat. The rules limiting women's participation in combat were first codified in 1948, with the passage of the Women's Armed Services Integration Act, or Public Law 625. While the main purpose of the law was to establish a permanent corps of women in the services, it also contained statutory exclusions for women in combat. Specifically, Public Law 625 prohibited the permanent assignment of Navy women to duty on vessels or aircraft that are "engaged in combat missions" or on other than temporary duty to vessels except hospital ships, naval transports and similar vessels not expected to be assigned to combat missions. The Marine Corps shared these restrictions. The restrictions for Air Force women prohibited their permanent assignment to duty in aircraft assigned in combat missions. The Army was not prohibited under Public Law 625 from assigning women to combat, however, it adopted its own policy of exclusion. These combat restrictions are commonly referred to as the combat exclusion laws.

With the numbers of women on active duty from 1948 to 1969 averaging 1.2 percent of the total force (never reaching the two percent limit set by Public Law 625), and the majority of women serving in medical and clerical jobs, the combat exclusion laws were not seriously challenged. However, by 1967, opposition to the draft and the move toward an all-volunteer force led to an expanded need for women. The 1948 Act was amended in 1967 by Public Law 90-130, which removed the two percent limit on numbers of servicewomen, and later in the 1970s by the federal courts, which removed a number of legal obstacles to women's participation. Some of these actions permitted the assignment of Navy women to limited sea duty, opened missile silo site assignments to Air Force women, opened the service academies to women, and accepted women into flight training.

A major problem with the combat exclusion laws (besides the fact that personnel were discriminated against on the basis of sex) was that each service had a different definition of combat. In 1988, the Department of Defense issued the DOD Risk Rule, for deciding which noncombatant positions and units were to be closed to women. Its purpose was to open more assignments to women by narrowing and standardizing each service's interpretation of combat.

Another problem with the exclusion laws is they have served as a barrier to the expansion of women in the services. By not allowing women to fill many combat and combat-related jobs, the services have been able to limit the number of women they accepted.

Recent conflicts, such as Operation Just Cause in Panama in 1989, and Desert Shield/Desert Storm in 1990-1991, renewed the debate on women in combat. The Fiscal Year 1992 House Defense Authorization Bill, passed in May 1991, repealed the exclusion laws banning military women from flying aircraft on combat missions. However, implementation was delayed while a Presidential Commission on the Assignment of Women in the Armed Forces was established to study and make recommendations on a wide range of issues relating to women in the armed forces. Among other recommendations, the Commission's report, completed in November 1992 (see **811**), recommended that there were circumstances where women might be assigned to combat roles, that women should be excluded from direct land combat units and positions, and by an eight to seven vote, that women should serve in combat aircraft.

In April 1993, then Secretary of Defense Les Aspin issued a memorandum regarding the Policy on the Assignment of Women in the Armed Forces, which directed the services to open more specialties and assignments to women. This included permitting women to compete for assignments in aircraft, specifically aircraft engaging in combat missions, and opened additional ships to women. The Navy was directed to develop a legislative proposal to repeal the combat exclusion laws and permit the assignment of women to combatant ship, which was accomplished in November 1993. In 1994, the USS *Eisenhower* became the first combat vessel to carry an integrated crew of men and women.

In January 1994, Secretary Aspin rescinded the DOD Risk Rule, and issued a new ground combat assignment rule. It stated that women were eligible to be assigned to all positions for which they were qualified, and were to be excluded from assignments to units below the brigade level whose primary mission was to engage in direct combat on the ground. This new rule has allowed the Marine Corps to open thirty-three additional specialties and nine new units to women, and the Army to open all units and positions except direct ground combat battalions and support units physically collocated with them, for a total of 32,699 new positions. The Navy and Air Force were largely unaffected.

BIBLIOGRAPHIES

734 *Hooper, Glenda. "Women at War: Should Mothers and Daughters, Sisters and Sweethearts Fight for Their Country: A Selected Bibliography." BARC Notes Supplement* 15: 1-12, March 1982.
A short bibliography of monographs, films, government documents, and magazine and newspaper articles on the issue of women in the military. Emphasis on women's role in combat. A very small number are annotated.

735 *White, Anthony G.* **U.S. Servicewomen--Air Combat Debate: A Selected Sourcelist.** Monticello, IL: Vance Bibliographies, 1986. 6p. See **559**.

736 *White, Anthony G.* **U.S. Servicewomen--Ground Combat Debate: A Selected Bibliography.** Monticello, IL: Vance Bibliographies, 1986. 9p. OCLC 17296165.
A very brief list of articles from military periodicals. Arranged alphabetically by author. No annotations.

GENERAL WORKS

737 *Becraft, Carolyn H.* **"Personnel Puzzle."** *Proceedings: U.S. Naval Institute* 115(4): 41-44, April 1989.
Discusses combat restrictions and policies of each service, as well as the role of technology in redefining the meaning of combat.

738 *Bolebruch, Lori.* **"Women in Combat: And the Walls Come Tumbling Down."** *Proceedings: U.S. Naval Institute* 118(2): 42-44, February 1992.
Reaction to repeal of some of the combat-exclusion statutes contained in Title X of the U.S. Code. Concludes that repeal is in the best interests of the United States.

739 *Campbell, D'Ann.* **"Combatting the Gender Gulf."** *Minerva* 10(3-4): 13-41, Fall/Winter 1992.
Gives a history of women and combat, evolution of the combat restriction laws, and a detailed discussion of women's performance in Desert Storm, including the problems they encountered. Concludes that it is unlikely the Department of Defense will open new roles for women.

740 *Campbell, D'Ann.* **"Women in Combat: The World War II Experience in the United States, Great Britain, Germany, and the Soviet Union."** *Journal of Military History* 57(2): 301-323, April 1993.
Interesting discussion of WAAC participation in an experiment during World War II, where WAACs were trained in searchlight units (see **430, 454**). Also discusses women in combat roles in Great Britain, the Soviet Union and Germany. Concludes that the prohibition against women in combat in the U.S. was not based on experimental research or on the consideration of the effectiveness of women in combat in other armies; restrictions were primarily political decisions.

741 *Cecil, Thomas H.* **Women in Combat: Pros and Cons.** Maxwell Air Force Base, AL: Air Command and Staff College, Air University, 1988. 18p. OCLC 20333109.
A pro and con discussion of women in combat. Author believes women in combat would increase their prestige while men's prestige would decrease. Includes a good discussion of the problems that would occur if women filled combat roles only as volunteers.

742 Conley, Kathleen M. **Integration of Women into Combat Units.**
Newport, RI: Naval War College, Department of Operations, 1992. 32p.
Analyzes the likely impact of the integration process for women
combatants to delineate key concerns for operational commanders. Not
a discussion of whether or not women should be in combat, rather an
attempt to examine how to minimize the disruption caused by women's
integration.

743 Corbett, Arthur J. **Women in Combat: The Case for Combat
Exclusion.** Newport, RI: Naval War College, 1993.
Responds to the assertion that the combat exclusion policy is arbitrary
and unjustly discriminatory. Examines the physiological differences
between men and women, the dilemma between trade-offs in military
efficiency and political expediency, and the philosophical distinction
between the proponents and opponents of women in combat.

744 D'Amico, Francine. **"Women at Arms: The Combat Controversy."**
Minerva 8(2): 1-19, Summer 1990.
Examines the combat exclusion policy. Provides good information about
women's roles in the 1986 air attack on Libya and Operation Just Cause
in Panama in 1989. Presents physiological, psychological, military-
strategic, and sociological-political arguments for excluding women from
combat. Asserts the combat exclusion policy is impractical and
inequitable.

745 Dean, Merrianne E. **"Women in Combat--The Duty of the Citizen-
Soldier."** San Diego Justice Journal 2(2): 429-460, Summer 1994.
Addresses the role of women as soldiers and the impact that the
limitations on this role has had on women to participate fully as citizens.
Details historical qualifications for citizenship, arguments for and against
women in combat, legal actions, and social changes. Concludes that if
women are excluded from the defense of their country, they are not full
citizens.

746 Devilbiss, Margaret Conrad. **Attitudes toward Women in Combat Roles.**
New Haven, CT: M.C. Devilbiss, 1983. 48p. OCLC 16258870.
Presents pros and cons of women in combat roles and research results.
Concludes that most debates on the issue center more on attitudes and
beliefs about gender roles rather than upon empirical or historical
evidence.

747 Devilbiss, M.C. **"Women in Combat: A Quick Summary of the
Arguments on Both Sides."** Minerva 8(1): 29-31, Spring 1990.
A brief list of five pro and five con arguments on women in combat.
Good quick introduction to the main issues.

748 DiLucente, A. **"Equality: A Step Backward."** Proceedings: U.S. Naval
Institute 118(2): 46-48, February 1992.
Author feels neither women nor the military will benefit from the repeal
of some combat exclusion laws. Women interrupt "male bonding" and

when they insist on competing in the male combat environment, they sacrifice their one unique and ultimate power--motherhood.

749   *Downing, T.M.* ***"Women in Combat: Just Say No!!"*** *Proceedings: U.S. Naval Institute* 118(2): 45-46, February 1992.
Argues that letting women integrate combat units will destroy the effectiveness of the military.

750   *Dunbar, Cynthia.* ***"Toward a Gender-Blind Military: A Comparative Look at Women in Combat."*** *Harvard International Review* 15(1):52-53, 58, Fall 1992.
Presents a fundamental rationale for putting women in combat roles: equal opportunity. Provides information on the role of women in the military in Canada, Great Britain, and Norway.

751   *Ferber, Martin M.* **Combat Exclusion Laws for Women in the Military: Statement of Martin M. Ferber.** Washington, DC: GAO, 1987. GAO/T-NSIAD-88-8. 16p. SuDocs GA1.5/2:T-NSIAD-88-8; OCLC 18927302.
Testimony providing background on the statutory restrictions enacted over forty years ago and the services' policies for implementing these restrictions. Good summary of combat restriction policies and how these affect the kinds of jobs open to military women.

752   *Fraser-Andrews, Linda J.* **Women in Combat: The Operational Impact of Meeting a National Security Necessity.** Newport, RI: Naval War College, 1991. 26p. OCLC 25604386.
An overview of women's role in the military and the arguments most often raised regarding women in combat. Discusses the possible degradation of combat unit integrity, public opinion, and the perceptions of America's allies and adversaries. Recommends the military objectively quantify combat job requirements, develop testing to assess individuals for jobs, and start a national desensitization program to women in combat.

753   *Gemmettee, Elizabeth Villiers.* **"Armed Combat: The Women's Movement Mobilizes Troops in Readiness for the Inevitable Constitutional Attack on the Combat Exclusion for Women in the Military."** *Women's Rights Law Reporter* 12(2): 89-101, Summer 1990.
Addresses possible governmental objectives in defense of the combat exclusion and writings from the feminist movement which challenge the government's assumptions. Covers sex-linked differences, mixed-sex units, and sex-neutral considerations. Good discussion of key issues.

754   *Gilder, George.* ***"The Case Against Women in Combat."*** *Parameters, Journal of the US Army War College* 9(3): 81-86, September 1979.
Reprinted article from the *New York Times Magazine* which suggests that even if expanded use of military women is desirable to relieve recruitment and attrition costs and to fill technical needs, removal of the combat exclusion laws might be unnecessary and unwise. Argues against women in combat.

755   *Goldman, Nancy Loring, editor.*   **Female Soldiers--Combatants or Noncombatants?   Historical and Contemporary Perspectives.** Westport, CT: Greenwood Press, 1982. 307p. OCLC 7876448; ISBN 0313231176.
A collection of chapters written by various authors examining case studies on the use of women in the military and their combat performance. Widely cited.

756   *Golightly, Niel L.* **"No Right to Fight."** *Proceedings: U.S. Naval Institute* 113(12): 46-49, December 1987.
Argues that letting women in combat would destroy unit cohesiveness. Men would become stilted and inhibited, and might become patronizing and compete with each other for women's attention. Generated many responses from readers of the journal (see **766**).

757   *Hart, Roxanne C.* **Women in Combat.** Patrick Air Force Base, FL: The Institute, 1991. 23p. OCLC 23377173.
Gives historical background of women in combat and includes a brief discussion of women's roles in the 1983 invasion of Grenada, the 1986 strike on Grenada, and Operation Just Cause in Panama in 1989. Presents the pros and cons of the biological, psychological and sociological issues of women in combat.

758   *Hixson, R.M.* **"Equal Rights, Equal Risks."** *Proceedings: U.S. Naval Institute* 111(9): 37-41, September 1985.
Issues surrounding women in combat are discussed. Good information on technology's role in opening opportunities for women, such as easing physical requirements for jobs. Concludes that technology enables most women to serve in most combat units and if women want equal rights they must take equal risks.

759   *Kirk, Kathleen F.* **Women in Combat?** Alexandria, VA: Defense Technical Information Center, 1988. 85p. OCLC 20802301.
A poorly prepared report for a master's degree project containing several factual errors. Recommends a review of the New Testament Epistles for guidance on the proper behavior for men and women.

760   *Kohn, Richard H.* **"Women in Combat, Homosexuals in Uniform: The Challenge of Military Leadership."** *Parameters, Journal of the U.S. Army War College* 23(1): 2-4, Spring 1993.
See **680**.

761   *Lett, David K.* **Equal Rights and the U.S. Combat Exclusion Policy for Women: A Congressional Lobby Confrontation.** Maxwell Air Force Base, AL: Air War College, Air University, 1988. OCLC 20233989.
A brief examination of the argument for passage of the Equal Rights Amendment.   Traces judicial and legislative decisions which have affected women's service on the armed forces. Concludes that an equal rights amendment will likely pass in the near future and combat exclusion laws will be rescinded.

762   *Luddy, Joan.* **"Two Wrongs Don't Make it Right. Women in Combat &**
Sexual Harassment." *Proceedings: U.S. Naval Institute* 118(11): 68-
70, November 1992.
Advocates maintaining the combat exclusion laws as the military is not
the place for social experimentation. Believes men and women fighting
together will damage the cohesiveness of the unit.

763   *Martin, Caroline Lucille.* **Women in Combat/The Military: An Analysis**
of Feminist and Anti-Feminist Rhetoric. Thesis (M.S.)--University of
Tennessee, Knoxville, 1992. 99p. OCLC 28355156.
The arguments of anti-feminists and feminists concerning the
participation of women in the U.S. military/combat from 1972-1992
were examined to see if the types of rhetoric had changed over the
years. Found that earlier articles by anti-feminists relied on tradition and
biology and were successful. The feminists relied on pragmatic and
educational approaches and were not successful.

764   *Mauck, Patrice.* **"Women in Combat": Is Warring a Male Occupation**
Only? Newport, RI: Naval War College, 1990. 138p.
The author, a major in the Marine Corps, studied the integration of
women in combat in the Canadian Army. Conducted an opinion poll of
Marine Corps officers on women in combat, and reviewed the major
arguments on women in combat.

765   **"No Right to Fight?"** *Proceedings: U.S. Naval Institute* 114(5): 133-
139, May 1988.
Collection of letters sent in reaction to the article by Lieutenant Golightly
(see **756**). Both pro and con views of women in combat are presented.

766   *Noone, Michael F., Jr.* **"Women in Combat: Changing the Rules."**
Naval Law Review 39: 187-195, Winter 1990.
Contends that any of the three branches of government could permit
women to serve in combat units. Provides discussion of how the laws
could be changed.

767   *Norton, Douglas M.* **"Women in Combat: It's Time."** *Proceedings: U.S.*
Naval Institute 118(2): 48-50, February 1992.
Endorses opening some combat roles for women, such as in aviation and
surface warfare and possibly submarines. Otherwise, women's talents
will be wasted. Highlights problems faced by Navy women.

768   *Peach, Lucinda J.* **"Women at War: The Ethics of Women in Combat."**
Hamline Journal of Public Law and Policy 15(2): 199-241, Spring 1994.
Examines the history and present legal status of women in combat, the
influence of gender ideology on the debate over women in combat, and
ethical perspective on the debate. A detailed analysis emphasizing the
legal aspects. Concludes that combat assignments should be made in
accordance with gender-neutral standards of fitness and capability for
the individual combat position, not on the basis of unfounded
assumptions about gender.

769   *Poyer, Joe.   "'GI Jane':   Should Women Be Allowed to Fight?"* International Combat Arms 54-57, 92, 93, November 1986.
Discusses combat restrictions on women in all of the services and reasons for restrictions, such as physical strength, pregnancy, fraternization, and parenthood. Suggests women deserve equality with men.

770   *Roush, Paul E.   "Combat Exclusion: Military Necessity or Another Name for Bigotry?"* Minerva 8(3): 1-15, Fall 1990.
Analyzes the writings of former Navy Secretary James Webb, Lt. Niel Golightly (see **756**), and Brian Mitchell (see **731**), as prime exclusionists, as they advocate retaining combat exclusion legislation. Refutes many of their assertions about why women are unsuitable for combat. Challenges the notion of gender based bonding, that combat consists solely of hand-to-hand combat, that women have more lost time than men, etc. Excellent rebuttal to exclusion arguments.

771   *Roush, Paul E.   "The Exclusionists and Their Message."* Naval Law Review 39: 163-170, Winter 1990.
Interesting analysis of the recurring themes used by exclusionists, those who want to exclude military women from combat. Describes four main arguments against women in combat and argues that the exclusionists perspective should be abandoned.

772   *Saimons, Vickie J.   Women in Combat: Are the Risks to Combat Effectiveness Too Great?* Fort Leavenworth, KS: Army Command and General Staff College, 1991. 53p.
Examines whether introducing women into combat units would negatively affect unit cohesion and effectiveness. Describes a model for building cohesion, then cites conclusions from studies on cohesion and combat effectiveness. Concludes that cohesion is too complex a phenomenon to isolate one factor, such as gender of unit members, as the cause of change in unit cohesion.

773   *Shapiro, Stephen J., Chairman.   "The Combat Exclusion Laws: An Idea Whose Time Has Gone."* Minerva 9(4): 1-55, Winter 1991.
A report by the Committee on Military Affairs and Justice of the Bar of the City of New York, on whether or not women should be allowed to serve in combat. Focuses on the federal laws which prohibit women from combat in the Navy and Air Force. An excellent, detailed discussion of all pertinent issues.

774   *Smith, Diana W. and Debra L. Mowery.   Women in Combat: What Next?* Newport, RI: Naval War College, 1992. 38p.
Presents discussion on how the combat commander should prepare for women integrating combat units. Suggests questions which must be considered, such as how integration will be achieved without reducing unit effectiveness.

775 *Stiehm, Judith H.* **"Women and the Combat Exemption."** *Parameters, Journal of the US Army War College* 10(2): 51-59, June 1980.
Presentation of issues of women in combat, including reasons for and implications of exempting women. Equates the exemption of women from combat with excluding women from full citizenship.

776 *United States. Congress. House. Committee on Armed Services. Military Forces and Personnel Subcommittee.* **Assignment of Army and Marine Corps Women under the New Definition of Ground Combat.** Washington, DC: GPO, October 6, 1994. 107p. SuDocs Y4.AR5/2A:993-94/50; ISBN 0160465443.
Hearing of testimony on the new assignment policy for Army and Marine Corps women under the new definition of ground combat. Discusses new positions which will be opened to women and which will remain closed.

777 *United States. Congress. House. Committee on Armed Services, Military Forces and Personnel Subcommittee.* **Women in Combat.** Washington, DC: GPO, May 12, 1993. 180p. SuDocs Y4.Ar5/2A:993/94-30; ISBN 0160435528.
Hearing to examine how the services plan to implement former Secretary Les Aspin's decision to let women compete for assignments to combat aircraft and to consider the Department of Defense's request that the statutory exclusion for combatant ships be repealed. Includes many statistics for women in Air Force and Naval aviation.

778 *United States. General Accounting Office.* **Women in the Military: Impact of Proposed Legislation to Open More Combat Support Positions and Units to Women.** GAO/NSIAD-88-197BR. Washington, DC: GAO, 1988. 16p. OCLC 18631677.
Addresses the impact of changes in the services' policies on jobs open to women, specifically those relating to a proposed bill to amend Title 10 of the U.S. Code to increase combat support positions open to women. Summarized data from all services on positions and units closed to women because of exclusionary laws and policies, ongoing service reviews of positions and units closed to women and the impact of new legislation on these positions and units.

779 *United States. General Accounting Office.* **Women in the Military: More Military Jobs Can Be Opened under Current Statutes.** GAO/NSIAD-88-222. Washington, DC: GAO, 1988. 56p. SuDocs Y4.AR5/2A:993-94/50; ED 300591.
A review of how service policies implementing the combat exclusion laws affect the number and assignment of women in the military and whether other factors limit job opportunities for women. Recommends the Marine Corps provide access without regard to gender when making noncombat assignments now prorated between men and women, the Air Force allow unrestricted pilot and navigation openings to be available equally to men and women, and the Army remove limits resulting from gender specific accession goals for enlisted women.

780   *Winters, Kathleen.   "Women in the US Armed Forces: A Short History."* Air Force Journal of Logistics 16(2): 1-4, Spring 1992.
A short history of women in the military and the development of the combat exclusion laws. Discusses the issues of women and combat in four different time periods, 1948-1960, 1961-1973, 1973-1980, and 1981-1990.

781   *Witherspoon, Ralph P. "Female Soldiers in Combat - A Policy Adrift."* Minerva 6(1): 1-28, Spring 1988.
Examines U.S. policy with regard to the use of female soldiers in combat, the sociological factors which affect that policy, and how it is changing over time. Concludes that women would generally perform as well as men in combat.

AIR FORCE

782   *Bateman, Sandra L.   **Female Air Force Pilots and Combat Aircraft: "The Right Stuff" Has No Gender.*** Maxwell Air Force Base, AL: U.S. Air University, Air Command and Staff College, 1987. 14p.
See **555**.

783   *Gordon, Marilyn A.   "A Constitutional Analysis of the Combat Exclusion for Air Force Women."* Minerva 9(2): 1-34, Summer 1992.
A very detailed analysis of the combat exclusion law, giving a historical and legislative summary. Concludes that the law, insofar as it prohibits women from flying combat aircraft, is unconstitutional.

784   *Gordon, Marilyn A. and Mary Jo Ludvigson. "The Combat Exclusion for Women Aviators: A Constitutional Analysis."* Naval Law Review 39: 171-185, Winter 1990.
Detailed discussion of the combat exclusion law as it applied to the Air Force. Provides information about testing the constitutionality of the exclusion and the arguments commonly employed against women in combat, such as pregnancy and physical strength. Concludes banning women from flying combat aircraft is unconstitutional.

785   *Oelke, Marion E. and Richard J. Vogt. **Women in Combat Roles: Past and Future.*** Maxwell Air Force Base, AL: Air War College, 1988. 120p. OCLC 20234013.
The authors, both lieutenant colonels in the Air Force, analyze U.S. law and Air Force policy regarding combat for women. Summarizes international laws and policies and presents arguments pro and con for women in combat. States that Congress probably won't modify the combat exclusion law.

786   *Peterson, Teresa Marne. **USAF Women Pilots: The Combat Issue.*** Maxwell Air Force Base, AL: Air Command and Staff College, Air University, 198. 50p. OCLC 19731241.
Written by a woman pilot, presents the results of the first survey

directed towards women Air Force pilots. One hundred percent of the women agreed that women can fly combat aircraft, ninety-three percent agreed that all Air Force aircraft and missions should be open to women, and eighty-one percent wanted to personally fly combat aircraft. A well presented, interesting study. Includes comments from women pilots.

787   *Shields, Patricia M., Landon Curry and Janet Nichols.* **"Women Pilots in Combat: Attitudes of Male and Female Pilots."** *Minerva* 8(2): 21-35, Summer 1990.
Addresses the questions surrounding women pilots as combatants, such as are women ready to fly combat missions and what are the attitudes of male pilots towards women as combatants? Used data from a survey conducted in 1987 of 224 women Air Force pilots and 162 male pilots. Found that over eighty percent of female pilots felt women should have a combat role and sixty-eight percent anticipated discrimination from male pilots if they assumed combat roles. Male pilots were marginally positive or accepting of female combat pilots.

788   *United States. Congress. House. Committee on Armed Services. Military Personnel and Compensation Subcommittee.* **Implementation of the Repeal of the Combat Exclusion on Female Aviators.** Washington, DC: GPO, January 29, 1992. 40p. SuDocs Y4.Ar5/2a:991-92/38; ISBN 016038835X.
Focuses on clarifying the Department of Defense's position and intended course of action in response to the repeal of the combat exclusion law prohibiting women from flying combat aircraft. Includes statements from each service regarding the role played by female aviators and planning for the expansion of women's roles.

789   *Winters, Kathleen M.* **USAF Women in Combat: Policy and Implementation in the All-Volunteer Force.** Wright-Patterson Air Force Base, OH: Air Force Institute of Technology, 1990. 75p.
A review of the policy on women in combat from 1948 to the present and how it was implemented by the Air Force. Does not discuss whether or not women should be allowed to fly combat aircraft. Suggests Air Force women are moving closer to a combat role.

ARMY

790   *Alderman, Marc I.* **Women in Direct Combat: What is the Price for Equality?** Fort Leavenworth, KS: United States Army Command and General Staff College, 1992. 61p.
Examines whether allowing women in direct combat assignments in the Army will adversely affect unit cohesion and degrade combat effectiveness. Examines historical precedents and current issues. Concludes allowing women into combat units would reduce cohesion and combat effectiveness.

791   *Andrews, Michael A.* **Women in Combat.** Fort Leavenworth, KS:
        United States Army Command and General Staff College, 1978. 10p.
        OCLC 4583242.
        Discusses attitudes towards women in combat. Concludes that the
        Army should simply specify what qualities are required for each job, then
        consider all qualified applicants, regardless of sex.

792   *Andrews, Michael A.* **"Women in Combat?"** *Military Review* 59(7):
        28-34, July 1979.
        Believes the Army of a democratic society must put women in combat.
        Equal opportunity won't exist in the Army until all jobs are open to
        anyone qualified to fill them and further research and study will not be
        useful in resolving the issue of women in combat.

793   *Berrong, Larry Boyd.* **A Case for Women in Combat.** Fort Leavenworth,
        KS: United States Army Command and General Staff College, 1977.
        11p. OCLC 4297645.
        Examines the question of why the Army does not allow women to serve
        in combat roles. Dated, but interesting in that the author concludes the
        exclusion has more to do with the infringement of women on a male role
        than women's abilities.

794   *Cook, Ralph J.* **The Combat Role of Women in the U.S. Army.**
        Washington, DC: Industrial College of the Armed Forces, 1973. 88p.
        OCLC 1933592.
        Conducted a study to examine, analyze, and evaluate the attitude and
        opinions of civilian and military communities relative to incorporating
        women in combat. The study was based on the assumption that the
        Equal Rights Amendment would be passed. Concludes enough women
        are interested in pursuing a combat role that the Army should allow them
        to do so.

795   *Geraci, Karen Sellars.* **"Women in Combat?"** *Minerva* 13(1): 19-35,
        Spring 1995.
        Good discussion of the Army's reaction to the rescinding of the DOD
        Risk Rule, which opened additional military occupational specialties to
        women. Writes that despite the directive to open positions to women,
        the Army is resisting. As women are so vital to Army readiness, it will
        be impossible to keep women separate and still perform team missions.

796   *Hooker, Richard D., Jr.* **"Affirmative Action and the Combat Exclusion:
        Gender Roles in the U.S. Army."** *Parameters, Journal of the US Army
        War College* 19(4): 36-50, 1989.
        Contrasts the Army's commitment to affirmative action with the
        exclusion of women from combat roles. Discusses current Army
        assignment policies, judicial intervention, and arguments for and against
        women in combat.

797   *Mosher, Mary Ann.* **Army Women in Combat: An Examination of
        Roles, Opportunities, Administration, and Social Acceptability.** Thesis

(DPA)--University of Alabama, 1993. 219p.
Conducted a survey of active duty personnel assigned to Fort Rucker, AL on women in the military, specifically of women in combat roles. Found that soldiers were less accepting of women in direct combat roles, such as infantry or armor, but thought that women should be allowed in combat aviation.

798   *Nyberg, James E.* **Should Women Be in the Field Artillery?** Carlisle Barracks, PA: United States Army War College, 1990. 21p. OCLC 22093447.
Good concise discussion of women's roles in the combat arms branches of the Army. Women were restricted in pursuing a career in the field artillery due to the limited number of positions open to them. The author advocates opening more artillery positions to women.

799   *Roy, Thomas M.* **The Combat Exclusion Policy: Myth or Reality for Women in Today's Army?** Carlisle Barracks, PA: United States Army War College, 1991. 33p.
Focuses on the issues of whether or not the Army's policy regulating the assignment of women through the use of the Direct Combat Probability Coding System will be effective or necessary in future combat operations.

800   *Spencer, Dorothy E.* **Toward the Army of the 1980s: A Study of Male Attitudes toward Women As Combatants.** Thesis (M.M.A.S.)--United States Army Command and General Staff College, 1978. 349p. OCLC 4084276.
Attitudes of male students of the U.S. Army Command and General Staff College, class of 1978, towards the issue of women in combat. Biggest concern of those surveyed was that women as combatants would reduce the unit's effectiveness. Traditional roles for women were favored.

801   *Woods, George T., III.* **Women in the Infantry - The Effect on the Moral Domain.** Fort Leavenworth, KS: United States Army Command and General Staff College, 1992. 54p.
Examines the effect of allowing women to serve in the infantry of the U.S. Army. Focuses on aspects of the moral domain cohesion, bonding, unit cohesion, morale, and stress. Specifically discusses the introduction of women into small level infantry units, such as squads and platoons. Concludes that there is sufficient evidence to proceed cautiously with allowing women to serve in the infantry.

NAVY

802   *Brown, Nancy E.* **Women in Combat in Tomorrow's Navy.** Carlisle Barracks, PA: United States Army War College, 1993. 34p.
Discusses issues of Navy women in combat, including mixed gender crews living together for extended periods, strength requirements, women prisoners of war, etc. Proposes solutions and recommendations.

803   *Coyle, Barry J.* **"Women on the Front Lines."** *Proceedings: U.S. Naval Institute* 115(4): 37-40, April 1989.
States the Navy's goal should be to assign women to any billet for which they qualify and volunteer. Author was the commander of a naval aviation squadron, where women were easily integrated. Rational discussion of issues such as physical strength, pregnancy, facilities and fraternization and sexual harassment.

804   *Kelly, James F., Jr.* **"Women in Warships: A Right to Serve."** *Proceedings: U.S. Naval Institute* 104(10): 44-52, October 1978.
Believes the law preventing the Navy from assigning women to ships with a combat mission should be changed. Women must be used due to a shortage of men. Good information about the changes necessary to combat ships so they can accommodate women.

805   *Levens, LuAnne K. and Deborah G. Meyer.* **"Navy Women in Combat: Who Needs Them?"** *Armed Forces Journal International* 117(8): 26-29, April 1980.
Written after a House Armed Services Personnel Subcommittee hearing (in November 1979) to hear testimony considering the repeal of the combat exclusion laws. Discusses the testimony and issues involved.

806   *Norton, Douglas M.* **"Women in Combat: It's Time."** *Proceedings: U.S. Naval Institute* 118(2): 48-50, February 1992.
See **767**.

PRESIDENTIAL COMMISSION ON THE ASSIGNMENT OF WOMEN

807   *Donnelly, Elaine.* **"Women in Combat: From a Commissioner."** *Proceedings: U.S. Naval Institute* 119(2): 55-56, February 1993.
Written by a member of the Commission on the Assignment of Women in the Armed Forces. A conservative member of the committee, writes of her opposition to the recommendation that combat roles for women should be opened. Felt the commission did a good job.

808   *Finch, Mimi.* **"Women in Combat: One Commissioner Reports."** *Minerva* 7(1): 1-12, Spring 1994.
Another member of the Presidential Commission, the author studied duty assignments available to servicewomen. Discusses the workings of the committee, including issues relating to women in combat.

809   *Lawrence, William P.* **"Women in Combat: The Commission."** *Proceedings: U.S. Naval Institute* 119(2): 48-51, February 1993.
An analysis of the recommendations made by the Presidential Commission. Discusses problems on the commission caused between the five conservatives and the other members. Believes the members appointed were not necessarily qualified, so the final report was useless.

810   *Sadler, Georgia C.   "Women in Combat: The Polling Data."*
Proceedings: U.S. Naval Institute 119(2): 51-54, February 1993.
Discusses the results of a survey conducted by the Presidential
Commission.   Found that overall, the American public was more
supportive of women in the combat than were members of the military.
A majority of both the general public and the military felt that women
should be drafted in a national emergency.

811   *United States.   Presidential Commission on the Assignment of Women
in the Armed Forces.   **Women in Combat: Report to the President.***
Washington, DC: Brassey's, 1993.   Not paged.   OCLC 028506119;
ISBN 002881097X.
The final report of the Commission containing a review of existing laws
and policies and recommendations for the future assignment of women
in the armed forces.   Defines seventeen critical issues, including many
questions of women in combat, and presents recommendations for each.

PRISONERS OF WAR

*For other materials on prisoners of war, see **203-214, 257-261**.*

812   *Booher, Alice A.   **"American Military Women Prisoners of War."***
Minerva 11(1):17-22, Spring 1993.
Brief discussion of women who have been prisoners of war and what
benefits they are entitled to.

813   *Cornum, Rhonda, as told to Peter Copeland.   **She Went to War: The
Rhonda Cornum Story.***   Novato, CA: Presidio Press, 1992.   203p.
OCLC 25410980; ISBN 089141630.
At the start of Desert Shield, Cornum was the Chief of the Crew Life
Support Branch at the U.S. Army Aeromedical Research Lab.   She went
to Saudi Arabia as a flight surgeon.   Includes many interesting details of
life in Saudi Arabia awaiting the start of the ground war.   On 27 February
1991, Cornum became the second woman POW when a helicopter in
which she was riding to rescue an F-16 pilot was shot down, and she
was released eight days later.   A unique account from a woman prisoner
of war.

814   *Dillingham, Wayne E.   **"The Possibility of American Military Women
Becoming Prisoners of War: A Challenge for Behavioral Scientists."***
Minerva 8(4):17-22, Winter 1990.
Suggests behavioral science research could provide insight and
assistance to help in predicting the consequences of American military
women as prisoners of war.   Some problems women prisoners of war
face might be sexual torture, pregnancy, and amenorrhea.

14

VETERANS

The number of women veterans has traditionally been small, with little attention paid to their needs by the Veterans Administration. This became apparent by the treatment of women Vietnam veterans. In the years following the end of the war, much attention was paid to problems faced by male vets, such as post-traumatic stress disorder (PTSD), while women veterans and their problems were virtually ignored. Fortunately, this situation has improved in recent years, as both the contributions and problems of women veterans have been recognized. Much of the research on women veterans, especially Vietnam veterans, has been conducted by women themselves.

According to the 1990 Census, there are 1.1 million women veterans, about four percent of the veteran population. Services for these women veterans have grown in the 1990s. The Women Veterans Health Program Act of 1992 authorized new and expanded services for women veterans. As a result of Public Law 102-585, four Women Veterans Comprehensive Health Centers were established in 1993, and four were added in 1994. Among other recent services is an outpatient treatment center for women with PTSD at the Women's Health Science Division at the Boston VA Medical Center. The various VA centers are listed in Appendix B.

This chapter contains general materials about women veterans, as well as about nurses who served in Vietnam and articles about their health, including post-traumatic stress disorder.

GENERAL WORKS

815 *Department of Veterans Affairs.* **Women Veterans, a Decade of Progress: July 1990 Report of the VA Advisory Committee on Women Veterans.** Washington, DC: Department of Veterans Affairs, July 1990. 16p. OCLC 22904881.
Presents a chronology of events of the Department of Veterans Advisory Committee on Women Veterans from 1980-1990. Also includes a brief discussion of issues and recommendation for women veterans, i.e., they are often unaware of their entitlement to benefits.

816 *Feitz, Robert H.* **Female Veterans' Usage of the Post-Korean Conflict G.I. Bill.** Washington, DC: Office of Information Management and Statistics, 1985. 12p. OCLC 12073314.
Presents statistical information on the participation of women in the Post-Korean G.I. Bill. Found that for the women who did use the G.I. Bill, they used more of their entitlement than did men.

817 *Harris (Louis) and Associates.* **Survey of Female Veterans: A Study of the Needs, Attitudes and Experiences of Women Veterans.** Washington, DC: Veterans Administration, Office of Information Management and Statistics, 1985. 299p. OCLC 12743118; ED 274798.
Results of a survey conducted in February 1984 by the Veterans Administration to study female veterans. Found that the female veteran population was relatively young, and only one percent had completed a military career (twenty years). Veterans of Vietnam and the post-Vietnam era were more likely than veterans of earlier eras to have adjustment problems. Includes many statistics.

818 *Mehay, Stephen L. and Barry T. Hirsch.* **The Post-Military Earnings of Female Veterans.** Monterey, CA: Naval Postgraduate School, Department of Administrative Sciences, 1993. 31p.
Examines the civilian labor market of women veterans, using traditional data sets and a survey. Found female veterans possess a higher level of measured earnings endowments than do non-veterans.

819 *United States Veterans Administration.* **Data on Female Veterans, Fiscal Year...** Washington, DC, GPO, 1983-. SuDocs VA1.2/12:year.
An irregular publication providing information on female veterans including age, period of military service, females in VA medical centers and hospitals, pensions and disability use, and educational benefits.

820 *United States Veterans Administration.* **The Woman Veteran: Readjustment Experience and Problems Met Three to Four Months after Separation, Survey of Enlisted Women Discharged from Army and Navy in February 1946.** Washington, DC: The Administration. 10p. SuDocs VA1.2:W84.
A study of women veterans after discharge discussing differences in their employment status before enlistment and after separation from active duty. Also surveys use of veterans benefits, such as the GI bill and home loans.

821 *Willenz, June A.* **Women Veterans: America's Forgotten Heroines.** New York: Continuum, 1982. 252p. OCLC 9686639; ISBN 0826402410.
Reviews the history and accomplishments of women veterans. Presents a collection of personal reminiscences by military women who served during and after World War II. Includes a discussion of benefits available for women veterans.

VIETNAM VETERANS

822   *Alexander, Susan K.   "The Invisible Veterans: Nurses in the Vietnam War."* Women's Studies Quarterly 12(2): 16-17, Summer 1984.
Very brief discussion of the shortage of books written by women veterans of Vietnam, problems of nurses in Vietnam, and lack of support for them from the Veterans Administration.

823   *Baker, Rodney R., Shirley W. Menard and Lois A. Johns.* **"The Military Nurse Experience in Vietnam: Stress and Impact."** Journal of Clinical Psychology 45(5): 736-744, September 1989.
Presents demographic, health, and psychosocial data from two studies on military nurses assigned to Vietnam. Surveyed sixty Army nurses in the first study and forty Army nurses and twenty Air Force and Navy nurses in the second study. Results of the two studies are compared. Both confirmed earlier reported problems and stress encountered by female military nurses in Vietnam.

824   *Denzler, Brenda.* **"Acceptance and Avoidance: The Women Vietnam Vet."** Minerva 5(2): 72-96, Spring 1987.
Reprints excerpts of interviews with women Vietnam veterans. The majority felt isolated from male veterans and were not accepted in veterans groups.

825   *Dienstfrey, Stephen J.* **"Women Veterans' Exposure to Combat."** Armed Forces and Society 14(4): 549-558, Summer 1988.
Analysis of data from the 1984 Harris Survey of 3,000 female veterans (see **817**). About one in twenty women veterans reported being exposed to combat. About three-quarters of those were nurses, most from the Army Nurse Corps. The second largest group were clerical, then administrative workers.

826   *Leon, Gloria R., Yossef S. Ben-Porath and Stephen Hjemboe.* **"Coping Patterns and Current Functioning in a Group of Vietnam and Vietnam-Era Nurses."** Journal of Social and Clinical Psychology 9(3): 334-353, 1990.
A group of thirty-six nurses who served in Vietnam were compared with a group of thirty-two Vietnam-era military nurses on patterns of coping during their duty tours, the impact of their experiences, and current functioning.

827   *McVicker, Sara J.* **"Invisible Veterans: The Women Who Served in Vietnam."** Journal of Psychosocial Nursing 23(10): 12-19, October 1985.
Discusses experiences of nurses serving in Vietnam, including types of assignments, working and living conditions, and problems faced by nurses after the war. Includes information about PTSD and treatment of women veterans at Veterans Centers.

828   *Paul, Elizabeth A. and Jacquelyn S. O'Neill.* **"American Nurses in Vietnam: Stressors and Aftereffects."** American Journal of Nursing 86(5): 526, May 1986.
Study to identify the environment in which nurses worked in Vietnam and to determine if they suffered and are still suffering adverse aftereffects. Surveyed 137 Vietnam veteran nurses. Found eight major stressors to women. Over one-third of the respondents had adverse aftereffects similar to PTSD. As in other studies, nurses remaining in the military had fewer problems than those who left the service.

829   *Renning, Judy Lyn.* **Vietnam Era Army Nurses: Perceptions of the Effect of the War on Closer Relationships.** Thesis (MSW)--California State University, Long Beach, 1992   74p.
An exploratory study to determine if Army nurses who served in Vietnam perceived this experience as having an effect on their close relationships. Surveyed twenty nurses, who were found to be very resilient and viewed their relationships in a positive manner.

830   *Salvatore, Maggie.* **"Concepts of Social Support and Social Networks Applied to the Population of Women Vietnam Veterans."** Minerva 9(3): 32-42, Fall 1991.
Discusses the network among a population of women Vietnam veterans consisting of varying groups which provide a variety of functions.

831   *Scannell-Desch, Elizabeth Ann.* **The Lived Experiences of Women Military Nurses in Vietnam during the Vietnam War.** Thesis (Ph.D.)--Georgia State University, 1992. 176p.
Purpose of the study was to explore common components of nurses' experiences in Vietnam and common experiences of their lives after Vietnam.   Twenty-four veterans were interviewed.   Found that the nurses struggled with the ethics of wartime nursing, but also felt a special bond with their wartime colleagues.

832   *Scuteri, Gina M.* **Casualties of War and Research: A Case Study of United States Women Veterans of Vietnam.** Thesis (Ph.D.)--Perdue University, 1993. 296p.
Presents research to obtain information on the experiences of women veterans in the Vietnam War.   Also briefly discusses the relationship between the veteran's experiences and the development of PTSD and other war related disorders.

833   *Stroud, Julia Meta.* **Adjustment Difficulties of Women Viet Nam Veterans.** Thesis (Ph.D.)--University of Montana, 1983. 83p. OCLC 16507201.
Fifteen female and fifteen male Vietnam veterans participated in a study designed to provide a description of the impact the Vietnam conflict had upon their lives. A control group of fifteen non-veteran women was also surveyed. Both male and female veterans were found to be more prone to depression and anxiety than members of the control group. Female

veterans had more difficulty in developing and maintaining relationships than the non-veteran women.

834 *Willenz, June A.* **"Women Veterans from the Vietnam War through the Eighties."** *Minerva* 6(3): 44-60, Fall 1988.
Estimates between 7,500-11,000 women served in Vietnam, three-quarters of whom were exposed to combat. Most were nurses or other medical personnel. Discusses their problems, society's response to them and their experiences at Veteran Centers.

HEALTH

835 *Carney, Caren Marie.* **Perceived Symptoms among U.S. Army Nurses: The Effects of Combat Environment, Gender, Control, and Social Support.** Thesis (Ph.D.)--George Washington University, 1985. 219p. OCLC 14126802.
Author surveyed 712 Army Nurse Corps members (about one-half were women) assigned to either Vietnam or who served in the Vietnam era on their current physical health status. Nurses who had served in Vietnam did report more current symptoms than nurses who had served elsewhere, but there was generally an absence of a meaningful difference between the two groups.

836 *Dvoredsky, Ana E. and William Cooley.* **"The Health Care Needs of Women Veterans."** *Hospital and Community Psychiatry* 36(10): 1098-1102, October 1985.
Presents data that suggests women veterans do not utilize their health care benefits as often as men, and when they do, they use it selectively for serious illnesses needing protracted care. Suggests VA hospitals need to plan better to provide for women's health care needs.

837 *Leda, Catherine, Robert Rosenheck and Peggy Gallup.* **"Mental Illness among Homeless Female Veterans."** *Hospital and Community Psychiatry* 43(10): 1026-1028, October 1992.
Examined sociodemographic and psychiatric diagnostic data from 19,313 veterans seen in a program for homeless, chronically mentally ill veterans to determine the proportion and characteristics of female veterans. 310 women were compared to the men and were found to be younger, less likely to be employed, more likely to have a major psychiatric illness, and less likely to have that illness diagnosed.

838 *LeDonne, Diane M.* **"Trends in Morbidity and Use of Health Services by Women Veterans of Vietnam."** *Navy Medicine* 79(3): 22-25, May-June 1988
Takes statistics from the Survey of Female Veterans (see **817**) to examine women veterans from the Vietnam era. Twenty-eight of the women had served in Vietnam. Found that a higher percentage of those who had served in Vietnam had chronic conditions and disabilities, had cancer, or had children born with defects.

839   *Rice-Grant, Sharon Kay.* **Does Anyone Care? About the Health of Women Who Served in Vietnam.** Thesis (M.S.W.)--California State University, Sacramento, 1986. 186p. OCLC 14922374.
An exploratory study addressing medical issues of women who served in Vietnam. 446 military and civilian women were surveyed to explore a range of health issues and collect data on the types of assignments held by military women and their exposure to toxic chemicals. The author concludes that there is no proof that Vietnam service damaged women's health.

840   *Rothman, Gene H.* **"Needs of Female Patients in a Veteran's Psychiatric Hospital."** *Social Work* 29(4): 380-385, July-August 1984.
Reviews the psychiatric and medical care of female veterans through sixty-nine interviews at a veterans psychiatric facility. Found that women are generally satisfied with their care.

841   *Schuler, Maureen P., Allan G. Barclay, Bruce Harrison and Paul Larson.* **"Psychological Services Offered to Female Veterans."** *Journal of Clinical Psychology* 42(4): 668-675, July 1986.
Results of a questionnaire completed by ninety-one chiefs of Veterans Administration psychology services to request information on services provided to female veterans. Found a significant correlation between the number of services offered routinely and the following four factors: the state population of women veterans, the income of the women veteran clients, the total number of psychologists on staff, and the annual number of clients.

Health - Post-Traumatic Stress Disorder (PTSD)

842   *Campos, Rhoda.* **Post-Traumatic Stress Disorder in Female Vietnam Veterans from 1973 to 1986.** Thesis (M.S.W.)--Louisiana State University, Baton Rouge, 1987. 43p. OCLC 24120564.
A literature review of post-traumatic stress disorder in female veterans, using Sociological Abstracts, Social Work Abstracts, Medline, Nursing and Allied Health Abstracts, etc. The literature indicates that female veterans have experienced personal, interpersonal and social difficulties due to PTSD. A good review with an extensive bibliography.

843   *Dean, Donna M.* **Warriors without Weapons: The Victimization of Military Women.** Thesis (Ph.D.)--The Union Institute, Cincinnati, OH, 1994. 255p.
See **689**.

844   *Dreeben, Jane.* **The Role of Pre-Service Interpersonal Experiences and Family Relationships in the Post-War Adjustment of Vietnam Veteran Nurses.** Thesis (Ph.D.)--Boston College, 1992. 191p.
Investigates variables related to the current psychological adjustment, measured by the presence or absence of PTSD in Vietnam nurse veterans. Found the women who currently had war related PTSD were

more likely than those who did not to have experienced pre-service trauma involving physical and/or sexual abuse, or an alcoholic parent. The PTSD women also were exposed to higher levels of trauma in Vietnam than those without PTSD.

845 *Engel, Charles C., Jr., et al.* **"Posttraumatic Stress Disorder Symptoms and Precombat Sexual and Physical Abuse in Desert Storm Veterans."** *Journal of Nervous and Mental Disease* 181(11): 683-688, November 1993.
Studies the association between precombat sexual and physical abuse and combat-related post-traumatic stress disorder in female and female Desert Storm veterans. Men reported significantly higher levels of combat exposure and women significantly more precombat abuse. Found that women describing precombat abuse reported much greater PTSD symptomatology than women denying precombat abuse.

846 *Jacobs, Marianne Scherer.* **The Best of Times, the Worst of Times: The Vietnam Experiences of and Post-Traumatic Stress Disorder among Female Nurse Veterans**. Thesis (Ph.D.)--University of Washington, 1990. 203p. OCLC 24278706.
An interesting and well written analysis of the Vietnam and readjustment experiences of 275 female nurse veterans, based upon questionnaires and personal interviews. Has a detailed discussion of post-traumatic stress disorder. The author served as an Army nurse in Vietnam from September 1970-September 1971.

847 *Norman, Elizabeth M.* **"Post-Traumatic Stress Disorder in Military Nurses Who Served in Vietnam during the War Years: 1965-1973."** *Military Medicine* 153(5): 238-242, May 1988.
Fifty nurses who served in Vietnam were interviewed about their war experiences and the presence of post-traumatic stress disorder. Found that the incidence of PTSD has dropped since the initial post-war years.

848 *Paul, Elizabeth A.* **"Wounded Healers: A Summary of the Vietnam Nurse Veteran Project."** *Military Medicine* 150(11): 571-576, November 1985.
The Vietnam Nurse Veteran Project was designed to identify stressors and after-effects experienced by nurse veterans. Article summarizes one of the first research studies conducted on women Vietnam veterans. Found that nurses who had served less than six months in the military before going to Vietnam had more problems coping than more experienced nurses. Other stressors were sexual harassment, and lack of some medical supplies.

849 *Rogers, Barbara and Janet Nikolaus.* **"Vietnam Nurses."** *Journal of Psychosocial Nursing* 25(4): 11-15, April 1987.
A brief discussion of PTSD in nurse Vietnam veterans and psychological treatment. Includes a case report of a nurse suffering from PTSD.

850   *Smith, Winnie.* **American Daughter Gone to War: On the Front Lines with an Army Nurse in Vietnam.** New York: William Morrow and Company, Inc., 1992. 352p.
See **231**.

851   *Stretch, Robert H., James D. Vail, and Joseph P. Maloney.* **"Posttraumatic Stress Disorder among Army Nurse Corps Vietnam Veterans."** *Journal of Consulting and Clinical Psychology* 53(5): 704-708, October 1985.
Presents results of a questionnaire completed by Vietnam veterans still on active duty in the Army. Found that 3.3 percent of the Vietnam nurses had post-traumatic stress disorder. Suggests the occurrence of PTSD is different among those who have maintained a military affiliation than among those who have left the military.

852   *Van Devanter, Lynda with Christopher Morgan.* **Home before Morning: The Story of an Army Nurse in Vietnam.** New York: Beaufort Books, 1983. 382p.
See **232**.

853   *Wolfe, Jessica, Pamela J. Brown, Joan Furey and Karen B. Levin.* **"Development of a Wartime Stressor Scale for Women."** *Psychological Assessment* 5(3): 330-335, September 1993.
Discusses prior research, which has shown the importance of stress measurement as a component of evaluating PTSD. Describes the development and preliminary psychometric analyses of the Women's Wartime Stressor Scale, designed to measure the self-report of wartime stressors by both theater and era veterans as well as civilian women who served in Vietnam.

854   *Wolfe, Jessica.* **"Female Military Veterans and Traumatic Stress."** *PTSD Research Quarterly* 4(1): 1-4, Winter 1993.
A literature review of publications on women Vietnam veterans and traumatic stress. Includes dissertations, journal articles, and book chapters. Good summary of important research. The author is the Director of the Women's Health Sciences Division of the National Center for PTSD at the Boston Veterans Administration Center.

855   *Wolfe, Jessica, Pamela J. Brown and John M. Kelley.* **"Reassessing War Stress: Exposure and the Persian Gulf War."** *Journal of Social Issues* 49(4): 15-31, 1993.
Surveyed 2,244 Persian Gulf War veterans (208 females) after their return from the Gulf to investigate three major categories; traditional wartime activities, nontraditional wartime activities, and nonwar-zone, deployment related experiences. Found only three percent of male and three percent of female returnees had high levels of traditional combat exposure. The prevalence of presumptive PTSD was low.

856   *Wolfe, Jessica, Pamela J. Brown, and Maria L. Bucsela.* **"Symptom Responses of Female Vietnam Veterans to Operation Desert Storm."**

American Journal of Psychiatry 149(5): 676-679, May 1992.
Examined the status of symptoms of PTSD in seventy-six women Vietnam veterans. Found veterans who had previously reported high levels of PTSD experienced the most intensification of stress symptoms during Desert Storm.

857 *Wolfe, Jessica, DeAnna Mori and Suzanne Krygeris.* **"Treating Trauma in Special Populations: Lessons from Women Veterans."** *Psychotherapy* 31(1): 87-93, Spring 1994.
Describes the planning and evolution of a specialized PTSD program for women veterans. The program emphasizes clinical services related to life stressors and accompanying symptomatology across all life periods.

APPENDIX A: ARCHIVAL RESOURCES

MILITARY HISTORICAL CENTERS

Albert F. Simpson Historical Research Center (Air Force)
Bldg. 1405
Maxwell Air Force Base, AL 36112
(205) 293-5958
Collects materials dealing with the history of the Army Air Forces and Air Force. Includes several collections relating to Air Force women, including records of the Office of the Director, Women in the Air Force, Women Air Force Service Pilots, and miscellaneous records on Women in the Military.

U.S. Army Center of Military History
1099 14th Street, NW
Washington, DC 20005-3402
(202) 504-5373
The central agency for the U.S. Army museum system. Divided into two sections, the Historical Division and the Museum Division. Many archival materials.

U.S. Army Military History Institute
Carlisle Barracks, PA 17103-5008
(717) 245-3434
Holds personal papers, photographs, taped interviews, etc. of non-official Army historical source materials. Has some personal papers of servicewomen, materials relating to the Army Nurse Corps during World War I, materials concerning servicewomen during World War II.

U. S. Coast Guard
Office of Coast Guard Historian, G-CP-4
2100 Second Street, SW
Washington, DC 20593-0001
(202) 267-0948
Holds nine boxes of materials on World War II SPARs, as well as miscellaneous separate items, including personnel rosters, photographs, class lectures,

correspondence, regulations, insignia, manuals, and newspaper clippings. Also hold video interviews with Coast Guard women.

U. S. Marine Corps Historical Center
901 M Street, SE
Navy Yard, Bldg 58
Washington, DC 20374-5040
(202) 433-3840
Collections on Women Marines in World Wars I and II, which include interviews with women marines, correspondence, articles, photographs, clippings, pamphlets, etc.

U.S. Naval Historical Center
Bldg. 108, Washington Navy Yard
901 M Street, SE
Washington, DC 20374-5060
(202) 433-2765
Operational Archives hold many collections relating to Navy women, including an oral history interview collection, official records pertaining to all aspects of the development of the WAVES, a two volume administrative history of the Women's Reserve, and a history of the Naval Reserve Midshipman's School in Northampton, Massachusetts.

U.S. Naval Institute Oral History Office
Annapolis, MD 21402
(301) 268-6110
Oral history interviews with many Navy women. Transcripts are available here as well as at the Naval Historical Center in Washington, DC.

OTHER ARCHIVES/HISTORICAL CENTERS

National Archives
Pennsylvania Avenue at 7th Street, NW
Washington, DC 20408
(202) 501-5400

National Archives II
8601 Adelphi Road
College Park, MD 20704-6001
(301) 713-6800
The National Archives and Records Administration preserves important records of agencies of the federal government. Records were originally housed at the Washington, DC location. A new repository, Archives II in College Park, MD, was completed in 1994 and will eventually house documents as well as all nontextual records (photographic, sound, etc.) The finding aid for these records is *American Women and the U.S. Armed Forces: A Guide to the Records of Military Agencies in the National Archives Relating to American Women* [**011**].

National Personnel Records Center
9700 Page Avenue
St. Louis, MO 63132
(314) 538-4246
Holds World War II personnel and related records.

PRESIDENTIAL LIBRARIES

The following Presidential libraries have records relating to military women, including some collections of personal papers:

Dwight D. Eisenhower Library
Abilene, KS 67410
(913) 263-4751

Franklin D. Roosevelt Library
511 Albany Post Road
Hyde Park, NY 12538
(914) 229-8114

Harry S. Truman Library
U.S. Highway 24 & Delaware Street
Independence, MO 64050
(816) 833-1400

MILITARY MUSEUMS

United States Air Force Museum
Wright-Patterson Air Force Base, OH 45433-6518
(513) 255-3284
The main museum for the U.S. Air Force. Owns women's uniforms, insignia and equipment.

United States Coast Guard Museum
U.S. Coast Guard Academy
15 Mohegan Road
New London, CT 06320-4195
(203) 444-8511
Covers the history of the Coast Guard. Holdings include a small number of SPAR materials.

United States Marine Corps Museum
Marine Corps Historical Center
Washington Navy Yard
Washington, DC 20374-5040
(202) 433-3840
Some holdings pertaining to women Marines, including uniforms.

United States Military Academy Museum
West Point, NY 10966
(914) 938-9478
Items of interest include uniforms and equipment for nurses and WACs.

United States Navy Museum
Washington Navy Yard
9th & M Street
Bldg. 76
Washington, DC 20374-0571
(202) 433-4882
Have items of Navy women from World War I to the present.

Women's Army Corps Museum
Building 1077, 3rd St and 5th Av
Ft. McClellan, AL 36205-5000
(205) 848-3512/5559; FAX: (205) 848-7323
The only museum devoted solely to military women. Covers the WAC as well as women in the other services. Holdings include uniforms and equipment. Oral histories, photographs, films, etc. are located in the archival holdings.

APPENDIX B: WOMEN'S MILITARY ASSOCIATIONS

*This list was compiled from a variety of sources. Information is provided for organizations when available. Note that addresses and names of organizations often change. Check the most recent issue of the **Encyclopedia of Associations** for further information.*

MILITARY WOMEN'S ORGANIZATIONS

Air Force Women Officers Association
P.O. Box 780155
San Antonio, TX 78278
(800) 805-8297, ext. 96

Alliance of Women Veterans
P.O. Box 48817
Los Angeles, CA 90048

Army Women's Professional Association (AWPA)
P.O. Box 46006
Washington, DC 20050-6006

Coast Guard/SPAR, Inc.
5904 Mt. Eagle Drive, Apt. 4-1616
Alexandria, VA 22303
(703) 960-2559

Hispanic Women Veterans Coalition
P.O. Box 25047
Harper Woods, MI 48225-1825
(313) 881-5514

National Navy Women's Reunion
P.O. Box 147
Golden Rod, FL 32733-0147
(407) 578-2794

National Organization of World War Nurses
10500 Rockville Pike, #213
Rockville, MD 20852
(301) 493-5153

National Women Veterans Conference, Inc.
2902 Irving Street
Denver, CO 80211-6756

Navy Nurse Corps Association
P.O. Box 1229
Oak Harbor, WA 98277-1229
(360) 675-9046
Holds biannual reunions for former, retired, active and reservist members of the
Navy Nurse Corps. Publishes a newsletter for members three times per year.

Retired Army Nurse Corps Association (RANCA)
P.O. Box 681026, Serna Station
San Antonio, TX 78218-1235
(210) 655-6905
Provides educational and social activities for over 2,000 members, and helps
preserve the history of the Army Nurse Corps. Publishes a quarterly newsletter,
The Connection. Some other activities include conducting oral histories with
Army Nurse Corps POW's from World War II, and holding biannual conventions.

Society of Retired Air Force Nurses
P.O. Box 681026
San Antonio, TX 78268

United Women Veterans
225 Larkin St
Madison, WI 53705
(608) 233-3105

WASP
4300 Caledonia Way
Los Angeles, CA 90065

WAVES National
1902 Dartmouth
Camp Hill, PA 17011
(717) 737-4254

Women Airforce Service Pilots World War II
Marty Wyall, President
P.O. Box 9212
Fort Wayne, IN 46809
(219) 747-7933
Over 900 members. Includes women who graduated from WASP training or flew in the WASP or WAF between 1942 and 1944. Provides information to researchers of the WASP. Maintains biographical archives, which are held in the WASP Collection at the Blagg-Huey Library, Texas Woman's University.

Women Marines Association (WMA)
P.O. Box 387
Quantico, VA 22314
(703) 979-1149
Members number 3,000. Women in the Marine Corps or Reserve, honorably discharged, or retired are eligible for membership. Promotes the welfare of women in the Marine Corps, provides assistance to hospitalized veterans, and maintains a charitable program. Hosts a biennial convention.

Women Military Aviators, Inc.
13541 Lord Baltimore Place
Upper Marlboro, MD 20771

Women Officers' Professional Association (WOPA)
Box 1621
Arlington, VA 22210
Supports the professional development of its members and serves as a forum for discussion about the sea services (USN, USMC, USGC, NOAA). Membership is available for officers of these services and chiefs. Affiliate membership (non-voting) is available to junior enlisted and other servicemembers.

Women Veterans of America
P.O. Box 290283, Homecrest Station
Brooklyn, NY 10229-0005

Women's Army Corps Veterans Association
P.O. Box 5577
Fort McClellan, AL 36205
4,000 members who are veterans of the Women's Army Corps and Women's Army Auxiliary Corps, women soldiers and officers on active duty or who have been honorably discharged, and members of the Army Reserve and National Guard. Conducts hospital and community service projects and supports the Women's Army Corps Museum. Holds an annual convention every August.

World War II Flight Nurses Association
02111 Spring Lake Road
Fruitland, FL 32731-5154
(904) 787-6064

VETERANS ORGANIZATIONS

The National Registry of Women Veterans
VA Medical Center (152)
2002 Holcombe Blvd.
Houston, TX 77030
phone: (713) 794-7903; fax: (713) 794-7103
The Registry is developing an electronic database to identify all women veterans separated from active military service since 1942 to enable the Department of Defense to communicate important health and health care information to women veterans.

WOMEN VETERANS HEALTH PROGRAMS

Office of Environmental Medicine and Public Health
VA Central Office
Washington, DC
(202) 535-7182

WOMEN VETERANS COMPREHENSIVE HEALTH CENTERS

Boston VA Medical Center
Boston, MA
(617) 232-9500, ext. 4276

Chicago Area Network
(Hines, Lakeside, North Chicago, and West Side VA Medical Centers)
(312) 666-6500, ext. 3382

Durham VA Medical Center
Durham, NC
(919) 286-6936

Minneapolis VA Medical Center
Minneapolis, MN
(612) 725-2030

Southeast Pennsylvania Network
(Coatesville, Lebanon, Philadelphia, and Wilmington VA Medical Centers)
(215) 823-4496

San Francisco VA Medical Center
San Francisco, CA
(415) 221-4810, ext. 2174

Sepulveda/West Los Angeles VA Medical Centers
Sepulveda and Los Angeles, CA
(818) 972-2000, ext. 3678

SPECIAL HEALTH PROGRAMS

Post-Traumatic Stress Disorder

National Center for PTSD
Women's Health Services Division
National Center for Post-traumatic Stress Disorder
VA Medical Center
Boston, MA
(617) 232-9500, ext. 4145

Womens' Inpatient PTSD Unit
VA Medical Center
Palo Alto, CA
(415) 493-5000, ext. 2274

Women's Stress Disorder Treatment Teams

Boston VA Medical Center
Boston, MA
(617) 232-9500, ext. 4145

Cleveland/Brecksville VA Medical Center
Brecksville, OH
(216) 526-3030, ext. 5835

New Orleans VA Medical Center
New Orleans, LA
(504) 568-0811, ext. 5835

Loma Linda VA Medical Center
Loma Linda, CA
(909) 825-7084, ext. 2595

OTHER ORGANIZATIONS

Defense Advisory Committee on Women in the Service (DACOWITS)
Pentagon, Rm. 3D769
Washington DC 20301-4000
Established in 1951 to assist and advise the Secretary of Defense on policies and matters relating to women in military service. Composed of civilian men and women appointed by the Secretary of Defense for a three year term. Meets each spring and fall to form recommendations to ensure the effective utilization of military women.

The Minerva Center, Inc.
Dr. Linda Grant De Pauw, Founder and President
20 Grenada Road
Pasadena, MD 21122-2708
(410) 437-5379
email: minervacen@aol.com
The Minerva Center is a non-profit organization dedicated to promoting women's military studies. It publishes *Minerva: Quarterly Report on Women and the Military* and *Minerva's Bulletin Board: The News Magazine on Women and the Military.* Operates an online discussion group, H-Minerva. To subscribe, send an email message to listserv@h-net.msu.edu: subscribe h-minerva, your first name, your last name.

Vietnam Women's Memorial Project, Inc. (VWMP)
2001 S Street, NW, Suite 302
Washington, DC 20009
phone: (202) 328-7253; fax: (202) 986-3636
The VWMP dedicated the Vietnam Women's Memorial, located in Washington, DC, in 1993. It currently is sponsoring project "Sister Search" to locate the military and civilian women who served during the Vietnam War to provide a network for these women and to assist research efforts on women Vietnam veterans.

Women in Military Service for America Memorial Foundation, Inc. (WIMSA)
Dept. 560
Washington, DC 20042-0560
phone: (800) 222-2294; fax: (703) 931-4208
email: wimsa@aol.com
The Women in Military Service Memorial will be the first national monument to honor all service women. Located at Arlington National Cemetery, it will include a computerized registry with information on all servicewomen who register, as well as a museum.

Women's Research & Education Institute (WREI)
1700 18th Street, NW, #400
Washington, DC 20009
phone: (202) 328-7070; fax: (202) 328-3514
WREI's Women in the Military Project was established in 1990 to gather, analyze and disseminate information about women in the military, as well as to advocate within the Department of Defense on behalf of military women, to monitor the progress of women veterans, and to consider legal and public policy strategies for challenging laws and policies that restrict military women's opportunities. Has a small number of short publications on military women.

APPENDIX C: CHRONOLOGY OF WOMEN'S SERVICE

1901: Army Nurse Corps established as an auxiliary of the Army. Nurses have no Army rank, officer status, or equal pay with men, or benefits such as retirement or veteran's rights.

1908: Navy Nurse Corps established.

March 19, 1917: Navy Department authorizes the enrollment of women in the Naval Reserve, in the ratings of Yeoman, Electrician (radio), or in other ratings that are considered essential.

October 8, 1917: General Pershing of the American Expeditionary Force in France, requests one hundred women telephone operators (later called "Hello Girls") who could speak French. The women are sent overseas as civilian contract employees working for the Army Signal Corps with privileges similar to the Army Nurse Corps. Other women follow, under contracts with the Quartermaster General, the Ordnance Department, and the Medical Corps, but none have military status. (Veteran's status was granted to these women in 1977.)

August 8, 1918: Secretary of the Navy, Josephus Daniels, authorizes the enrollment of women in the Marine Corps Reserve for clerical duty at Headquarters, U.S. Marine Corps, Washington, DC, and at other Marine Corps offices in the United States where they could replace men qualified for field duty.

November 11, 1918: World War I ends. More than 10,000 nurses served overseas in the Army and Navy Nurse Corps, and almost 15,000 more women served under contract to the Army or as civilian volunteers. 305 women enlisted as Marines and nearly 12,000 in the Navy as Yeomen (F).

May 7, 1942: Sixty-six nurses and eleven Navy nurses held in Japanese prison camps in the Philippines after the fall of Corregidor. Five Navy nurses captured in Guam are interned in a military prison in Japan.

May 15, 1942:   President Roosevelt signs Public Law 77-554, An Act to Establish a Women's Army Auxiliary Corps (WAAC) for service with the Army of the United States. On May 16, Mrs. Oveta Culp Hobby is sworn in as Director, WAAC. Women in the WAAC served with the Army, not in it, and did not receive full military benefits.

July 30, 1942:   Public Law 689 is signed, establishing the Navy Women's Reserve (WAVES) and the Marine Corps Women's Reserve (Women Marines). Women in the Navy and Marine Corps Reserve served in their respective services, not as an auxiliary (as the WAAC), and received full military benefits.

September 1942:   The Women's Auxiliary Ferrying Squadron (WAFS) is formed with Nancy Love appointed as its director of pilots. Jacqueline Cochran is named to head the Women's Flying Training Detachment (WFTD), based in Houston, Texas, to train women for the WAFS.

November 23, 1942: Women's Reserve of the U.S. Coast Guard (SPAR) established.

December 1942: First WAAC officers (five) sent overseas to General Eisenhower's Headquarters in North Africa. Their troopship is torpedoed and sunk one day out of port from England, but the women are rescued.

January 1943: First contingent of enlisted WACs is sent overseas to Algiers, North Africa. They serve primarily as stenographers, typists, telephone operators, bakers and cooks, and drivers.

July 1, 1943: Bill to establish a Women's Army Corps (WAC) *in* the U.S. Army is passed. More than seventy-five percent of women in the WAAC chose to reenlist in the WAC. Women in the WAC receive full military benefits.

August 1943: Women's Airforce Service Pilots (WASP) formed, encompassing women of the WAFS and WFTD.

December 20, 1944: The WASP is inactivated.

February 1945:   Army and Navy nurses held as prisoners of war in the Philippines are liberated.

May 8, 1945: End of World War II in Europe.

September 2, 1945: End of World War II in Japan. 350,000 women served in the military during the war.

April 1947: Army-Navy Nurse Act (Public Law 36-80C) establishes the nurse corps as a permanent part of their services.

June 12, 1948:   President Truman signs Public Law 80-625, the Women's Armed Services Integration Act, which among other provisions, gives permanent status to women in all the armed forces, both Regular and Reserve, imposes a two percent ceiling on the proportion of women on active duty, and in the Navy and Air Force, prohibits women from service on aircraft engaged in combat missions and in the Navy, from service on vessels except hospital ships and naval transports. Women serve in the Air Force, Army, Marine Corps, and Navy, but the Coast Guard Women's Reserve (SPAR) is disbanded in 1946.

1950-1953: Korean conflict. Total strength of women's units reaches less than 49,000.

August 1951: The Defense Advisory Committee on Women in the Service (DACOWITS) is formed of outstanding civilian leaders, including the first director of the WAC, Mrs. Hobby and former directors of the WAVES, Mildred McAfee Horton and the women Marines, Dorothy Streeter. Their mission is to suggest ways to help the military meet its recruiting goals for women. (DACOWITS now advises the Department of Defense on issues relating to women's military service.)

1964-1974: Vietnam War. Estimates of the number of women serving in Vietnam range from 6,000-12,000. Primarily nurses, this includes nine Navy officers, 36 women Marines, 700 WACs, and 500-600 Air Force women. Eight Army nurses are killed, mainly in air crashes, but one, First Lieutenant Sharon A. Lane, dies of shrapnel wounds during an enemy rocket attack.

November 8, 1967: Public Law 90-130 is passed, the first major policy change affecting military women since the Women's Armed Services Integration Act in 1948. Removes rank limitations and the two percent limitation on numbers of women serving.

1969: Air Force ROTC opens to women.

June 11, 1970: The first women are promoted to the rank of Brigadier General; Anna Mae Hays, Chief of the Army Nurse Corps, and Elizabeth P. Hoisington, Director of the WAC.

1972: Army and Navy ROTC open to women.

February 23, 1972: Title of WAVES abolished.

May 14, 1973: In *Frontiero v. Richardson*, a class action suit brought by Air Force First Lieutenant Sharron Frontiero, the Supreme Court rules it is unconstitutional to require female service members to prove spousal dependence to receive benefits. Women are now treated equally with men in matters of dependence and benefits.

February-June 1974: Six women earn their wings as Naval aviators, becoming the first women pilots in any branch of the U.S. military.

June 1974: First Army woman pilot receives her wings.

1974: Coast Guard begins recruiting women.

1975: Women admitted to the Coast Guard Academy.

May 15, 1975: Involuntary discharge for pregnancy/parenthood is discontinued.

October 7, 1975: Public Law 94-106 signed, admitting women to the U.S. Air Force, Military, and Naval Academies. The first women enter in June 1976 in the class of 1980.

August 1976: The Air Force begins training women pilots.

1977: Women Airforce Service Pilot's (WASP) World War II service is recognized to have been active duty in the armed forces for purposes of laws administered by the Veterans Administration, making them eligible for veterans benefits.

1977: First women assigned as permanent crew on two Coast Guard ships.

August 1978: Coast Guard removes all assignment restrictions based on sex.

October 20, 1978: President Ford signs Public Law 95-584, abolishing the Women's Army Corps as a separate corps. Department of the Army issues General Order 20 the same day, discontinuing the WAC. Women are integrated into the regular Army.

October 1983: Women are deployed with the American forces during Urgent Fury, the invasion of Grenada.

December 1989: 770 women participate in Operation Just Cause in Panama.

1990-1991: Operation Desert Shield/Desert Storm becomes the largest ever deployment of military women. Depending on the source, between 27,066 to over 40,000 military women were deployed. Thirteen women were killed, two were taken as prisoners-of-war. Renews controversy over women in combat and parenting issues.

May 1991: Fiscal Year 92 House Defense Authorization Bill passes, repealing the exclusion laws banning military women from flying aircraft on combat missions. Implementation is delayed while a Presidential Commission on the Assignment of Women in the Armed Forces is tasked to study and make recommendations on a wide variety of issues relating to women in the military.

September 8-12, 1991: 35th Annual Symposium of the Tailhook Association held at the Las Vegas Hilton Hotel. Ninety victims of indecent assault are identified by an investigation by the Office of the Inspector General, Department of Defense. Renews debate over sexual harassment in the military.

November 1992: Report of the Presidential Commission on the Assignment of Women in the Military is released. Recommends, by an eight to seven vote, that women should serve in combat aircraft.

April 1993: Secretary of Defense Les Aspin issues a memorandum regarding the Policy on the Assignment of Women in the Armed Forces, directing the services to open more specialties and assignments to women, including assignments to aircraft engaging in combat missions and opening additional ships to women.

November 1993: Exclusion laws prohibiting women from serving in Navy combatant ships are repealed.

January 1994: Secretary Aspin rescinds the Department of Defense "Risk Rule," and issues a new ground combat assignment rule, making women eligible for assignment to all positions for which they are qualified, except for assignment to units below brigade level whose mission is to engage in direct ground combat.

October 20, 1994: The USS *Eisenhower* becomes the first aircraft carrier to deploy with women as permanent members of the crew.

November 1994: Two Navy women F/A-18 pilots become the first U.S. women to fly combat sorties, patrolling the no-fly zone in southern Iraq.

April 1995: The USS *Eisenhower* returns to port after completing a six month deployment in the Mediterranean and Persian Gulf. Becomes not only the first combat ship to deploy with a mixed sex crew, but the first to launch naval women aviators on a combat mission.

APPENDIX D: MILITARY WORLD WIDE WEB PAGES

This list provides a sample of information about military women available on the World Wide Web. Web sites are frequently updated. Use a search engine to find the most recent information and other military pages.

OFFICIAL SERVICE HOMEPAGES

U.S. Air Force Link
address: http://www.dtic.mil/airforcelink/
The U.S. Department of the Air Force Homepage. A very well done page, with information such as biographies of Air Force leaders, photographs, fact sheets, current Air Force news and information, and a library of speeches, issues, and Air Force news.

U.S. Army Homepage
address: http://www.army.mil/
Links to Army installations, the Center of Military History, recruiters, personnel locator, BosniaLink, etc.

U.S. Coast Guard
address: http://www.dot.gov/dotinfo/uscg/
Basic information about the Coast Guard. Includes two historical articles on women; one a general history of Coast Guard women and the other on women in World War II.

MarineLink: The Official WWW Information Service of the United States Marine Corps
address: http://www.usmc.mil/
Gives press releases and other news about the Corps, recruiting information, fact sheets on weapon systems, and historical information. A fact sheet on women in the Marine Corps discusses the role of women Marines during World War II.

DefenseLINK
The Department of Defense Homepage
address: http://www.dtic.mil/defenselink/
Links to the homepages of each service, as well as official news releases and photos, publications, and information about the Department of Defense. Many statistics are presented. Military Manpower Statistics, including those for women, are available through the Publications link.

MILITARY MUSEUMS

U.S. Air Force Museum
address: http://www.am.wpafb.af.mil/museum/usaf_museum.html/
Very well done homepage of the U.S. Air Force museum. Good information about women in the Army Air Force during WWII and WASPs, with photographs.

The Navy Museum
address: http://www.his.com/~tom/navymu.html/
Homepage for the Navy museum in Washington DC. Photos and short descriptions of some of the displays.

Women's Army Corps Museum
address: http://www-tradoc.monroe.army.mil/mcclellan/wac.html/
A brief page from the WAC museum.

SERVICE ACADEMIES

U.S. Air Force Academy
address: http://www.usafa.af.mil/
Homepage of the Air Force Academy. Not much information.

U.S. Coast Guard Academy
address: http://www.dot.gov/dotinfo/uscg/hq/uscga/uscga.html/
Information on Coast Guard Academy missions and activities. Has links to the other service academies as well as to foreign service academies.

U.S. Military Academy
address: http://www.usma.edu/
Homepage of the U.S. Military Academy.

U.S. Naval Academy
address: http://www.nadn.navy.mil/
Brief description of the academy.

VETERANS

Department of Veterans Affairs
address: http://www.va.gov/
Homepage of the Department of Veterans Affairs. A wealth of information for and about veterans. Includes a link to the National Registry of Women Veterans and to statistical data of estimated number of female veterans from 1970 through 1994.

The National Registry of Women Veterans
address: http://www.va.gov/womenvet/index.htm/
This registry promotes improvements in health and health care of women veterans. The goal is to identify all women veterans separated from active duty since January 1, 1942.

ONLINE SERVICE MAGAZINES

Airman: The Magazine of America's Air Force
address: //www.dtic.dla.mil/airforcelink/pa/new/airman/cover.htm/
The official magazine of the Air Force. Use to access current and back issues.

Airpower Journal: The Professsional Journal of the United States Air Force.
address: http://www.cdsar.af.mil/apje.html/
Includes current and past issues.

Marines Magazine: Official Magazine of the U.S. Marine Corps
address: http://www.usmc.mil/marines/default.htm/
Source of articles from Marines Magazine.

Soldiers: The Official U.S. Army Magazine
address: http://www.redstone.army.mil/soldiers/home.html/
Electronic version of Soldiers Magazine. Past and present issues available.

HISTORICAL/ARCHIVAL SITES

U.S. Army Military History Institute
address: http://carlisle-www.army.mil/usamhi.htm/
The U.S. Army archive for documents relating to military history. Can search archives and manuscript holdings. Links to other historical sites. Searching for information on women yields an extensive bibliography of articles, books, and archival holdings at the Institute.

U.S. Center of Military History (CMH)
address: http://imabbs.army.mil/cmh-pg/
An excellent, highly detailed web site, with a wealth of information on the CMH as well as military history. Includes publications index, ordering information, Army history frequently asked questions, list of Army Record depositories, and links to other military history web sites.

National Archives and Records Administration
address: http://www.nara.gov/
Homepage of the National Archives. Links to Presidential libraries, regional archives, and Federal Records Center.

OTHER GOVERNMENT SOURCES

General Accounting Office
address: http://www.gao.gov/
Can search for reports issued by the GAO and read online or electronically order. The first copy of each report is free.

U.S. Government Printing Office
address: http://www.access.gpo.gov/
Source of information on the GPO. Has ordering information for government documents as well as an online version of subject bibligraphies.

MISCELLANEOUS WEB SITES

H-Minerva: Women and War
address: http://h-net.msu.edu/~minerva/
Minerva homepage. Links to academic programs, conference announcements, archival and manuscript collections, grants, etc.

Military Woman
address: http://ourworld.compuserve.com/homepages/military_woman/
A non-official web site with many sources of information about military women.

The Women's Memorial
address: http://www.clark.net/pub/wimsa/wimsa.html/
Homepage of the Women in Military Service for America Memorial. Discusses the memorial project, fundraising, the education center, and details of charter membership.

Women's Research and Education Institute (WREI)
address: http://www.nas.edu.cwse/wrei.html/
Homepage of WREI. Gives contact information only.

AUTHOR INDEX

Page numbers, e.g., p.5, refer to pages in the bibliography; citation numbers refer to sequentially numbered citations throughout the bibliography.

TITLE INDEX

Page numbers, e.g., p.5, refer to pages in the bibliography; citation numbers, e.g., 305, are used to refer to the sequentially numbered citations throughout the bibliography.

SUBJECT INDEX

Page numbers, e.g., p.5, refer to pages in the bibliography; citation numbers, e.g., 305, refer to sequentially numbered citations throughout the bibliography.

About the Compiler

VICKI L. FRIEDL graduated with a degree in history from the University of California, where she held a three-year ROTC scholarship. She served as an active duty Army officer in the Transportation Corps from 1980 to 1984. Her most recent job as a librarian was as history bibliographer at Boston University.

ISBN 0-313-29657-X

90000>

EAN

9 780313 296574

HARDCOVER BAR CODE